Liability

Liability
Perspectives and Policy

Robert E. Litan and Clifford Winston
editors

The Brookings Institution
Washington, D.C.

Copyright © 1988 by

THE BROOKINGS INSTITUTION

1775 Massachusetts Avenue, N.W., Washington, D.C. 20036

Library of Congress Cataloging-in-Publication Data

Liability: perspectives and policy / Robert E. Litan and Clifford
    Winston, editors.
        p. cm.
    Includes bibliographical references and index.
    ISBN 0-8157-5272-5   ISBN 0-8157-5271-7 (pbk.)
    1. Liability (Law)—United States.   2. Insurance, Liabil-
ity—United States.   3. Torts—Economic aspects—United
States.
I. Litan, Robert E., 1950–   . II. Winston, Clifford,
1952–   .
KF1250.L53 1988
346.7303—dc19
[347.3063]   88-7254
                                                       CIP

9 8 7 6 5 4 3 2 1

THE BROOKINGS INSTITUTION is an independent organization devoted to nonpartisan research, education, and publication in economics, government, foreign policy, and the social sciences generally. Its principal purposes are to aid in the development of sound public policies and to promote public understanding of issues of national importance.

The Institution was founded on December 8, 1927, to merge the activities of the Institute for Government Research, founded in 1916, the Institute of Economics, founded in 1922, and the Robert Brookings Graduate School of Economics and Government, founded in 1924.

The Board of Trustees is responsible for the general administration of the Institution, while the immediate direction of the policies, program, and staff is vested in the President, assisted by an advisory committee of the officers and staff. The by-laws of the Institution state: "It is the function of the Trustees to make possible the conduct of scientific research, and publication, under the most favorable conditions, and to safeguard the independence of the research staff in the pursuit of their studies and in the publication of the results of such studies. It is not a part of their function to determine, control, or influence the conduct of particular investigations or the conclusions reached."

The President bears final responsibility for the decision to publish a manuscript as a Brookings book. In reaching his judgment on the competence, accuracy, and objectivity of each study, the President is advised by the director of the appropriate research program and weighs the views of a panel of expert outside readers who report to him in confidence on the quality of the work. Publication of a work signifies that it is deemed a competent treatment worthy of public consideration but does not imply endorsement of conclusions or recommendations.

The Institution maintains its position of neutrality on issues of public policy in order to safeguard the intellectual freedom of the staff. Hence interpretations or conclusions in Brookings publications should be understood to be solely those of the authors and should not be attributed to the Institution, to its trustees, officers, or other staff members, or to the organizations that support its research.

Foreword

IN RECENT years the United States has witnessed an unprecedented growth in personal injury lawsuits. State and federal courts have been flooded with litigation involving medical malpractice, unsafe products, and environmental hazards. Jury awards and out-of-court settlements for medical expenses, income losses, and the pain and suffering of victims have routinely amounted to hundreds of thousands of dollars. At the same time, premiums for liability insurance have risen steeply, and some companies have refused to cover new clients or withdrawn coverage entirely. These developments have threatened the functioning of the entire civil litigation process and touched off a national debate over what should be done to bring order to our system of dealing with personal accidents and injuries. Some critics have urged fundamental reform of the civil liability system to limit awards. Others have contended that more extensive regulation of the insurance industry would reintroduce stability.

In this book Robert E. Litan, Clifford Winston, and a team of economists and lawyers evaluate the issues underlying this debate and suggest policies to ameliorate the problems of both the courts and the insurance industry. They examine the functions of tort law in providing compensation and deterring harmful behavior, the apparent liberalization of tort doctrines that has contributed to higher damage awards and affected the availability and cost of insurance, and the ways in which changes in the system have affected the provision of medical services, the development of safer products, the maintenance of safety in the workplace, and the protection of the environment. The authors also identify critical gaps in knowledge that need to be filled before any sweeping changes can be advanced. Thus, although they provide specific policy recommendations, they are cautious about calling for radical changes, such as replacing the tort system with broad administrative compensation programs, unless sound evidence supporting such programs becomes available.

Robert E. Litan and Clifford Winston are senior fellows in the Brookings Economic Studies program. Robert Litan is also counsel to Powell, Goldstein, Frazer and Murphy. Other contributors are John Calfee, assistant professor of management, University of Maryland; Patricia M. Danzon, professor of health care systems, University of Pennsylvania; Scott E. Harrington, associate professor of insurance, University of Pennsylvania; Peter Huber, private consultant, Washington, D.C., and senior fellow, the Manhattan Institute; George L. Priest, professor of law, Yale University; Peter Swire, associate, Powell, Goldstein, Frazer and Murphy; and W. Kip Viscusi, professor of economics, Northwestern University.

The editors wish to thank Paul L. Joskow and participants in the June 1987 Brookings Civil Liability Conference for helpful comments on the chapters.

Various individuals made useful contributions to specific chapters. Chapters 1 and 8 benefited from research assistance by Theo Correl. Chapter 2 benefited from the comments of Ralph Winter, Marilyn Simon, and Richard Craswell. Chapter 3 benefited from the comments of David Brummond and Chuck Berry; research assistance was provided by Chong Lee. Chapter 4 received data on malpractice rates from Benson L. Dutton, Jr.; research assistance was provided by Jan Mills. Chapter 7 benefited from research provided by Scott Brooks and Jon Lewis.

James R. Schneider edited the manuscript, Victor M. Alfaro and Almaz S. Zelleke verified its factual content, and Margaret Lynch prepared the index.

Funding for this project was provided in part by the A. V. Starr Foundation, Dow Chemical Company, Bell Atlantic, the Alex C. Walker Foundation, and the Aetna Foundation.

The views expressed in this book are those of the authors and should not be ascribed to those persons or organizations whose assistance is acknowledged or to the trustees, officers, or other staff members of the Brookings Institution.

BRUCE K. MACLAURY
President

April 1988
Washington, D.C.

Contents

Tables

CHAPTER ONE

The U.S. Liability System: Background and Trends

Robert E. Litan, Peter Swire, and Clifford Winston

THE AMERICAN civil litigation system, in recent years, has been placed on trial. Critics charge that the explosive growth in the number of liability lawsuits, coupled with dramatic increases in jury awards and settlements, has caused an insurance crisis—steeply higher premiums for liability insurance and, in some instances, coverage curtailed or withdrawn. For many lines of commercial liability insurance, including products liability and medical malpractice, premiums have skyrocketed in just a few years. For other lines, notably those covering nurse-midwives, municipalities, and day care centers, coverage is simply no longer available in some areas. As a result, the crisis may be dampening productivity growth and pushing up prices for a broad range of goods and services, crippling the international competitiveness of the American economy at a time when it can ill afford it. Only fundamental reform of the nation's civil justice system, critics warn, will make liability insurance more available and affordable.

This outlook is not universally shared. Skeptics acknowledge that property and casualty insurance companies suffered unusually large losses in 1984 and 1985—$1.9 billion and $3.8 billion, respectively—but they attribute these setbacks to excessive rate cutting in earlier years and to falling returns from the industry's portfolio investments. These critics also deny that the civil justice system needs fundamental overhaul. The liability insurance industry, they charge, has launched a "tort reform" campaign to cover its own underwriting mistakes and even perhaps its collusive behavior. The only reform required in their view is more intensive regulation of the industry.

The controversy is not a new one. Public concern over the efficiency and fairness of the civil liability system ebbs and flows with the apparentlycyclical performance of the property and casualty insurance industry. The previous insurance "crisis," for example, occurred in the mid-1970s, when liability premiums also escalated and coverage was curtailed. The events prompted Congress and state legislatures to examine possible reforms to the nation's tort laws. But relatively little change at either the federal or state levels resulted.

More has happened during the current crisis. Although Congress has thus far failed to agree on any reforms to the civil justice system, most states have recently modified their liability laws—imposing caps on awards and adjusting tort doctrines so that they do not unduly favor plaintiffs—in an attempt to reduce liability costs. In the meantime, however, many customers have abandoned their insurers and chosen to form insurance syndicates of their own or even to self-insure. This has led to a vicious cycle. Because the customers who drop their insurance tend to be low-cost risks, insurers are left with servicing higher-risk customers. This "adverse selection" process forces premiums up still further and in turn induces still more low-risk customers to seek alternative ways of meeting their liability costs.

Nevertheless, calls for reforming the system of civil justice are less urgent now then they have been in recent months. As in previous insurance cycles, increases in premiums have moderated. In some instances, coverage that was withdrawn has reappeared. In 1986 the property and casualty industry earned 11.6 percent on its equity, a return lower than the manufacturing sector average of 13 percent during the past decade but still considerably better than the disappointing performance of the previous two years.

The issues raised by the most recent crisis, however, will not disappear. If nothing else, the dramatic increases in premiums and curtailments of coverage have called greater attention to the nation's civil justice system—whether it is working satisfactorily, and if not why—than at any point in recent memory. Moreover, interest in these issues will intensify if and when the underwriting cycle reverses course and turns against the industry once again.

It is essential therefore that there be a framework within which to evaluate and develop policies that merit consideration. This book attempts to supply that framework by bringing together analyses of the major issues raised by the recent crisis. It also examines certain underlying causes of the recent dramatic changes in insurance markets, assesses the merits of conflicting opinions, and identifies critical gaps in knowledge that must be filled before fundamental disputes can be resolved and sound public policy developed.

The Changing Function of Tort Law

Injuries pose three different and potentially conflicting challenges for all societies. One is efficiently to *deter* behavior that causes injuries. A second and related objective is to exact *retribution* against those responsible. Most societies use some combination of criminal and civil penalties—jail sentences and fines—to meet these goals. The third challenge is to *compensate* victims for their injuries. Compensation may be supplied by the government or by the private sector (through insurance), and may or may not be linked to specific injuries or types of accidents. *Tort law*—rules allowing accident victims to seek compensation through the judicial system from the parties responsible—can be considered a mechanism for meeting all three of these challenges.

Tort rules will efficiently deter accident-causing behavior if responsibility for the costs of injuries is imposed on those who can avoid or prevent accidents most cheaply. If they are well designed, liability rules encourage "cheapest-cost avoiders" to take efficient precautions, unless it is less expensive simply to pay for the cost of injuries. For example, suppose that the plaintiff in a lawsuit could have avoided a $10,000 injury only by taking precautionary measures costing $1,000 but that the defendant manufacturer could have avoided the accident by spending just $100. Holding the defendant—the cheapest-cost avoider—responsible for the costs of the injury would encourage others similarly situated to take efficient precautions to prevent future such accidents.

Of course, tort law administered in this fashion imposes higher costs on those whose activities entail the risk of injury—say, manufacturers of hazardous substances—which requires them to charge higher prices on their products or services to cover the costs of preventing future accidents. Some producers or organizations might even decide not to offer certain products or services because of the liability risks. But if producers and other participants in the economy are not charged for the costs they impose on others through accidents and injuries, resources will be misallocated toward activities that create or perpetuate risks.

Tort law also provides a means for compensating injured parties or *spreading losses* by making individuals or firms with greater resources, either on their own or through their liability insurance policies, pay for the costs of injuries. Misfortune can strike suddenly and unpredictably. A car accident can paralyze and forever change the life of an injured driver or passenger. A drug once thought to be totally safe can later be discovered to cause cancer among many who use it. All societies must choose how these and similar losses should be borne, either solely by victims or spread in some way among other parties.

One method for spreading losses is to have government-administered (and taxpayer-financed) programs for compensating injured parties, as is the case in New Zealand and Sweden and to a limited extent in the United States through the disability component of the social security system. Compensation through the tort system is an alternative means. In practice, tort law administers compensation through private third-party insurance, which individuals and firms purchase to cover the costs they might owe to injured victims. Liability insurance spreads losses not only among all policyholders but, in the case of business purchasers, among consumers, in the form of higher prices of products or services, and workers, in the form of lower wages. If premiums are based on experience or risk, liability insurance can also deter activities that create risks.

A third objective of the tort system is to exact retribution against wrongdoers regardless of cost. The idea here, of course, is that justice requires wrongdoers to pay a price for their harmful behavior. Criminal laws are designed to accomplish this by punishing those who intentionally inflict harm on others. Many legal scholars argue that the common-law tort system, which requires negligent parties to compensate those they injure, should also be used to assign culpability. Given its focus on the economic functions of the civil liability system, however, this book concentrates primarily on the objectives of deterrence and spreading loss.

As it turns out, these two objectives can conflict. If individuals may recover only those losses that defendants could more cheaply avoid, then the loss-spreading function of the civil liability system will be limited. In particular, injured parties who could have avoided their accidents more cheaply than potential defendants may receive no compensation at all, even in cases where the defendants may have been able to take practical preventive measures. Conversely, if the system is to be used liberally to spread losses, many individuals and firms will be forced to bear costs they may have no way of preventing. Thus, for example, losses may be easily spread by requiring manufacturers to pay for injuries that scientists may some day link to their products. But if the manufacturers have no way at the time to prevent the injuries, then requiring them to shoulder the cost many years later will do nothing to promote deterrence.

The discussions in this book broadly suggest that, in fact, changes in tort law and the growth of third-party insurance during the past two decades have sharply increased the use of the tort system to spread losses, but at the cost of reducing the system's ability to deter harmful activities efficiently. It was not always this way: a variety of tort doctrines formerly limited the ability of plaintiffs to recover. From the mid-nineteenth century until very recently, for example, plaintiffs could win a tort action only by proving that their injuries were "proximately caused" by the defendant's negligence or by behavior that a "reasonable man" would not have displayed. And plaintiffs could only recover for purely economic damages or medical costs and lost income; they could not be compensated for pain and suffering or emotional distress. At one time, plaintiffs injured by defective products could recover only from the retailers from whom they purchased the products (in legal terms, those with whom they were "in privity"), not from manufacturers. Even when defendants were negligent, plaintiffs could not recover at all if through their own negligent conduct they contributed to their predicament. And some potential defendants, notably federal, state, and local governments, were immune from suit.

Americans have gradually grown more receptive, however, to using the tort system as a vehicle for compensation. Having enjoyed significant advances in living standards, many Americans could afford to pay more attention to the environmental, health, and safety effects of industrial growth. In the 1960s and 1970s Congress responded by authorizing major programs to regulate exposure to harmful substances in the workplace, in products sold to consumers, and in the general environment.[1] During the same years, judges and juries eased the availability and raised the levels of compensation provided through the tort system. Finally, individuals have increasingly sought compensation from the courts because existing insurance policies or government compensation funds have offered less generous compensation prospects.

The increasing importance of the loss-spreading objective of the tort system has been manifested in three ways. Changes in tort doctrines have made it easier for plaintiffs to recover in any given litigation. Successful plaintiffs in certain classes of tort cases have enjoyed larger damage awards and settlements. And the combination of both trends appears to have induced many more individuals to file lawsuits.

Liberalization of Tort Doctrines

Tort law in the United States is largely based not on statutes but on common law, a body of legal principles developed case by case by judges, primarily those in state courts. It is difficult therefore to generalize about

1. See Robert E. Litan and William D. Nordhaus, *Reforming Federal Regulation* (Yale University Press, 1983), pp. 34–58.

the status of tort law in all jurisdictions. Nevertheless, certain important changes in doctrines have occurred in the past several decades, all of which have expanded the system's function in spreading losses:

—Whether by applying the negligence test in a flexible fashion or by imposing liability on parties whose behavior is causally related to accidents but who are not necessarily negligent (so-called strict liability), the courts have increased manufacturers' liability for defective products. Early in the twentieth century courts began to weaken the privity doctrine by allowing plaintiffs and then members of their families to recover directly from manufacturers for injuries caused by defective products. More recently, certain courts have held that a product can be defective even if it conforms to prevailing regulatory standards and if the manufacturer had no knowledge at the time of design or production that it would entail the risks later attributed to it in litigation.

—The negligence standard itself has been extended through litigation to impose liability on a wide class of service providers not previously accustomed to being sued. Day care centers, ski lift, ice rink, and amusement park operators, taverns and restaurants, and not-for-profit organizations have all been taken to court for failures to warn of certain dangers and for the careless conduct of their employees. The exposure of these defendants to liability claims has been widened by the doctrine of joint and several liability, which allows prevailing plaintiffs to recover up to the full amount of a total damage award from any single defendant if the other defendants are unable to pay, and by the collateral source rule, which prohibits juries from reducing damages by subtracting insurance monies or other compensation plaintiffs receive from other sources.

—The concept of contributory negligence has been relaxed in many states so that negligent plaintiffs are no longer totally barred from recovery. Instead, they find their damages reduced by the proportion by which their negligence contributed to their injury. In addition, beginning with the Federal Tort Claims Act of 1946, which waived the federal government's sovereign immunity, courts have made state and local governments liable for tort suits.

—Courts have relaxed the standards plaintiffs must satisfy in proving, under either the negligence or strict liability doctrine, that defendants have caused their injuries. This trend has been manifested primarily in product liability and so-called toxic tort cases, which have frequently required courts to decide whether plaintiffs' injuries have been caused by their exposure, often over long periods of their lives, to substances recently discovered to be associated with the development of cancer or other serious diseases. Courts have adopted a range of rules to determine causation in such cases. Some have placed liability on the first or last source to which plaintiffs can establish they were exposed; others have made *all* manufacturers of the substance jointly and severally liable. In one noted case involving the exposure of Vietnam veterans to the chemical Agent Orange, a federal court actively encouraged a $180 million settlement even though no hard scientific evidence had been uncovered that linked the chemical to the medical infirmities claimed by the plaintiffs.

—Finally, courts in certain jurisdictions have liberally interpreted statutes of limitation, which bar plaintiffs from recovering if they wait too long after suffering injury (typically more than three or four years) to file suit. In many toxic tort, product liability, and medical malpractice cases, it is difficult to determine when injury actually occurs. It could occur with the first exposure to a substance or operation, or it could develop decades later when the symptoms of disease become observable. Although jurisdictions differ widely on this issue, the trend has been for courts not to invoke the statute of limitations to bar suits involving long-latent injuries.

Higher Damage Awards and Settlements

The tort system allows for compensation to injured parties through lawsuits and, far more importantly, through claims resolution by liability insurance companies. Indeed, of the millions of insurance claims filed each year, typically only 2 percent are resolved through litigation. Of cases brought to court, less than 5 percent are tried to verdict; the rest are settled.[2]

In addition, the amounts actually received by successful plaintiffs are often much smaller than those originally awarded by juries. Trial judges and appellate courts may, for instance, override jury verdicts; or in some cases the defendant may not have sufficient resources (even with insurance) to satisfy the judgment. One recent study of 198 tort verdicts in 1984 and 1985 that resulted in awards of $1 million or more found that the successful plaintiffs received the original jury award in only 51 cases; the final distributions to plaintiffs in the other cases were, on average, 30 percent less than the amount originally awarded.[3]

In short, jury awards represent only the tip of the tort system and

2. William E. Bailey, "The High Cost of Insurance: Who's to Blame?" *The Brief,* vol. 16 (Winter 1987), pp. 15–18.

3. Ivy E. Broder, "Characteristics of Million Dollar Awards: Jury Verdicts and Final Disbursements," *Justice System Journal,* vol. 11 (Winter 1986), p. 353.

Table 1-1. *Average Jury Awards in Cook County, Illinois, and San Francisco, Selected Periods, 1960–84*
Constant 1984 dollars unless otherwise specified

Type of Case	1960–64	1975–79	1980–84	Average annual percentage increase 1960–64 to 1975–79[a]	Average annual percentage increase 1975–79 to 1980–84[a]	Average annual percentage increase 1960–64 to 1980–84[a]
Medical malpractice						
Cook County	52,000	324,000	1,179,000	13.0	29.5	16.9
San Francisco	125,000	644,000	1,162,000	11.5	12.5	11.8
Product liability						
Cook County	265,000	597,000	828,000	5.6	6.8	5.9
San Francisco	99,000	308,000	1,105,000	7.9	29.1	12.8
All personal injury						
Cook County	59,000	130,000	187,000	5.4	7.5	5.9
San Francisco	66,000	133,000	302,000	4.8	17.8	7.9
Real GNP	...	...	...	3.6	2.3	3.2
Real price of medical services	...	...	...	1.9	1.1	1.7

Sources: Mark A. Peterson, *Civil Juries in the 1980's: Trends in Jury Trials and Verdicts in California and Cook County, Illinois* (Rand Corporation, Institute for Civil Justice, 1987), pp. 22, 35, 51; and *Economic Report of the President, January 1987.*
a. Compiled from midpoints of each five-year period.

may not even accurately reflect the actual levels of compensation received by plaintiffs. Nevertheless, verdicts set benchmarks for nonlitigated claims and tort settlements. As jury awards increase, claimants and litigants have greater incentives to hold out for larger settlements in return for not proceeding with litigation. Accordingly, no analysis of the tort system can be complete without examining trends in jury verdicts.

Unfortunately, there are no comprehensive nationwide data on jury awards. The only reliable data that do exist for a relatively long period are those collected by the Rand Corporation's Institute for Civil Justice, which has assembled civil jury verdicts over a twenty-five year period in two large metropolitan areas: Cook County, Illinois, and San Francisco.[4] These data do not reflect appellate court revisions, although they are adjusted for inflation. Key statistics from the institute's data base are shown in table 1-1, which presents average jury awards in the two jurisdictions for selected five-year periods. Over the entire twenty-five

4. Mark A. Peterson, *Civil Juries in the 1980s: Trends in Jury Trials and Verdicts in California and Cook County, Illinois* (Santa Monica, Calif: Rand Corp., Institute for Civil Justice, 1987).

years, average awards in tort cases brought in Cook County and San Francisco increased sharply, considerably faster than the growth in real GNP and real prices of medical services. The average annual rate of increase in awards for all lawsuit categories was more rapid in the recent period closely associated with the insurance crisis.

The data shown in table 1-1 reflect two other important trends. First, awards in medical malpractice and product liability cases were significantly higher and increased at a faster pace than those for personal injury cases generally. This pattern is consistent with the recent survey of jury verdicts in ten states between 1981 and 1985 conducted by Stephen Daniels and Joanne Martin, which also found award levels in malpractice and product liability cases to be higher than for other categories of tort cases.[5]

Second, much of the increase in medical malpractice and product liability awards in Cook County and San Francisco, especially in recent years, has been caused by an explosive growth in jury awards of $1 million or more. In Cook County, for example, there were only two verdicts of $1 million or more (in 1984 dollars) from 1960 to 1964, and these accounted for only 4 percent of personal injury awards. By 1980–84, sixty-seven verdicts of $1 million or more had been handed down, accounting for 85 percent of awards. In San Francisco from 1980 to 1984 only 3.8 percent of all personal injury cases produced verdicts of $1 million or more, but these accounted for almost half of the total amounts awarded. The increase in large awards is confirmed in other studies as well.[6]

Some have argued that although the relatively small number of large dollar verdicts apparently has been very instrumental in driving up the average tort award, *median* awards have increased less dramatically.[7]

5. Stephen Daniels and Joanne Martin, "Jury Verdicts and the 'Crisis' in Civil Justice," *Justice System Journal,* vol. 11 (Winter 1986), p. 339. However, the study also found that malpractice and product liability cases generally make up less than 10 percent of total tort litigations and are more difficult for plaintiffs to win (p. 333).

6. One recent survey of product liability claims greater than $100,000 that were closed in 1985 revealed a sharp increase in the proportion of claims that have yielded payments of at least $1 million: from none in 1975 to 6 percent in 1979 to 13 percent in 1985. See Lawrence W. Soular, *A Study of Large Product Liability Claims Closed in 1985* (Schaumberg, Ill., and New York: Alliance of American Insurers, and American Insurance Association, 1986), p. 3.

7. By definition, half of all awards are above and half are below the median. With a relatively small number of large dollar awards, the median will typically fall below the average, which gives greater weight to the large dollar figures.

The data from the Institute for Civil Justice presented in table 1-1 do, in fact, show

However, this observation ignores two problems that liability insurers face when deciding whether to offer coverage and how to set premiums: insurers can only remain profitable if they set their premiums to cover total expected claim costs, and large dollar claims increase uncertainty about the range of possible losses.

The greater frequency of large dollar awards can be partly explained by increases in noneconomic damages—those for pain and suffering— as well as increases in punitive awards in certain cases. George Priest finds that noneconomic damages generally account for 30 to 40 percent of all tort damage awards and for even higher proportions of very large awards.[8] Patricia Danzon documents a similar trend for jury awards in medical malpractice cases in chapter 4 of this volume. Meanwhile, the Cook County and San Francisco data reveal dramatic increases in the dollar value of punitive awards: from averages of $7,000 and $166,000 in constant 1984 dollars between 1960 and 1964 to averages of $729,000 and $381,000 between 1980 and 1984.[9]

To be sure, it is difficult to infer a nationwide pattern from data on jury awards on just two, albeit large, metropolitan areas. Nevertheless, the trends in these two areas are consistent with the pattern of underwriting losses recently experienced nationwide by liability insurers.

The Litigation Revolution

As with jury verdicts, there are no comprehensive data for tort lawsuits filed in federal and state courts in the United States. The information that is available, however, suggests that the number of certain types of tort cases has risen sharply. This is to be expected, given the expansive functions for spreading loss that have been assigned the tort system by judges and juries.

It is clear, for example, that the volume of medical malpractice and

---

that median jury awards increased in both Cook County and San Francisco at a slower pace than average awards. The median inflation-adjusted medical malpractice and product liability awards in Cook County, for example, increased over the 1960–84 period by 245 percent and 82 percent, respectively; the corresponding increases for the average awards were 2,167 percent and 212 percent. Similarly, in San Francisco, median awards in the two types of cases advanced by 144 percent and 641 percent over the twenty-five-year period; the average awards ballooned by 830 and 1,016 percent.

8. George L. Priest, "The Current Insurance Crisis and Modern Tort Law," *Yale Law Journal,* vol. 96 (June 1987), pp. 1521–90.

9. Mark Peterson, Syam Sarma, and Michael Shanley, *Punitive Damages: Empirical Findings* (Rand Corp., Institute for Civil Justice, 1987), p. 15.

products liability cases filed in federal court have increased sharply. Between 1976 and 1985, filings in these categories roughly trebled, to more than 1,800 malpractice cases and 13,500 products liability lawsuits. A significant part of the increase in products liability claims has been the result of a sharp rise in the number of suits involving toxic torts (notably asbestos) and medical products.

Limited evidence suggests that tort filings in state courts have mirrored the trends at the federal level.[10] State court data for medical malpractice, for example, show a jump of 123 percent in cases filed between 1979 and 1983, to a nationwide total of more than 23,500. A similar trend—an increase of 141 percent—occurred during this period in claims filed against officials of municipal and county governments.[11]

Compensation through Tort Law: Blessing or Curse?

Even if more expansive liability doctrines and awards were not efficiently deterring accidents and injuries, they conceivably could be justified as means for filling gaps in existing compensation programs and devices. For example, even though medical insurance is available through medicare to all American citizens aged sixty-five and older and to more than 80 percent of younger Americans through private insurance or medicaid, more than 30 million people still remain uninsured for medical expenses at any given time, and perhaps more than 20 million are

10. Of the approximately 866,000 tort suits terminated in the United States in 1985, 827,000 were in state courts and only 39,000 in federal courts. James S. Kakalik and Nicholas M. Pace, *Costs and Compensation Paid in Tort Litigation* (Rand Corp., Institute for Civil Justice, 1986), p. 15.

11. *Report of the Tort Policy Working Group on the Causes, Extent and Policy Implications of the Current Crisis in Insurance Availability and Affordability* (Government Printing Office, 1986). The data cited in a recent report by the National Center for State Courts prove nothing to the contrary, in contrast to what some observers have claimed. See National Center for State Courts, *State Court Caseload Statistics: Annual Report, 1984* (Williamsburg, Va.: NCSC, 1986). According to this study, which surveyed court filings in thirteen states, the total number of all types of tort filings increased by only 9 percent between 1978 and 1984, or roughly the same rate as the general population (8 percent). But as the Tort Policy Working Group has pointed out, the National Center data do not include cases at all levels of state courts (California municipal court statistics, which show, for instance, much larger rates of increase, are excluded). In addition, the center's figures conceal the fact that suits involving automobile accidents, the cause of over half of all tort actions, have declined in recent years because of fewer accidents and the adoption of no-fault insurance in many states. See Tort Policy Working Group, *An Update on the Liability Crisis* (GPO, 1987), pp. 42–46.

uninsured throughout a given calendar year.[12] In addition, many of those with insurance have limited coverage, especially for the catastrophic medical expenses often associated with major tort litigations.[13]

Gaps also exist in programs designed to compensate for income losses, although it is likely that the coverage provided by public and private disability insurance programs has increased over time.[14] Workers' compensation statutes now in effect at the state level cover both medical and income losses due to disability, but only for occupationally related injuries. Furthermore, as Kip Viscusi shows in chapter 6, workers' compensation programs have infrequently covered losses caused by disease. The social security system provides disability benefits for medical or mental impairments from any cause, but only for those disabled longer than one year or if the condition can be expected to result in death. Moreover, although the average benefit of $30,000 (present discounted value) is substantial, it is far less than the compensation available for pain and suffering in many tort actions.[15] Finally, many employers provide disability insurance for their employees, but coverage is typically limited to only 50 to 60 percent of current earnings.

The merits of each of the purported justifications of recent trends in tort law, however, raise significant questions. While they have broadened the availability of compensation, more liberal liability doctrines and larger damage awards and settlements may have overdeterred, forcing socially worthwhile products, services, and activities to be curtailed, withdrawn from the market, or eliminated. Patricia Danzon discusses in chapter 4 the increasing reluctance of doctors, especially obstetricians, to offer medical services because of liability risks. Peter Huber in chapter 5 notes that all but two insurance carriers have withdrawn liability coverage for operators of hazardous waste facilities, forcing many to

12. Margaret B. Sulvetta and Katherine Swartz, *The Uninsured and Uncompensated Care* (Washington, D.C.: George Washington University National Health Policy Forum, June 1986), p. 3.

13. One leading study has found that at least a quarter of the nonelderly population— perhaps more than 50 million people—is inadequately protected against exposure to large medical bills. See Pamela J. Farley, "Who Are the Underinsured?" *Milbank Memorial Fund Quarterly/Health and Society,* vol. 63 (Summer 1985), p. 479.

14. Lawrence Summers and Chris Carroll, "Why Is U.S. National Saving So Low?" *Brookings Papers on Economic Activity,* 2:1987, pp. 607–35.

15. For average benefits see Jerry L. Mashaw, *Bureaucratic Justice: Managing Social Security Disability Claims* (Yale University Press, 1983), p. 18. Disability benefits under social security are also not well linked to previous earnings of the victim, nor are they provided to those who are only partially disabled.

shut down. Similarly, liability concerns reportedly have caused drug companies to reduce research and development of new vaccines.[16]

Meanwhile, there is little evidence that expanded tort liability has efficiently filled in the gaps left by the existing public and private network of compensation plans. In fact, as George Priest has persuasively argued, the trend toward compensation of noneconomic injury through the tort system may be *undermining* the compensation objective by inducing private insurers to withdraw coverage and to raise premiums at the expense of low-income consumers.[17] As noted earlier, the pain and suffering component of jury verdicts appears to account for much of the increase in personal injury awards, especially those in product liability and medical malpractice cases. But perhaps even more important, given the subjective nature of decisions to award these kinds of damages, is the uncertainty about the probable amount of the awards, which makes it increasingly difficult for liability insurers to write coverage profitably. Insurers have raised premiums for commercial lines to compensate for the increased risk, but as rates climb, lower-risk customers are finding it cheaper to self-insure. Liability insurers are therefore increasingly plagued with the problem of adverse selection—insuring only the poorest risks—which drives up premiums even further, and in extreme cases compels insurers to withdraw altogether from providing coverage.[18]

Finally, delivering compensation through the tort system is very expensive. According to the Institute for Civil Justice, the United States spent between $29 billion and $36 billion on tort litigation in 1985. Of this amount, only $14 billion to $16 billion, or less than half the total, was paid to plaintiffs as damage awards; the rest went to lawyers and court administrators.[19] Researchers at New York University, using a variety of methodologies, have arrived at similar estimates for administrative costs.[20]

Precisely because these transactions costs are so high, interest has grown in supplementing or replacing the tort system with alternative means of compensation. Most suggestions would place some sort of cap

16. Institute of Medicine, *Vaccine Supply and Innovation* (Washington, D.C.: National Academy Press, 1985).

17. See Priest, "Current Insurance Crisis and Modern Tort Law," pp. 1585–86.

18. Ibid., pp. 1563–90.

19. Kakalik and Pace, *Costs and Compensation Paid in Tort Litigation,* pp. ix–x.

20. Andrew Schotter and Janusz Ordover, "The Cost of the Tort System," unpublished paper (New York University, Starr Center for Applied Economics, March 1986).

on total compensation—especially for pain and suffering—in return for automatic eligibility. More ambitious proposals envision separate funds, financed by taxes on employees or employers or both, to pay compensation awarded to victims of medical malpractice or exposure to toxic substances.

But the discussions in this book conclude that the limited experience with alternative compensation programs in the United States has not been encouraging. The federal black lung program, for example, was established in 1969 to provide temporary compensation for an estimated 100,000 retired miners with pneumoconiosis, a disease caused by long exposure to coal dust. But just as some courts have liberalized the tort standard of causation, Congress broadened eligibility criteria under the black lung program in both 1972 and 1978. Accordingly, 542,000 miners, spouses, and dependents had received benefits under the program by the end of 1981.[21] Because of this experience, future proposals to establish compensation programs are unlikely to be given serious consideration by Congress or state legislatures unless they are accompanied by convincing demonstrations that their costs can be contained.

Outline of the Book and Key Conclusions

The balance of this book addresses the issues raised above in greater detail and depth. In the next chapter, John Calfee and Clifford Winston set forth a methodological framework for evaluating the debate over the current liability system. They explain formally why the objectives of efficient deterrence and compensation may conflict and therefore why no liability rule or policy can achieve both goals.

Scott Harrington follows in chapter 3 with a detailed examination of the performance and behavior of the property and casualty insurance industry. Concentrating on the first half of the 1980s, he finds that increases in premiums and cutbacks in coverage reflect a sharp rise in losses.

Chapters 4 through 7 document the trends toward liberalized liability and rising damage awards in the specific areas of tort law in which the insurance crisis has been most pronounced: medical malpractice (Patricia Danzon), environmental liability (Peter Huber), occupational liabil-

---

21. John S. Lopatto, "The Federal Black Lung Program: A 1983 Primer," *West Virginia Law Review*, vol. 85, no. 4 (1983), pp. 677–78.

ity (Kip Viscusi), and products liability (George Priest). These chapters demonstrate how, in moving toward broader compensation, the tort system has affected the medical system, the environment, the workplace, and the development of products.

In the concluding chapter, Robert Litan and Clifford Winston summarize the policy recommendations made in each of the previous chapters. First, given Harrington's findings that property and casualty insurance markets have simply reflected underlying trends in the civil liability system, they find that calls for stiffer regulation of the insurance industry would accomplish very little and by inducing insurers to withdraw coverage would likely be counterproductive. Second, tort law would more efficiently deter undesirable behavior if judges encouraged juries, in deciding which parties should bear the loss of accidents, to balance the costs and benefits of the behavior of both plaintiffs and defendants. Third, much of the uncertainty about the size of damage awards could be removed if schedules were established for pain and suffering that base recoveries on the age of the injured party and the severity of the injury. Finally, given the limited data available, we simply know too little about the total costs and benefits of the current liability system to be confident that any radical change—in particular, replacing the tort system with a government-administered compensation program—would produce benefits to society that would outweigh the costs.

CHAPTER TWO

Economic Aspects of Liability Rules and Liability Insurance

John E. Calfee and Clifford Winston

T HE U.S. liability system may be seen as an attempt to use one mechanism, a payment for damages, to perform two functions: providing an incentive to prevent injury and compensating for injury (insurance). Using this mechanism for both tasks may succeed if all information on risks to be insured against is available to producers and buyers. But a primary reason for having liability rules is to offset a lack of information about risk. Information can be imperfect in many ways. Consumers may misperceive risks. Insurers cannot prevent moral hazard, the tendency for those who are insured to become careless because they know they are insured. Insurers are also subject to adverse selection, the tendency at given rates for high-risk individuals or groups to buy more coverage than low-risk individuals or groups, thus exposing insurers to much higher payouts per policy. Finally, courts cannot know appropriate levels of precaution and producers often do not know what constitutes appropriate standards of due care. In these situations the means for achieving the two goals of compensation and prevention tend to diverge: what works well for achieving one goal will work poorly for achieving the other. We argue that no liability rule or policy can optimally handle both compensation for and deterrence of injury under the conditions encountered in most economic environments.

A Simple Model of Liability

An easy way to see the commonality of many of the problems discussed in this book is to work with a model of liability and insurance. The model simplifies various complex issues that arise in actual liability disputes, but still reveals the major difficulties in applying liability rules and provides a framework for understanding the primary issues discussed in the chapters that follow. The model and its results are summarized in a nontechnical manner in the text and stated mathematically in the appendix.

In the section that follows we apply our model to various standards of liability. We seek to determine the conditions under which each of these rules meets the objectives of both deterrence and compensation for each of the types of losses that injuries may produce. For convenience our discussion focuses on injuries resulting from defective products. However, the results are easily generalized to injuries resulting from services such as medical care and to such other activities as handling hazardous materials.

The analysis considers three types of losses individuals may suffer when an injury occurs: *monetary losses,* which deprive the victim of money or income; *pure nonmonetary losses,* such as pain and suffering not explicitly valued in the marketplace; and *changes in the marginal utility of income or money,* which may occur if an injury renders some activities impossible—driving a car, for example—or, at its most serious, restricts individual mobility completely.[1]

Nonmonetary or noneconomic losses roughly correspond to those described by the term "pain and suffering." If no nonmonetary damages are involved and injured parties can reasonably be assumed risk-neutral toward monetary losses (that is, indifferent as to whether a payout is certain or only expected from a gamble), there is no need to consider marginal utility of income or money at all, and the analysis can proceed in terms of dollar losses and gains.[2] Many analyses of the economic effects of liability rules work this way.[3] But some of the most troublesome aspects of prod-

1. For a theoretical exposition of the distinction between monetary and nonmonetary commodities (also called nonpecuniary or irreplaceable commodities) see Philip J. Cook and Daniel A. Graham, "The Demand for Insurance and Protection: The Case of Irreplaceable Commodities," *Quarterly Journal of Economics,* vol. 91 (February 1977), pp. 143–56.

2. William M. Landes and Richard A. Posner, "A Positive Economic Analysis of Products Liability," *Journal of Legal Studies,* vol. 14 (December 1985), p. 536, argue that liability rules can reasonably be analyzed while assuming risk-neutrality. The term risk-aversion usually refers to a willingness to pay a premium for insurance against monetary losses. Michael Spence, "Consumer Misperceptions, Product Failure and Producer Liability," *Review of Economic Studies,* vol. 44 (October 1977), pp. 561–72, uses the term to cover situations in which there are nonmonetary losses, regardless of whether consumers would wish to insure against such losses.

3. See, for instance, John Prather Brown, "Toward an Economic Theory of Liability," *Journal of Legal Studies,* vol. 2 (June 1973), pp. 323–49; Steven Shavell, "Strict Liability versus Negligence," *Journal of Legal Studies,* vol. 9 (January 1980), pp. 1–25; William M. Landes and Richard A. Posner, "The Positive Economic Theory of Tort Law," *Georgia*

ucts liability and the liability insurance crisis stem from treatment of nonmonetary losses. As the discussion will show, the presence of nonmonetary losses tends to place a wedge between the two basic goals of compensation and deterrence and strongly affects the relations between such alternative bases for standards as the doctrines of strict liability and negligence.[4]

In essence, the model developed and used in this chapter determines conditions that characterize optimal levels of safety (deterrence or prevention) and compensation for injury, thus enabling one to assess whether these conditions are satisfied by particular liability standards. Optimal levels of deterrence and compensation maximize social welfare, which is dependent on consumers' expected utility from goods and services and producers' competitive profit. The concept of social welfare could be expanded to include the necessity for social justice and compensation for the costs of litigation (transactions costs), but doing so would not change the basic problems.

We emphasize, however, that the model contains a number of simplifying assumptions. We usually assume that prevention efforts affect only the occurrence of injury, not its extent and nature, and that only producers of products, not those who are at risk of injury, are able to affect the probability of loss. For the time being we assume insurance is available at cost, by which we mean that insurance paying a given amount in case of injury is available for an actuarially fair premium. We usually assume there are no administrative costs for compensating victims and no problems of adverse selection and moral hazard in the insurance market. But we point out where these assumptions are likely to fail and the resulting implications. We do not model the problem of scope of liability, an issue that arises when many factors combine to cause injury, but do note where the model can be extended to treat this problem. We also ignore the possibility that potential injurers and victims can write contracts to bypass the liability system. Finally, an important aspect of the liability system not modeled is the informational requirements of the legal system. Again, where it is relevant, we note the implications of the model for informa-

Law Review, vol. 15 (Summer 1981), pp. 851–924; and Landes and Posner, "Positive Economic Analysis of Products Liability."

4. This is discussed in the context of workmen's compensation by Samuel A. Rea, *Disability Insurance and Public Policy* (University of Toronto Press, 1981); and Rea, "Nonpecuniary Loss and Breach of Contract," *Journal of Legal Studies,* vol. 11 (January 1982), pp. 35–53.

tional and other demands on the liability system. If these issues were considered in the model, the difficulties of achieving both appropriate deterrence and compensation would be exacerbated.

Liability Rules

Liability standards provide guidance for courts to evaluate the legality of the behavior of litigants when defendants are claimed to have inflicted some type of damage on plaintiffs. The standards that have been applied in the United States are first-party liability, strict liability, and negligence.

First-Party Liability

A first-party liability rule makes injured parties responsible for their losses unless producers voluntarily provide compensation. The efficiency of first-party liability depends greatly on the extent to which consumers are aware of the risks inherent in using a given product, that is, on the information available to them.

MONETARY LOSSES. Suppose there are no nonmonetary losses and that consumers know both the probability that products fail when properly used and the monetary losses such failures will cause. Economic theory suggests that producers operating in a competitive market will take actions to prevent injuries and will provide compensation at levels that maximize consumers' expected utility, that is, consumers' preferred trade-off between compensation, price, and risk, subject to normal profits.[5] Alternatively, if producers do not offer compensation, buyers will purchase insurance from third parties that will yield a level of compensation equal to that which producers should have provided.

As shown mathematically in the appendix, appropriate compensation will be achieved when consumers use insurance, either voluntarily supplied with the product or sold separately by third parties, to transfer income between situations in which a loss occurs and those in which no loss occurs in order to equalize the rates at which income provides satisfaction in each situation.[6] This condition is met when consumers are fully insured

---

5. More precisely, producers will maximize consumer utility subject to a profit constraint or other constraints that may involve nonmonetary factors. See Patricia M. Danzon, "Tort Reform and the Role of Government in Private Insurance Markets," *Journal of Legal Studies,* vol. 13 (August 1984), pp. 517–49; and the appendix to this chapter.

6. If the price of insurance includes a premium to cover insurers' costs, as all insurance

against monetary losses. Producers in a fully competitive market of informed consumers will also adjust the level of product safety or precaution to maximize consumer utility. As demonstrated in the appendix, this occurs when the marginal cost of prevention is equated with the marginal benefit of prevention.[7]

In short, when consumers know the probability of loss, first-party liability should efficiently handle both prevention of and compensation for injury.

Several conditions may disturb this efficiency, however. Producers' compensation plans could suffer from adverse selection—too many high-risk consumers—and, if potential victims can affect the probability or magnitude of loss, compensation plans could encounter moral hazard—too much consumer carelessness in using the product. The result in either instance could be that inadequate compensation would be provided for injuries caused by the product. These problems may be mitigated if consumers can buy insurance instead of using the liability system for insurance. In principle, insurers are likely to have greater ability and experience in providing compensation, and thus exhibit greater efficiency in satisfying consumers. Nevertheless, first-party insurance will produce efficient incentives for purchasers to take proper precautions only if the premiums charged are explicitly linked to purchases of the risky products. Yet in practice, first-party insurance policies such as medical insurance typically cover numerous products and events at the same time; the insurance covers its purchasers, not specific products or activities. Imperfections of this sort keep market prices from providing consumers an incentive to shop for safer products. How, after all, can a consumer distinguish potential differences in levels of risk for two products that perform the same function if insurance costs for using them are the same?

When consumers are unaware of the risks, the market will behave imperfectly in several ways, and first-party liability clearly is not an efficient rule. Producers have no incentive to offer compensation or incur prevention costs for risks that consumers do not perceive. Thus for most risky products the price will be too low and the product itself will be

---

does, consumers will purchase less than the amount of insurance necessary to equalize marginal satisfaction from income between situations of injury and no injury; see Danzon, "Tort Reform," appendix A. If consumers are not risk-averse—that is, if the utility of wealth is simply proportional to wealth so that the marginal utility of wealth is a constant—then consumers will have no reason to purchase insurance even if it is priced at an actuarially fair level.

7. See Brown, "Toward an Economic Theory of Liability."

consumed in larger than optimal quantities. But if the product actually reduces risk from its "natural" state (obstetrical services, for example, reduce risks for both mother and infant), the absence of liability does not necessarily lead to overconsumption of the product. Appropriate levels of consumption depend on the perceived reduction in risk.[8]

Consumers may be aware that a risk exists, but their perceptions of its magnitude or duration may be inaccurate. In such a situation their marginal utility of income before and after an injury will not be equal even after the purchase of insurance (see the appendix). In particular, if consumers underestimate risk, producers will provide insufficient compensation. The effect of underestimating risk on prevention depends on how perceptions change in response to reductions in risk from product improvement. On the whole, consumers' underestimation of risk probably leads producers to underinvest in risk reduction (see the appendix).

Again, the effect of imperfect consumer information on price and consumption depends partly on whether the product does itself reduce risks. Risky products are likely to have a price that is too low and therefore will be overconsumed. If the risky product itself reduces risk (again, as in the case of obstetrical services), price and consumption depend on the perceived reduction in risk, and the product might not be overconsumed.

NONMONETARY LOSSES. Nonmonetary losses occur when an injury affects a victim's utility for wealth in such a way that the same level of income does not produce the same level of satisfaction as before the loss. The effects of the availability of consumer information on the efficiency of first-party liability are qualitatively the same for nonmonetary losses as they are when only monetary losses are involved.

Again, consider the situation in which consumers are fully informed of the risks entailed in using a product. The possibility of nonmonetary losses makes it difficult to know the appropriate level of insurance or precaution. This difficulty is not a market imperfection, however, because the parties involved have an incentive to determine appropriate precautions without external rules. Consumers will attempt to purchase what is for them optimal insurance, and producers will compete to meet consumers' demands for the optimal level of prevention.

Nevertheless, the potential for nonmonetary losses poses special problems even when consumers and producers know the risks. One problem is the asymmetry of information: consumers may have reasonably certain

8. See John E. Calfee and Paul H. Rubin, "Liability for Reducing Risk," paper presented at the 1987 annual meeting of the Western Economic Association.

knowledge about the magnitude of their nonmonetary losses if they are injured, but producers may be far less certain and thus make inappropriate investments in prevention.[9] To the extent that nonmonetary losses are insured, the problems of adverse selection and moral hazard are more difficult to assess. When losses are primarily nonmonetary and the marginal utility of wealth is unaffected, little insurance is desired, as when pain and suffering follow necessary surgery. But if the nonmonetary loss increases the marginal utility of wealth, as when the loss requires major expenses just to achieve a normal life, a large amount of insurance may be sought. Then the informational requirements could be particularly difficult for insurers to meet, simply because of the tenuous nature of the loss and the possibility that consumers will overinsure.

Now suppose consumers are not aware of product failure rates. The implications for the desirability of first-party liability are complex but qualitatively similar to those for monetary losses. Again, producers will not incur prevention costs and will not pay compensation, and consumers will underinsure. Product prices will be too low because all the costs of using products will not be reflected in their prices, and most products will be consumed in larger than optimal quantities. Again, however, this result is not necessarily true for products that reduce risks.[10] If consumers are aware that a risk exists, but their perceptions are inaccurate, the effect on the level of prevention undertaken by producers again depends on the marginal relation between actual and perceived risk (see the appendix).

SOLUTIONS TO THE INFORMATION PROBLEM. The problems posed by imperfect consumer information could in principle be solved by having the government provide all relevant information.[11] But this would require that vast quantities of highly dispersed information be centralized, maintained, and distributed in a timely fashion. An alternative would be to require producers to provide risk information, perhaps through warnings on product labels and in product advertising. This would not eliminate the need for governmental collection of information, however, because the nature

9. Problems also arise when a heterogeneous body of consumers is considered. See Jerry Green, "On the Optimal Structure of Liability Laws," *Bell Journal of Economics,* vol. 7 (Autumn 1976), pp. 553–74.

10. With products that reduce risks, consumers will underinsure. But the degree of underinsurance could be less than when consumers forego use of the product, assuming that they do not accurately assess the risk they face if they do not use the product. See Calfee and Rubin, "Liability for Reducing Risk."

11. See W. Kip Viscusi, Wesley A. Magat, and Joel Huber, "Informational Regulation of Consumer Health Risks: An Empirical Evaluation of Hazard Warnings," *Rand Journal of Economics,* vol. 17 (Autumn 1986), pp. 351–65.

and amount of risk information provided by producers would have to be monitored.[12] Hence the main justification for imposing a liability rule on the market is that consumers lack information and find it costly to negotiate for its provision.

Strict Liability

The second rule of the liability system, strict liability, is the opposite of first-party liability in that it requires the producer to compensate a victim for all losses caused by the producer's conduct, regardless of the steps the producer has taken to prevent accidents. When injuries cause only monetary losses, strict liability is theoretically the optimal rule, although its efficiency may be compromised by market imperfections such as moral hazard and adverse selection. When injuries cause nonmonetary losses, however, strict liability will usually have the effect of requiring consumers to pay for more than their desired level of insurance. This can substantially increase the price of a product and have adverse effects on consumer choices among products.

MONETARY LOSSES. If a consumer's potential losses are exclusively monetary, a strict liability standard in effect requires producers to sell insurance against failure when they sell their products. Analytically, the situation is identical to first-party liability except that compensation is provided by the producer rather than by a third party (see the appendix). The producers absorb all costs and therefore will minimize expected losses from consumer injuries by taking optimal measures to prevent accidents and by purchasing appropriate insurance.[13] If the classic insurance problems of moral hazard and adverse selection do not arise, product prices will correctly reflect risk and the quantity purchased will be appropriate.

Beneath the superficial similarities between first-party liability and strict liability for monetary losses, however, there are significant differences. Informational requirements are more narrowly focused under strict liability. Only the producer (and the liability insurer, if any) must know the level of risk; consumers may remain uninformed. But the amounts and kinds of information needed by producers can be significant. This can be seen by looking at the insurance aspect of liability. Under strict liability, insurance classes are necessarily based on specific

---

12. If information provided by producers is not monitored except when injuries occur, the effect is much like that induced by a liability standard.
13. Brown, "Toward an Economic Theory of Liability."

products or activities rather than on specific types of consumers. For example, all users of home swimming pools, careful and careless alike, would form a single insurance class under a rule that made swimming pool manufacturers and installers strictly liable for all injuries suffered by pool users. This could frustrate insurers' attempts to take account of adverse selection and moral hazard, which are likely to arise if consumers can affect the size or probability of loss.[14] This involuntary formation of insurance classes could also have adverse effects when consumers have diverse tastes and incomes. In particular, strict liability generally requires poorer consumers to subsidize insurance for the well-off because they pay the same amount for the product but wealthier people will collect larger damage payments.[15]

Finally, and perhaps most importantly, the efficiency of strict liability in preventing and compensating injury critically depends on whether the scope of liability can be limited when there are multiple possible causes of injury, as there could be in cases involving long-term illnesses such as cancer. The key issue is whether liability efficiently encourages the incentive to reduce the probability of loss. If the injurer could not efficiently have taken precautions to reduce risk, it makes little sense to argue that he should nonetheless be held liable because he "caused" the loss.[16]

NONMONETARY LOSSES. Now suppose injury involves a nonmonetary loss for which the product's producer must also provide compensation. An immediate problem is the size of the payment. Nonmonetary damages by definition have no obvious monetary equivalent, and thus it is

14. See Richard A. Epstein, "The Legal and Insurance Dynamics of Mass Tort Litigation," *Journal of Legal Studies,* vol. 13 (August 1984), pp. 475–506; Epstein, "Products Liability as an Insurance Market," *Journal of Legal Studies,* vol. 14 (December 1985), pp. 645–69; and George L. Priest, "The Current Insurance Crisis and Modern Tort Law," *Yale Law Journal,* vol. 96 (June 1987), pp. 1521–90.

15. Priest, "Current Insurance Crisis," pp. 1559–60.

16. See Steven Shavell, "An Analysis of Causation and the Scope of Liability in the Law of Torts," *Journal of Legal Studies,* vol. 9 (June 1980), pp. 463–516; Shavell, "Uncertainty over Causation and the Determination of Civil Liability," *Journal of Law and Economics,* vol. 28 (October 1985), pp. 587–609; William M. Landes and Richard A. Posner, "Causation in Tort Law: An Economic Approach," *Journal of Legal Studies,* vol. 12 (January 1983), pp. 109–34; and Robert Cooter, "Prices and Sanctions," *Columbia Law Review,* vol. 84 (October 1984), pp. 1523–60. On proposals to limit liability in accordance with the probability of causation, see Naomi Sheiner, "Comment: DES and a Proposed Theory of Enterprise Liability," *Fordham Law Review,* vol. 46 (April 1978), pp. 963–1007; and David Rosenberg, "The Causal Connection in Mass Exposure Cases: A 'Public Law' Vision of the Tort System," *Harvard Law Review,* vol. 97 (February 1984), p. 851.

not clear how the courts can measure them. Surprisingly, this problem has largely been ignored in the relevant literature. A reasonable approach would be that courts would assess damages equal to the sum of two factors: the greatest amount the victim would have paid to avoid the injury (given that compensation will be paid for monetary loss) plus desired compensation, which is the amount of insurance the consumer would willingly have purchased to compensate for an injury that occurs despite precautions. Requiring the producer to pay this amount would make certain that he is treating potential consumer losses as if they were his own and thus would provide the appropriate incentive for preventing them (see the appendix).[17]

Such an approach entails two problems, however. The first relates to insurance. Compensation to be paid in event of injury is essentially an insurance policy that applies only if the injury occurs. Under a strict liability rule, a premium for this insurance will be reflected in the product price, which also includes costs of production and injury prevention. But the insurance a producer provides under a rule of strict liability will exceed the desired level by the amount that a typical consumer would be willing to pay for prevention, an amount that could be quite large. Although the extra insurance will be worth something, it will be worth less to many consumers than the premium producers pay and pass on to all consumers.

The second, and related, problem is that this overinsurance will make product prices too high. Prices will have three components: costs of production (including costs of prevention), a premium for desired insurance, and a premium for the undesired insurance payout for nonmonetary losses that is set equal to the amount consumers would have paid toward prevention. Optimal amounts of the products will not be purchased. Moreover, faced with the possibility of paying out this extra insurance, producers will further increase prevention activities, and necessarily their attendant costs, which will increase prices still further beyond the efficient level.

A number of analyses have nevertheless argued that strict liability could retain the producer's incentive to prevent injuries without requiring buyers to pay prices that include the unwanted insurance premium.[18]

---

17. Spence, "Consumer Misperceptions," p. 566.

18. Ibid. Spence points out that if consumer perceptions of risk are taken into account, the optimal fine may be less than the amount consumers would be willing to pay toward prevention, because awareness of risk provides some incentive for them to prevent accidents.

They propose that damages actually paid to victims consist only of the desired insurance payout, while the amount consumers have in effect paid toward prevention be paid as a fine to the state, with the fine used to subsidize the product price. Although some nonliability enforcement systems resemble this approach, the courts have not operated in this way for ordinary tort cases.[19] Currently, courts appear to award damages that include both the insurance payout and a penalty levied against the producer to compensate for pain and suffering.

There is no reason to think this two-part proposal will produce an appropriate price, either. If the undesired insurance premium is not included in the price of the product, the price will not reflect the risk of using the product. In this sense the price will be too low. There is no known solution to this problem. For products that reduce risk, however, the lower price brought about by the two-part arrangement is not necessarily bad, because this price may accurately reflect the fact that using the product is less risky than not using it.[20]

Negligence

A third liability rule, the negligence standard, requires producers who fail to achieve a prescribed level of prevention to compensate victims for all losses. Because it requires additional information to assess the required level of prevention and does not yield a price that reflects risk, the negligence standard is theoretically inferior to strict liability when injuries cause only monetary losses. But when injuries also cause nonmonetary damages, the negligence standard tends to avoid the involuntary overinsurance associated with strict liability.

MONETARY LOSSES. Under a negligence standard, courts determine whether the performance of the product or service at issue violates a standard of due care. If a defendant fails to take due care, he must compensate the victim for losses; otherwise, losses are borne by the victim. If the due care standard is set at the optimal level, producers have an incentive to take optimal safety precautions because they know that if they fail to do so they must absorb potential losses by victims. Thus producers that take optimal precautions but do nothing further will not be negligent and will pay no compensation.[21] This result must

19. An example of such a nonliability system would be one with regulations that use fines to support a government agency providing subsidized services to the industry.
20. Calfee and Rubin, "Liability for Reducing Risk."
21. Brown, "Toward an Economic Theory of Liability."

be modified, however, when there is uncertainty about the level of prevention required. Risk-neutral producers who are uncertain about what constitutes due care in a given situation are likely to spend more on prevention than consumers would wish to pay.[22]

If consumers are aware of the risks, they will secure desired levels of compensation by purchasing insurance from third parties. As a result the product price, if perceived as including the insurance premium, represents full social costs and leads to correct levels of output. As noted earlier, however, consumers normally purchase products separately from insurance. This reduces the ability of insurance to promote efficiency.

If consumers are unaware of the risks they run in using a product, producers will undertake optimal injury-prevention measures anyway because they will still be required to meet the due care standard. But uninformed consumers will underinsure and thus overconsume the product because the perceived price will not include a reserve for risk.[23] (Consumers' lack of information, it will be recalled, does not affect economic efficiency under a strict liability standard for monetary damages.) At the same time, however, a negligence rule is more effective than a strict liability rule in delineating the scope of liability. Enforcing a negligence rule requires courts to assess the optimal precaution level in terms of the effect of prevention on the probability of failure, and such an inquiry necessarily asks whether the producer was in a position to reduce the probability of failure. In contrast, a strict liability rule focuses on the consequences of the injury and pays little attention to the marginal costs and benefits of prevention efforts by the manufacturer.

A negligence rule also has specific implications for the informational requirements of courts and insurers. Courts must assess the appropriate degree of precaution, which requires information on consumer losses and the costs of prevention. But this information is required by courts only when injury occurs and is litigated. With a well-functioning negligence rule, most producers are not negligent and are not involved in litigation.[24] Informational problems such as adverse selection may arise

---

22. Richard Craswell and John E. Calfee, "Deterrence and Uncertain Legal Standards," *Journal of Law, Economics, and Organization*, vol. 2 (Fall 1986), pp. 279–303; and Steven Shavell, *Economic Analysis of Accident Law* (Harvard University Press, 1987), ch. 4.

23. Shavell, "Strict Liability versus Negligence," p. 4.

24. This suggests that comparing the costs of operating a liability system based on negligence with compensation actually paid to victims provides a misleading estimate of the efficiency of the tort system. Most benefits of the system are unobserved precautions taken by producers and unobserved third-party insurance payments to consumers.

in connection with insurance but are dealt with primarily by insurance companies rather than by non-negligent producers, who do not provide compensation.

Finally, if potential victims can affect the probability of loss, the negligence standard can become prey to careless consumers unless the due care standard takes account of appropriate precautions by consumers. Traditionally, most courts have taken account of precautions through the contributory negligence rule, which bars plaintiffs from recovering any compensation if they have not exercised due care in using a product. More recently, a number of courts have turned to a comparative negligence standard, which requires them to consider the behavior of both plaintiff and defendant and to award damages on the basis of how well the plaintiff observed due care standards in comparison with how well the defendant observed them.[25]

NONMONETARY LOSSES. A negligence standard tends to avoid consumers' overinsurance for nonmonetary losses, the most severe problem of strict liability.[26] If due care is set at the optimal level and the penalty for violations includes both compensation for monetary losses and a pain and suffering award equal to what consumers would have paid to prevent the injury, producers will have an incentive to take optimal precautions and, having met the due care standard, will not be found negligent. Because compensation is not actually paid, consumers are not forced to purchase more than the desired level of insurance.

But as with monetary losses, the extent to which the negligence rule promotes efficiency in the context of nonmonetary losses may change if producers are uncertain about what constitutes due care. Indeed, uncertainty could make the negligence rule highly inefficient because potentially large damage awards for pain and suffering caused by negligence can easily lead to expensive overcompliance with the standards on the part of producers. This potential for overcompliance could explain why the law sometimes uses a gross negligence standard, under which producers are liable only if their safety precautions fall far short of the

---

25. On contributory negligence, see Brown, "Toward an Economic Theory of Liability"; and George B. Assaf, "The Shape of Reaction Functions and the Efficiency of Liability Rules: A Correction," *Journal of Legal Studies,* vol. 13 (January 1984), pp. 101–11. David Haddock and Christopher Curran, "An Economic Theory of Comparative Negligence," *Journal of Legal Studies,* vol. 14 (January 1985), pp. 49–72, provide a recent analysis that includes a discussion of comparative negligence. None of these analyses take nonmonetary damages into account.

26. As noted earlier, strict liability for nonmonetary losses also encourages overinvestment in precautions.

Table 2-1. *Effects of Liability Rules under Simple Market Conditions*

Liability standard	Perfect consumer information	Imperfect consumer information
First-party liability		
Monetary losses	Optimal prevention Fully self-insure Appropriate price	Nonoptimal prevention Too little compensation Price too low
Nonmonetary losses	Optimal prevention Optimal self-insurance Appropriate price	Nonoptimal prevention Too little compensation Price too low
Strict liability		
Monetary losses	Optimal prevention Full compensation Appropriate price	Optimal prevention Full compensation Appropriate price
Nonmonetary losses	Too much prevention Involuntary overinsurance Price too high	Too much prevention Involuntary overinsurance Price does not reflect risk
Negligence		
Monetary losses	Optimal prevention Fully self-insure Appropriate price	Optimal prevention Too little insurance Price too low
Nonmonetary losses	Optimal prevention Optimal self-insurance Appropriate price	Optimal prevention Too little insurance Price does not reflect risk

optimal level. If there is producer uncertainty about due care, replacing a negligence standard with a gross negligence standard may increase social welfare.[27]

Consumers aware of risk can presumably obtain a desired level of protection through third-party insurance. If consumers are unaware of risk, market failures parallel those already described: consumers do not purchase levels of insurance they would otherwise want and, because the perceived price of a product does not include a risk reserve, the product will be produced in larger than optimal quantities. Again, products that reduce risk may be an exception because they are not necessarily overconsumed even if sold at a price that does not reflect risk.

Summary

This theoretical discussion has omitted much that would make the analysis more realistic. The analysis assumes, among other things, that

---

27. On uncertainty and the standard of gross negligence, see Craswell and Calfee, "Deterrence and Uncertain Legal Standards," pp. 284–85.

most informational problems are solved, that liability rules are well established in advance and are not rewritten by the courts or legislatures, and that juries look dispassionately at costs and benefits. But even in this intellectually streamlined world where problems should be far more manageable than in actual practice, fundamental problems arise. Rules of negligence and strict liability are both likely to operate imperfectly and may not even improve upon first-party liability. Table 2-1 summarizes the basic findings from our analysis.

Liability Theory and Liability Issues

The theory of liability rules is useful for illuminating aspects of liability law that are of major concern, including injuries attributable to malpractice, hazardous substances, occupational accidents, and unsafe products. In particular, the following discussion analyzes the potential inefficiencies associated with the current liability system and identifies the issues that require resolution before alternative policies can be confidently advanced. These issues are given further attention in the remainder of this book.

Professional Malpractice

As Patricia Danzon shows in chapter 4, liability claims of malpractice by physicians and other professionals have increased substantially in recent years. Although negligence is the predominant standard, strict liability has also been applied in particular situations. Available evidence suggests that neither rule has been especially effective in providing appropriate compensation and deterrence because the key problems that arise in malpractice are ones these rules are not well equipped to handle.

In situations that could lead to malpractice, consumers are frequently unaware of risks and producers are uncertain about appropriate levels of care. Imperfect information poses problems for negligence rules that can result in too many precautions taken or too many services—tests, consultations, operations—provided or both. Moreover, a large proportion of the claims that arise from alleged malpractice involve nonmonetary damages, which, as the theoretical discussion indicated, present problems for strict liability that also result in too much precaution and excessive involuntary insurance. These responses in turn raise the costs and price of professional care and could ultimately cause physicians to withdraw useful services.[28]

Given the problems with both rules, how do we determine which is better or whether an alternative is needed? Danzon's chapter identifies the difficulties in evaluating the benefits of the current malpractice system and in identifying superior alternatives. The chapter makes a point particularly important for the discussion here: the goals of compensation and deterrence should be separated, with modifications in the system made to satisfy each goal independently.

Optimal deterrence and compensation in connection with nonmonetary damages require accurate estimates of potential victims' willingness to pay to prevent injury. These estimates are difficult to obtain in practice, and current rules have generated levels of compensation that are probably nowhere near the theoretical ideal. Thus reforms in setting damages must be made directly. Danzon suggests that awards for pain and suffering be scheduled according to the severity of the injury and the age of the victim. A rule of liability based on fault could then be used to reduce uncertainty about risk and encourage an efficient level of care.

Toxic Torts

In chapter 5 Peter Huber documents the significant expansion in recent years of liability suits that involve hazardous materials, so-called toxic torts. This expansion raises several issues. What is the appropriate scope of liability? What effect did the defendant's actions have on the probability of loss? What are appropriate monetary and nonmonetary damage payments?

The courts have been inclined to apply a rule of strict liability in dealing with environmental hazards caused by producers. Theory indicates, however, that this rule does not effectively delineate the scope of liability, which leads to excessive precaution or the abandonment of risky activities (even those that reduce risk) because of the unavailability of insurance at a price that producers and ultimately consumers are willing to pay.

A negligence rule has an advantage over strict liability because prac-

---

28. These distortions could have particularly deleterious effects in the market for risky products that reduce risk. See Calfee and Rubin, "Liability for Reducing Risk."

tical application of a negligence standard tends to pin down the scope of liability. If courts must assess the effects of producers' investments in preventive measures on the likelihood of creating an environmental hazard, then the courts will also determine whether the producers were in a position to reduce the likelihood of a hazard. Thus a standard of negligence probably comes closer than one of strict liability to providing optimal deterrence. In addition, a negligence standard avoids involuntary overinsurance for nonmonetary losses.

Neither, however, is likely to provide optimal compensation in the circumstances in which toxic tort suits typically arise. As Huber's chapter emphasizes, there are serious ambiguities involved in linking exposure to a hazard, especially exposure long in the past, with a plaintiff's current disease or injury. Obviously, optimal compensation requires that this issue be resolved. Liability rules in and of themselves cannot effectively contribute to this resolution.

Occupational Accidents

Liability in the workplace, discussed by Kip Viscusi in chapter 6, provides an interesting comparison with other areas of liability. After controlling for wage adjustments, the employers' cost of workers' compensation has remained fairly stable during the past several years, suggesting that current rules may do an adequate job of providing compensation and deterrence.

Compensation for job-related accidents is determined by a payment schedule set in advance. This is a form of strict liability that operates largely outside the civil liability system. Because workers' compensation programs reimburse victims only for monetary damages and because they require considerably less information than negligence-based adjudications, it is theoretically plausible that such programs could provide optimal compensation. Indeed, Viscusi shows that the workers' compensation system has provided accident benefits at close to the optimal level in recent years. As is the case with compensation for injury from environmental hazards, however, compensation for health hazards in the workplace remains controversial because cause and effect is difficult to establish.

In addition, the workers' compensation system does not provide incentives for employers and workers to take optimal precautions against accidents because the system has never been truly based on data that reflect incidence of injuries by job category or type of employer. As a result, some combination of market forces (workers' underlying preference for degrees of risk), direct government regulation, and the residual deterrent effects of workers' compensation is needed to ensure adequate levels of safety.

Products Liability

The recent surge in products liability suits, documented by George Priest in chapter 7, can be attributed mostly to the broadening of the scope of liability and the shift from a negligence standard to one of strict liability. These changes have led not only to spectacular compensation awards but possibly also to serious inefficiencies in products markets.

Products liability law should be designed so that, at minimum cost to society, the law effectively deters the introduction of unsafe products into the marketplace, moderates the risk associated with the use of marketable products, and provides optimal compensation to consumers who are injured by such products. Theory, however, predicts that a standard of strict liability will lead to excessive compensation, especially for nonmonetary damages, and excessive involuntary insurance, in turn distorting market prices according to the likelihood of injury from product use. If the expected liability cost is too high, products may simply be withdrawn or never introduced.

As Priest notes, economic distortions created by current policy can be reduced by applying a negligence standard based on cost-benefit principles.[29] Such an action would place some reasonable bounds on the scope of liability standards and curb excessive awards for nonmonetary damages, but at the cost of increasing the informational requirements of litigation.[30] If strict liability for products is favored, however, it should probably resemble the workplace liability system by limiting scope and establishing damage schedules, while using means other than torts to encourage optimal safety.

Insurance Industry Performance

This overview of liability theory can also shed light on the insurance industry's financial performance. The recent slump in earnings and increase in premiums can be partly attributed to the cyclical nature of the

29. Priest points out that the negligence standard that applied before 1965 did not correspond to the cost-benefit approach associated with the negligence standard in theory.

30. When nonmonetary damages are involved, however, even strict liability imposes formidable information requirements on the courts.

industry's investment returns, but liability rules also affect industry performance. The adoption of strict liability standards and the enlarged scope of liability in many areas have led to higher premiums. As Scott Harrington warns in chapter 3, if changes are unanticipated, the industry suffers losses before premiums can be adjusted. In such an environment the problems of adverse selection and moral hazard can lead to the elimination of coverage.

Given the insurance industry's strong cyclical pattern of earnings, a stable liability system is necessary for adequate performance. The recent trends in the liability system identified in the introductory chapter have not provided this stability.

Final Comments

Our theoretical analysis has identified the strengths and weaknesses of various liability standards under well-specified conditions. We can see why applications of these rules, and variants of them, in practice have created inefficiencies. The institutional complexities of liability issues, the critical departures from theoretical conditions that are needed for analytical tractability, and the absence of essential empirical information unfortunately make it impossible to provide definitive recommendations on how to achieve optimal compensation and deterrence in specific areas of liability. Analysis with an eye toward this goal must be based on knowledge of specific institutions and experiences. The remaining chapters of this volume take up this task.

Appendix: Mathematical Derivations

This appendix derives in a formal manner the main results presented in the preceding discussion. The mathematical notation is as follows.[31] Let r = the level of prevention, safety, caution, or so forth taken by the producer; $p(r)$ = the probability of product failure ($p' < 0$, $p'' > 0$); $c(r)$ = the cost of r ($c' > 0$, $c'' > 0$); L = the monetary loss if the product fails;[32] M = the payment to victim if the product fails; $V_n(w)$ =

---

31. See Danzon, "Tort Reform." Many of the results outlined below were first reached in Spence, "Consumer Misperceptions," pp. 561–72. We cite other sources as appropriate.

32. Recall that we are assuming the magnitude of loss does not depend on r, the level of safety or prevention.

the utility of wealth when there is no product failure; $V_f(w)$ = the utility of wealth when there is a product failure; w_0 = the initial wealth of consumers; and s = production cost of the product, exclusive of $c(r)$.[33]

First-Party Liability

MONETARY LOSSES. When all losses are monetary, subscripts are not needed to distinguish the utility of income before and after the injury, so that $V_n(w) = V_f(w) = V(w)$. Suppose consumers know the failure probability, p. Then competitive market outcomes will be the theoretical optimum. Producers operating in a competitive market will set prevention level, r, and compensation, M, so as to maximize consumers' expected utility subject to normal profits. (Alternatively, if producers do not offer compensation, buyers will purchase the same amount of insurance from third parties.) Because pM is the cost of insurance to provide compensation, M, consumers' expected utility, EV, is

$$EV = (1-p)V(\text{no failure}) + pV(\text{failure})$$
$$= (1-p)V[w_0 - s - c(r) - pM]$$
$$+ pV[w_0 - s - c(r) - pM - L + M].$$

This expression is at a maximum when the partial derivatives with respect to r and M are equal to 0. Let r^* and M^* denote the optimal values of r and M. Working with M yields this expression in terms of marginal utilities: V' (no failure) = V' (failure), or

$$V'[w_0 - s - c(r^*) - pM^*] =$$
$$V'[w_0 - s - c(r^*) - pM^* - L + M^*].$$

Thus consumers will use insurance (voluntarily supplied with the product or sold separately by third parties) to equalize the marginal utility of income between situations in which a loss occurs and those in which no loss occurs.[34] Clearly this condition is met when $M^* = L$, that is, when consumers are fully insured against the monetary loss.

---

33. Other models (for example, Danzon, "Tort Reform") use one variable to represent total price, including costs of prevention, bundled insurance, and so forth. We keep these separate for expositional ease.

34. If the price of insurance includes a loading factor, as all insurance does, consumers will purchase less than the amount of insurance necessary to equalize marginal utility across states; see Danzon, "Tort Reform," appendix A. If consumers are not risk-averse— that is, if the utility of wealth is simply proportional to wealth, so that V' is a constant—

With full insurance, consumers are indifferent between the two states of failure and no failure, so

$$EV = V(\text{no failure}) = V(\text{failure}) = V[w_0 - s - c(r) - pL].^{35}$$

In addition to setting M, producers will adjust r, the level of safety or precaution, to the utility-maximizing level. This yields a condition relating the marginal cost of safety and the marginal probability of failure. Letting MC denote marginal cost and MP marginal probability yields

$$\frac{MC \text{ (prevention)}}{MP \text{ (failure)}} = \frac{c'(r^*)}{-p'(r^*)} = M = L.$$

This result, familiar in analyses that consider only monetary losses,[36] may be rewritten as

$$MC \text{ (prevention)} = MP \text{ (failure)} \times L$$
$$= \text{marginal benefit of prevention.}$$

When consumers are unaware of the risks, the market will behave imperfectly in several ways and first-party liability is not an efficient rule. Now suppose consumers are aware that a risk exists, but their perceptions are inaccurate. Let $h(p)$ = consumer perceptions of p. Spence derives the result that after consumers purchase desired insurance, the marginal utility of income in the different states will deviate in the following way:

$$V'\text{ (no failure)} = V'\text{ (failure)} \left[\frac{(1-p)h}{p(1-h)}\right].^{37}$$

If consumers underestimate risk ($p > h$), sellers provide no compensation and consumers purchase too little self-insurance. Competitive sellers

---

then they will have no reason to purchase insurance even if it is priced at an actuarially fair level.

35. If consumers are risk-neutral and do not purchase insurance, one can work directly in terms of changes in wealth rather than utility of wealth and will reach the same result as the one that follows.

36. See, for example, Brown, "Toward an Economic Theory of Liability." In the present model, total expected social costs, TC, consist of the costs of producing the product, subsumed in price s; costs of prevention, $c(r)$; and expected loss from failure, pL, so that $TC = s + c(r) + pL$, which is minimized when the derivative with respect to r is equal to 0: $c'(r) = -p'(r)L$.

37. Spence, "Consumer Misperceptions," p. 564.

will now set the level of safety according to an expression that involves costs of prevention, $c(r)$, and perceived failure probability, $h(p)$:

$$\frac{MC \text{ (prevention)}}{\text{perceived } MP \text{ (failure)}} = \frac{c'(r)}{-h'[p(r)]} = L.$$

The resulting level of prevention, r, is likely to be less than optimal for reasonable specifications of $c(r)$, $h(p)$, and $p(r)$.

NONMONETARY LOSSES. With nonmonetary losses the impact of consumer information on the effects of first-party liability is qualitatively the same as with monetary losses. Suppose consumers know p, the probability of failure. Again, competitive producers will maximize consumer utility. With nonmonetary losses in addition to monetary losses, consumers' expected utility is

$$EV = (1-p)V_n \text{ (no failure)} + pV_f \text{ (failure)}$$

$$= (1-p)V_n [w_0 - s - c(r) - pM]$$

$$+ pV_f [w_0 - s - c(r) - pM - L + M].$$

Again let r^* and M^* denote the optimal values of r and M. The first-order condition with respect to M again yields this expression in terms of marginal utilities: V_n' (no failure) $= V_f'$ (failure), or

$$V_n'[w_o - s - c(r^*) - pM^*] = V_f'[w_o - s - c(r^*) - pM^* - L + M^*].$$

Thus consumers will use insurance to equalize the marginal utility of income among situations in which a loss occurs and those in which no loss occurs, just as they did for monetary losses. But without knowing more about how the loss affects the utility function, it is impossible to know how large M^* will be; it could even be negative if the injury sufficiently decreases the marginal utility of money (death being an extreme example).[38]

Adjusting r, the level of safety or precaution, yields a condition relating the marginal cost of safety and the marginal probability of failure. Letting MC denote marginal cost and MP marginal probability yields

---

38. A consumer who purchases an annuity is essentially purchasing negative insurance against death in the sense of providing for less wealth in case of "failure" and more in case of nonfailure.

$$\frac{MC \text{ (prevention)}}{MP \text{ (failure)}} = \frac{c'(r^*)}{-p'(r^*)}$$

$$= \left[\frac{V_n(\text{no failure}) - V_f(\text{failure})}{(1-p)V_n'(\text{no failure}) + pV_f'(\text{failure})} \right] + M^*.$$

Because insurance, M^*, is chosen to equate marginal utility between states, $V_n' = V_f'$. Therefore the bracketed expression in the denominator can be denoted as simply V', the marginal utility of wealth in either situation (failure or no failure). Then

$$\frac{MC \text{ (prevention)}}{MP \text{ (failure)}} = \frac{c'(r^*)}{-p'(r^*)}$$

$$= \left[\frac{V_n(\text{no failure}) - V_f(\text{failure})}{V'(w)} \right] + M^*$$

$$= U + M^*,$$

where U denotes willingness to pay to prevent the utility loss from the failure.[39] This term applies because the expression in brackets is total utility loss divided by the marginal utility of wealth. So the previous equation may also be viewed as

$$\frac{c'(r)}{-p'(r)} = U + M^*$$

$$= \begin{bmatrix} \text{willingness to pay} \\ \text{to prevent injury} \end{bmatrix} + \begin{bmatrix} \text{amount of insurance} \\ \text{consumers wish to pay for} \end{bmatrix}.$$

Again, without knowing more about how the injury affects the utility function, we can say little about the level of prevention, r^*, or the costs of prevention, $c(r^*)$. In the present situation, however, in which consumers know the probability of failure, manufacturers will simply choose r^* in order to maximize profits, and $c(r^*)$ will be willingly paid by consumers along with production costs, s, and an insurance premium, pM^* (possibly paid to a third party). The amount $(V_n - V_f)/V'$ is of course never actually paid unless there is an opportunity to reduce the probability of failure from 1 to 0. Rather, the willingness to avoid the loss induces the producer to invest $c(r^*)$ and the buyer to pay this amount. Thus when consumers are fully informed, the presence of

---

39. U is related to the "compensating variation" used in welfare analysis; see P. R. G. Layard and A. A. Walters, *Microeconomic Theory* (McGraw-Hill, 1978), p. 151. We are indebted to Ralph Winter for this point.

nonmonetary losses makes it difficult to know the optimal level of insurance or precaution but does not create a market imperfection because individual actors have an incentive to solve the problem without external rules.

If consumers do not know the failure probability, p, the market imperfections that arise are qualitatively similar to those that obtained in the case of monetary losses. If consumers are aware that a risk exists but their perceptions are inaccurate, the effect again depends on the marginal relation between actual and perceived risk. Again, let $h(p)$ = consumer perceptions of p. Spence's result continues to obtain:

$$V' \text{ (no failure)} = V' \text{ (failure)} \left[\frac{(1-p)h}{p(1-h)} \right].{}^{40}$$

As when losses are entirely monetary, consumer underestimation of risk results in too low a level of compensation. The effect of imperfect information on the level of safety provided by producers depends on the *marginal* relation between actual and perceived risk. As Spence shows,

$$\frac{MC \text{ (prevention)}}{MP \text{ (failure)}} = \frac{c'(r^*)}{-p'(r^*)}$$

$$= h'(p) \left[\frac{V_n \text{ (no failure)} - V_f \text{ (failure)}}{(1-p)V_n' \text{ (no failure)} + pV_f' \text{ (failure)}} \right] + M^*.$$

This is equivalent to the condition for optimal prevention only when $h' = 1$, that is, when consumers correctly assess marginal changes in risk. The effect of consumer underestimation of risk is ambiguous: it can lead to either too little or too much prevention.

Producers' utility, $U(w)$, can also be taken into account. Again, a product failure may impose nonmonetary as well as monetary losses on producers and may affect marginal utility. The condition for optimal prevention is

$$\frac{c'(r^*)}{-p'(r^*)} = \left[\frac{V_n - V_f}{(1-p)V_n' + pV_f'} \right] + \left[\frac{U_n - U_f}{(1-p)U_n' + pU_f'} \right] + M^*.$$

This expression reflects the willingness of both consumers and producers to pay to prevent the nonmonetary losses associated with product failure. Analyzing producer utility rather than just producer wealth might be relevant for certain kinds of producers such as physicians or day-care

40. Spence, "Consumer Misperceptions."

centers, whose skills cannot easily be converted to other uses or who may suffer a utility loss of their own as a result of product failure.[41]

Strict Liability

MONETARY LOSSES. If losses are exclusively monetary, strict liability essentially requires the producer to sell insurance against failure. Again, expected consumer utility is

$$EV = (1-p)V(\text{no failure}) + pV(\text{failure})$$
$$= (1-p)V[w_0 - s - c(r) - pM]$$
$$+ pV[w_0 - s - c(r) - pM - L + M].$$

Analytically, the situation is identical to first-party liability except that compensation is necessarily provided by the producer rather than by a third party. The producer absorbs all costs and therefore minimizes expected liability costs by undertaking optimal prevention, r^*, and optimal insurance, M^*. If the classic insurance problems of moral hazard and adverse selection do not arise, product price will correctly reflect risk, and thus the quantity purchased will be appropriate.

NONMONETARY LOSSES. Nonmonetary damages by definition have no obvious monetary equivalent, and thus it is not clear how the courts would measure them. A plausible measure is the sum of two factors: U, which is the amount the victim would have paid to avoid the injury (given that compensation will be paid for monetary loss), and desired compensation if injury occurs despite precautions. So let $D = U + M$, where D equals damages payment.

As noted previously, M depends on monetary losses and on how injury affects marginal utility of wealth, and it may be zero or negative. We also noted that the condition for optimal prevention is

$$\frac{MC \text{ (prevention)}}{MP \text{ (failure)}} = \frac{c'(r^*)}{-p'(r^*)}$$

$$= \left[\frac{V_n \text{ (no failure)} - V_f \text{ (failure)}}{(1-p)V_n' \text{ (no failure)} + pV_f' \text{ (failure)}} \right] + M^*$$

$$= U + M^*.$$

41. Patricia M. Danzon, "Liability and Liability Insurance for Medical Malpractice," *Journal of Health Economics*, vol. 4 (December 1985), p. 311, notes that liability can impose uninsurable costs on physicians for loss of time and reputation.

Because this equation defines the optimal degree of prevention, requiring the producer to pay the amount $D = U + M^*$ has the effect that the producer treats potential consumer losses as his own and thus provides the correct incentive for prevention.[42] But this damages rule distorts product price. The price will include costs of production, costs of prevention, and the insurance premium: price $= s + c(r^*) + p(U + M^*)$.

But the insurance premium, $p(U + M^*)$, does not correspond to the amount of insurance the consumer would prefer to purchase, which is only M^*. Consumers are thus forced to pay for extra insurance, the value of which is (by the definition of M^*) less than the premium. Spence showed that this problem can be solved by splitting the payment into two parts, with M^* going to victims and U being paid to the state, which would then use the payment to subsidize product price.[43] This solution would avoid compulsory overinsurance but would not solve the pricing problem because price would not reflect the risks of using the product. This dilemma has not been solved.

42. See Spence, "Consumer Misperceptions," p. 566.
43. Ibid., pp. 561–72.

CHAPTER THREE

Prices and Profits in the Liability Insurance Market

Scott E. Harrington

Cᴏᴍᴍᴇʀᴄɪᴀʟ liability insurance premiums increased dramatically in 1985 and 1986. The growth for general liability insurance was especially pronounced: net premiums written increased from $6.5 billion in 1984 to $20 billion in 1986. During this time, limits of coverage were shrinking for many of those insured, and cancellations and denials of renewal were widespread for some types of business in some states. Premium growth had moderated substantially by the end of 1986, but the large increases in the previous two years undoubtedly imposed high costs on many businesses and professionals. Insurers reported large accounting losses on operations in 1984 and 1985. The causes of the premium increases—whether rapidly escalating and unpredictable claim costs, severe underpricing of business written before 1985 because of cyclical influences in the industry, or both—have been vigorously debated, as has the extent to which industry operations actually were unprofitable. While widespread deregulation of commercial insurance rates occurred during the 1970s, a few states have enacted new forms of rate regulation in response to recent experience.

This chapter provides an overview of prices and profitability in the commercial liability insurance market to examine the nature and causes of recent experience. It describes the structure of the market and possible causes of underwriting cycles and reviews financial and operating results for recent years. Detailed information is provided about growth rates in losses for general liability and other major liability lines. A model of breakeven (that is, zero-profit) insurance prices is used to provide evidence of whether increases in general liability premiums were commensurate with increases in the discounted value of losses and expenses. The chapter does not deal directly with tort reform, nor with allegations of collusion recently raised in several lawsuits against major liability insurers, but the analysis sheds light on some of the key issues.

The findings suggest that overall financial results for the property and liability insurance industry deteriorated substantially in 1984 and 1985, regardless of the accounting conventions used to measure income. Losses for commercial liability coverage, especially general liability insurance, were largely responsible for this decline. Growth in several measures of insured losses for general liability coverage increased significantly relative to GNP. The results also suggest that the total increase in premiums since 1981 can largely be explained by increases in the discounted value of reported losses. However, premium increases appear to have been much smaller than cost increases through 1984, with the result that substantial increases were needed to catch up with the growth in the discounted value of losses. While questions remain concerning why premiums failed to keep pace with losses through 1984, the analysis suggests that, based on what we know, significant changes in regulatory policy for the industry are not warranted.

Overview of the Market

Table 3-1 presents national market shares for the largest property and liability insurer group, the four largest groups, and the twenty largest groups by line of business. The low concentration levels indicate that the commercial liability insurance market is competitively structured.[1] The

---

1. See Paul L. Joskow, "Cartels, Competition and Regulation in the Property-Liability Insurance Industry," *Bell Journal of Economics and Mangement Science,* vol. 4 (Autumn 1973), pp. 375–427, for an early analysis of market structure in the property-liability industry. The competitive structure of the industry also has been emphasized by the Department of Justice, *The Pricing and Marketing of Insurance: A Report of the U.S. Department of Justice to the Task Group on Antitrust Immunities* (Washington, D.C., 1977). Also see the discusion in Tort Policy Working Group, *Report of the Tort Policy Working Group on the Causes, Extent and Policy Implications of the Current Crisis in Insurance Availability and Affordability* (Washington, D.C.: Department of Justice, 1986); and the Herfindahl-Herschmann indices reported by the Department of Justice, Antitrust Division, "The Crisis in Property-Casualty Insurance," in Tort Policy Working Group, *An Update on the Liability Crisis* (Washington, D.C.: Department of Justice, 1987), appendix. For some coverages, a more appropriate definition of the market might be the state. Average statewide concentration levels probably would not be much higher than those shown in table 3-1. Based on data reported on *Best's Insurance Management Reports: Property-Casualty Edition* (weekly), the mean market share of the largest firm across states for general liability was 12 percent in 1985; the maximum was 27 percent (these figures

Table 3-1. *Shares of National Net Premiums Written for Leading Property and Liability Groups, 1985*
Percent unless otherwise specified

Line of business	Estimated 1986 net premiums written (billions of dollars)	Market share (1985)		
		Largest group	Largest 4 groups	Largest 20 groups
General liability	20.0	9.0	22.4	66.1
Medical malpractice	3.6	19.9	38.6	73.7
Commercial multiperil	16.0	7.7	23.4	68.8
Commercial auto liability	9.5	5.1	18.5	59.9
Private passenger auto liability	34.3	18.8	39.8	62.5
Workers' compensation	19.6	10.0	24.8	65.4
All property and liability	176.4	9.8	22.1	55.1

Sources: Market shares calculated from data in *Best's Aggregates and Averages: Property-Casualty, 1986* (Oldwick, N.J.: A. M. Best, 1986). Net premiums written are from estimates in Paul E. Wish, "Review and Preview: Up from the Ashes," *Best's Review: Property/Casualty Insurance Edition,* vol. 87 (January 1987), p. 12. Separate estimates for commercial and private passenger auto liability were not provided; the figures for these two lines are based on 1985 proportions.

data suggest that the minimum efficient scale of operations is small relative to the size of the market.[2] Most premiums are written through independent agents and brokers. There would appear to be no major barriers to companies entering this distribution channel, although some modest barriers exist because of such regulations as minimum capital and surplus requirements and other licensing requirements.[3]

---

exclude Michigan, in which a subsidiary of General Motors had a 41 percent market share because it provided insurance for its parent). For commercial multiperil insurers, who sell property and liability coverage as a package to small and medium-sized businesses, the mean market share was 12 percent and the maximum was 21 percent. The single-firm shares reported by *Best's* were much higher for medical malpractice, but they often do not reflect experience of provider-owned mutual companies.

2. Some studies have suggested that average costs of production in the property-liability insurance industry decrease as the size of the firm decreases. See, for example, Joseph E. Johnson, George B. Flanigan, and Steven N. Weisbart, "Returns to Scale in the Property and Liability Insurance Industry," *Journal of Risk and Insurance,* vol. 48 (March 1981), pp. 18–45. These studies have, however, been plagued by the lack of information about average account size and other factors that could produce a bias toward finding decreasing costs.

3. Patricia Munch and Dennis E. Smallwood, "Solvency Regulation in the Property-Liability Insurance Industry: Empirical Evidence," *Bell Journal of Economics,* vol. 11 (Spring 1980), pp. 261–79. Joskow, "Cartels, Competition and Regulation," suggested the possibility of entry or growth barriers for direct-writing distribution methods. Whether this is likely has been disputed; see, for example, Mark Pauly, Howard Kunreuther, and Paul Kleindorfer, "Regulation and Quality Competition in the U.S. Insurance Industry,"

The insurance industry is largely exempt from federal antitrust legislation as a result of the McCarran-Ferguson Act of 1945. The exemptions allow insurers to pool loss data through various rating organizations or bureaus. In most states, rating bureaus promulgate premium rates for most lines of business, and subscribers may use the rates. The available data for at least private passenger auto insurance nevertheless suggest that despite these pooling arrangements insurers display considerable pricing independence. The key exceptions are small companies that tend to use bureau rates to economize on costs.[4] The evidence and concern about underwriting cycles also suggest vigorous price competition in commercial liability lines, regardless of the existence of rating bureaus.[5]

Price information is likely to be readily available to consumers through agents and brokers, and there is considerable standardization of coverage as a result of both the influence of rating bureaus and state regulation of policy forms, especially for small to medium-sized buyers. Little information is available, however, for consumers to assess differences in claim settlement practices. To the extent that consumer preferences for quality of claim service differ, independent agents may play some role in placing coverage with appropriate insurers. Most states also have laws dealing with unfair claim practices, and consumers may seek tort recoveries in the event of arbitrary treatment.

Many consumers may not be aware of differences in financial strength among insurers, and both consumers and agents may find it difficult to assess whether an insurer will be able to pay claims. This problem has generally been used to justify state regulation designed to reduce the number of insurance company failures and to protect consumers from the consequences of defaults that do occur.[6] Before 1970, regulations

in Jörg Finsinger and Mark V. Pauly, eds., *The Economics of Insurance Regulation: A Cross-National Study* (St. Martin's Press, 1986), pp. 75–78.

4. See Department of Justice, *Pricing and Marketing of Insurance;* Patricia M. Danzon, "Rating Bureaus in U.S. Property-Liability Insurance Markets: Anti- or Pro-Competitive?" *Geneva Papers on Risk and Insurance,* vol. 8 (October 1983), pp. 371–402; and Scott Harrington, "The Impact of Rate Regulation on Prices and Underwriting Results in the Property-Liability Insurance Industry: A Survey," *Journal of Risk and Insurance,* vol. 51 (December 1984), pp. 578–623.

5. As is discussed later, at one time rating bureaus and the antitrust exemption may have facilitated cartel behavior. See also Joskow, "Cartels, Competition and Regulation."

6. Jörg Finsinger and Mark Pauly, "Reserve Levels and Reserve Requirements for Profit-Maximizing Insurance Firms," in Günter Bamberg and Klaus Spremann, eds., *Risk and Capital* (Berlin: Springer-Verlag, 1984,) pp. 160–80, consider whether consumer failure to base purchasing decisions on the probability of default leads to excessive risk

emphasized direct controls of pricing, product mix, and investment policy. Since then they have emphasized monitoring, primarily through the National Association of Insurance Commissioners (NAIC) Insurance Regulatory Information System, and paying the claims of insolvent insurers through state guaranty funds.[7] The extent to which state guaranty funds have increased insurer risk taking by reducing the incentives of buyers to purchase coverage from financially sound companies is not known.

Information problems facing insurers are also substantial. First, for a given average expected loss per unit of coverage in a given line of business, considerable heterogeneity exists among consumers. For liability insurance, rates generally vary by industry and state. Rating plans also commonly allow underwriters to apply credits and debits on the basis of firm-specific characteristics and judgment. While such experience rating commonly is used for medium and large corporate risks, the low frequency of liability claims for most businesses and professionals and the resulting lack of statistical credibility of a risk's own loss experience often seriously limits the extent to which experience rating can reduce problems of adverse selection and moral hazard.[8]

Adverse selection is the tendency for high risks to buy more coverage than low risks at any given rate. Because insurers cannot identify differences in risk with perfect accuracy and those insured often will have more knowledge about their risk than insurers, some adverse selection

---

taking by insurers; see also Patricia Munch and Dennis Smallwood, "Theory of Solvency Regulation in the Property and Casualty Insurance Industry," in Gary Fromm, ed., *Studies in Public Regulation* (MIT Press, 1981), pp. 119–67. Compulsory coverage requirements might also lead buyers of third-party coverage with few assets at risk to seek coverage from insurers with low premiums but a high probability of default. For detailed discussion of the insolvency problem and associated regulation, see Scott E. Harrington and Patricia M. Danzon, "An Evaluation of Solvency Regulation in the Property-Liability Insurance Industry," report to the Alliance of American Insurers, American Insurance Association, and National Association of Independent Insurers (University of Pennsylvania, Wharton School, June 1986).

7. All states have guaranty funds for property and liability insurance. New York prefunds its plan through assessments on insurers. The remaining states assess surviving companies following a default. The maximum claim payable through the funds for liability coverage commonly is no more than $500,000. A recent amendment to the NAIC model legislation allows guaranty funds to seek recovery from corporations with net worth greater than $50 million for liability claims paid on their behalf.

8. General liability insurance rating procedures are described in Michael F. McManus, "General Liability Ratemaking: An Update," *Proceedings of the Casualty Actuarial Society,* vol. 67 (November 1981), pp. 144–80.

will exist and will tend to become more pronounced as heterogeneity among buyers in a rate class increases.

The theory of competitive insurance markets with adverse selection has emphasized the existence and characteristics of market equilibrium when insurers can identify the total amount of coverage owned by each buyer and compete by offering different combinations of price and coverage.[9] But it is not clear that this theory describes reality in liability insurance markets. Adverse selection could cause the market for particular types of coverage to disappear.[10] For a given rate, low risks might be unwilling to buy coverage. As they drop out of the pool, the rate must go up, causing more risks with low expected loss relative to the group average to drop out, and so on. Given expense loadings in premiums, the highest risks may not be willing to insure unless subsidized by low risks. If so, no market would exist.[11] Whether this is true is not known, but adverse selection may help explain instances in recent years in which coverage has been alleged to be unavailable at any price.

Moral hazard is the tendency for the presence and characteristics of insurance coverage to produce inefficient changes in buyers' loss prevention activities, including carelessness and fraud, which are often emphasized in the insurance literature. If insurance prices were to reflect perfectly the influence of loss prevention activities on expected losses, moral hazard would not exist. But while experience rating, deductibles, and other forms of copayment by buyers may mitigate moral hazard, the inability of insurers to monitor loss prevention activities accurately leads to too little prevention and too many losses.

Prices are also determined by the average expected loss per unit of exposure in a given rating class and for all classes combined, which may vary considerably over time. Liability insurance contracts sold on an occurrence basis promise to pay all claims that arise out of actions during the policy period, regardless of when the claim is made. The ong time that can elapse before all claims are paid for such coverage requires companies to predict payments that often will not be made for

9. Michael Rothschild and Joseph Stiglitz, "Equilibrium in Competitive Insurance Markets: An Essay on the Economics of Imperfect Information," *Quarterly Journal of Economics,* vol. 90 (November 1976), pp. 629–49.

10. George A. Akerlof, "The Market for 'Lemons': Quality Uncertainty and the Market Mechanism," *Quarterly Journal of Economics,* vol. 84 (August 1970), pp. 488–500. Also see George L. Priest, "The Current Insurance Crisis and Modern Tort Law," *Yale Law Journal,* vol. 96 (June 1987), pp. 1521–90.

11. For liability coverage, high-risk buyers with few assets to protect also could be unwilling to buy coverage unless subsidized by low risks.

many years.[12] As is discussed later, difficulty in accurately estimating future claims may cause coverage to be priced below expected costs. This difficulty may be a principal cause of underwriting cycles in the liability insurance market.

The possibility of destructive competition has been closely associated with regulation of property-liability insurance prices. Before the Mc-Carran-Ferguson Act was passed in 1945, allegations of destructive competition were used to justify cartel behavior. Rating bureaus were effective in controlling prices and commissions, at least in property insurance where deviations from bureau rating schemes could be detected. Following the enactment of McCarran-Ferguson, most states passed laws that required prior approval of rates by regulators for all property-liability lines. These laws often encouraged insurers to use bureau rates by making it difficult or costly to obtain approval of independent rate filings. A period of rate deregulation began in the late 1960s. With the exception of workers' compensation rates, which remain heavily regulated in most states, property-liability insurance rates are now subject to some form of prior approval in just under half of the states. Regulation in these states, however, probably has not had much impact on rates for commercial lines in recent years because of passive administration of the laws, pricing flexibility provided to underwriters by rating plans, and other influences.[13] In contrast, there is considerable evidence that rate regulation has lowered average prices for private passenger auto liability insurance in recent years.[14] Evidence also suggests that restrictive rate regulation is more likely in states with high losses per insured driver.[15]

12. This so-called tail reflects lags between the time that rates are made and their effective date for all policies, between the accident date and the date the claim is made, and between the date the claim is made and the date it is paid.

13. For a review of the impact of rate regulation, see Harrington, "Impact of Rate Regulation." Also see Richard E. Stewart, *Remembering a Stable Future: Why Flex Rating Cannot Work* (New York: Insurance Services Office and Insurance Information Institute, 1987).

14. See Henry Grabowski, W. Kip Viscusi, and William N. Evans, "The Effects of Regulation on the Price and Availability of Automobile Insurance," paper presented at the Nineteenth Atlantic International Economic Conference in Rome, 1985; Pauly and others, "Regulation and Quality Competition"; and Scott E. Harrington, "A Note on the Impact of Auto Insurance Rate Regulation," *Review of Economics and Statistics,* vol. 69 (February 1987), pp. 166–70.

15. Scott E. Harrington, "Cross-Subsidization and the Economics of Regulation: Theory and Evidence from Automobile Insurance," working paper 87-12 (University of Pennsylvania, Center for Research on Risk and Insurance, August 1987), develops a model that suggests consumer pressure for lower prices is likely to increase with costs if

As a result of recent experience in the liability insurance market, a few states have reregulated rates for commercial lines. These so-called flex-rating laws require prior approval only for rate changes in excess of a given statutory benchmark. Whether rate regulation is likely to be an appropriate response to the problems of the liability insurance market is discussed later in this chapter and again in the concluding chapter of this volume.

Overview of Financial Results

Table 3-2 shows reported income, capital structure, and insolvencies for the property-liability insurance industry from 1972 to 1986. Ratios of several alternative measures of income to both earned premiums and statutory surplus adjusted for prepaid acquisition expenses are shown in table 3-3.[16] All the income measures shown in tables 3-2 and 3-3 reflect calendar year losses, which equal losses paid plus the change in the loss reserve during the given year. As a result, the income measures for each year reflect revisions in the loss reserve for claims from previous years as well as loss experience for new claims during the year.[17]

The time period shown in tables 3-2 and 3-3 allows recent experience to be compared with that of the insurance crisis of 1974–75. Operating losses have been the major cause of problems in 1984–85; unrealized capital losses were the principle factor leading to the sharp declines in surplus in 1973–74. While unrealized capital gains contributed to rapid

---

demand is inelastic. The model provides a possible explanation of regulatory emphasis on affordability of coverage.

16. An introduction to insurance accounting and profit measurement using both statutory accounting principles (SAP) and generally accepted accounting principles (GAAP) is provided in appendix A. The underwriting income measures in table 3-3 are calculated with the combined ratio, which is defined as the sum of the ratio of incurred losses and policyholder dividends to earned premiums and the ratio of underwriting expenses to written premiums. As discussed in appendix A, 1 minus the combined ratio approximately equals the pretax GAAP underwriting profit margin relative to earned premiums. The income measures shown are divided by the average of the beginning and end-of-year values of adjusted surplus. Adjusted surplus is defined as SAP surplus plus the average underwriting expense ratio for the current and preceding year times the unearned premium reserve. GAAP surplus, which would also reflect items such as deferred taxes, generally is not reported for the aggregate industry.

17. Throughout the chapter *loss* refers to the sum of insurer loss-adjustment expenses and losses payable to claimants.

Table 3-2. *Selected Financial Results for the Property-Liability Industry, 1972–86*
Millions of dollars unless otherwise specified

Item	1972	1973	1974	1975	1976	1977	1978	1979	1980	1981	1982	1983	1984	1985	1986[a]
Combined ratio (percent)	96.2	99.2	105.4	107.9	102.4	97.1	97.4	100.6	103.1	106.0	109.6	112.0	118.0	116.3	108.6
Ratio of net investment income/earned premiums	7.1	7.6	8.3	8.2	8.1	8.5	9.3	10.7	11.8	13.6	14.6	14.9	15.4	14.6	13.0
Before-tax operating income[b]	3,724	3,100	959	−322	2,405	6,928	8,586	7,978	7,729	6,960	4,617	2,651	−3,609	−5,780	4,500
After-tax operating income[b]	2,895	2,631	1,284	232	2,256	5,913	7,197	7,083	7,137	6,906	5,333	3,869	−1,942	−3,822	6,000
Realized capital gains	301	412	−154	139	286	329	57	300	533	276	572	2,110	3,063	5,483	5,500
Unrealized capital gains	2,836	−4,915	−6,999	4,035	3,803	−1,083	41	2,030	4,274	−2,666	2,908	1,358	−2,848	5,227	4,500
Net capital and surplus paid in[c]	−458	−1,084	−185	17	−78	−72	−736	−1,199	−1,495	−1,775	−1,248	−1,945	233	5,561	1,300
Surplus at yearend[b]	23,812	21,389	16,270	19,712	24,631	29,300	35,379	42,395	52,174	53,805	60,395	65,606	63,809	75,511	91,000
Percent change in surplus	24.9	−10.2	−23.9	21.2	24.9	18.9	20.7	19.8	23.1	3.1	12.2	8.6	−2.7	18.3	20.5
Percent change in net premiums written	10.1	8.1	6.2	11.0	21.8	19.8	12.8	10.3	6.0	3.9	4.7	4.8	8.4	22.0	22.3
Ratio of net premiums written/surplus	1.63	1.97	2.75	2.52	2.45	2.47	2.31	2.13	1.83	1.85	1.72	1.67	1.86	1.92	1.94
Ratio of liabilities/surplus	2.12	2.64	3.70	3.47	3.29	3.32	3.21	3.10	2.79	2.95	2.84	2.80	3.15	3.12	n.a.
Ratio of loss reserves/surplus	1.12	1.42	2.13	2.00	1.91	1.94	1.94	1.91	1.77	1.90	1.85	1.87	2.11	2.05	n.a.
Number of insolvencies	2	2	5	20	4	6	6	3	4	6	9	4	20	20	n.a.

Sources: *Best's Aggregates and Averages: Property-Casualty*, 1986; and earlier years; and Wish, "Review and Preview." Number of insolvencies provided by National Committee on Insurance Guaranty Funds.

a. Estimated.

b. Income and surplus calculated according to statutory accounting principles.

c. Net capital and surplus paid in equals new capital and surplus paid in less dividends to stockholders.

Table 3-3. *Adjusted Income Measures as a Percentage of Earned Premiums and Adjusted Surplus, 1972–86*

Income measure[a]	1972	1973	1974	1975	1976	1977	1978	1979	1980	1981	1982	1983	1984	1985	1986[b]
Earned premiums															
Pretax underwriting income	3.8	0.8	-5.4	-7.9	-2.4	2.9	2.6	-0.6	-3.1	-0.6	-9.6	-12.0	-18.0	-16.3	-8.6
Pretax operating income	10.9	8.4	2.8	0.3	5.6	11.4	11.9	10.1	8.7	7.6	5.0	2.9	-2.6	-1.7	4.4
After-tax operating income	8.7	7.2	3.6	1.4	5.4	9.9	10.1	9.0	8.1	7.5	5.7	4.0	-1.2	-0.2	5.3
After-tax operating income plus realized capital gains	9.5	8.2	3.2	1.7	5.9	10.4	10.2	9.4	8.6	7.8	6.3	6.0	1.5	3.9	8.7
After-tax operating income plus realized and unrealized capital gains	17.0	-3.8	-12.8	10.2	12.5	8.8	10.2	11.7	13.2	5.1	9.1	7.3	-1.0	7.8	11.4
Adjusted surplus															
Pretax underwriting income	5.5	1.2	-9.7	-15.9	-4.8	5.9	5.1	-1.1	-5.1	-9.3	-14.5	-17.3	-26.8	-25.9	n.a.
Pretax operating income	15.6	12.4	5.1	0.5	11.3	23.0	23.4	18.5	14.4	11.8	7.5	4.2	-3.9	-2.7	n.a.
After-tax operating income	12.5	10.7	6.5	2.9	10.8	20.0	19.9	16.6	13.4	11.7	8.6	5.8	-1.8	-0.3	n.a.
After-tax operating income plus realized capital gains	13.6	12.2	5.8	3.5	11.8	21.0	20.0	17.2	14.3	12.1	9.4	8.6	2.2	6.2	n.a.
After-tax operating income plus realized and unrealized capital gains	24.5	-5.6	-23.0	20.5	25.2	17.8	20.1	21.5	21.9	7.9	13.7	10.5	-1.5	12.5	n.a.

Sources: *Best's Aggregates and Averages: Property-Casualty*, 1986 and earlier years; and Wish, "Review and Preview."
n.a. Not available.
a. Underwriting income, operating income, and surplus are adjusted for prepaid acquisition expenses. Taxes do not include deferred income taxes.
b. Estimated.

surplus growth in both 1975–76 and 1985–86, realized capital gains also had a major impact in the latter period. New inflows of capital accounted for over 40 percent of the growth in surplus in 1985. Increases in premiums written in 1985 and 1986 were larger relative to the preceding few years than those in 1975 and 1976. However, the absolute increases in 1985 and 1986 are only slightly greater than those that occurred in 1976 and 1977. The percentage increases in surplus following the decline in 1984 have been smaller than those following the steeper declines in 1973 and 1974, but the data indicate that large unrealized capital gains played a relatively greater role in rebuilding surplus during the earlier period.

If unrealized capital gains are not included, 1984 ranks as the worst year for all of the income measures in table 3-3. When unrealized capital gains are included, results were worse in 1973 and 1974. If all capital gains are excluded, 1985 ranks second to 1984 as the worst year during the period. In fact, 1984 and 1985 are the only two years with negative income exclusive of capital gains. As will be discussed later, whether capital gains should be included in income has been a major issue in the debate about whether operations actually were unprofitable in recent years.

The three measures of financial leverage shown in table 3-2 indicate that the highest values occurred in 1974. The ratios of premiums to surplus and total liabilities to surplus are substantially higher for 1974 and 1975 than for 1984 and 1985. Part of this difference reflects higher premium levels in the earlier period, which have a direct impact on both ratios.[18] The ratio of loss reserves to surplus is about the same during both periods. A major problem in comparing results for the two periods is that small differences in reserve adequacy over time can have a large impact on reported income and measures of leverage.[19] In both periods a historically large number of insolvencies occurred, with the total number in 1984 and 1985 much larger than in 1974 and 1975. While detailed data are not yet available, the number of insolvencies most likely remained high in 1986. Premium increases also were much larger

18. Premium levels influence the magnitude of the unearned premium reserve as well as net premiums written.

19. George M. Gottheimer, Jr., "Crisis of Confidence," in Numan A. Williams, ed., *Crisis Avoidance: Insurance Responsibilities* (Malvern, Pa.: Society of Chartered Property and Casualty Underwriters, 1986), pp. 67–84, provides an illustration of the potential impact of underreserving on the premium-to-surplus ratio in 1985.

for commercial liability lines during 1985 and 1986 than in 1976 and 1977.

Table 3-4 presents calendar year combined ratios and operating ratios for each insurance line from 1977 to 1986.[20] Since more net investment income and realized capital gains are allocated to the longer-tailed lines, the difference between the combined ratio and the operating ratio is greater for general liability and medical malpractice than for commercial multiperil and auto business.[21] With the exception of workers' compensation, the data show gradually increasing ratios through 1984. For general liability, medical malpractice, and private passenger auto liability, the ratios increased through 1985. The operating ratios generally began to exceed 100 percent in 1981 and 1982. These results indicate substantial accounting losses for commercial liability lines after investment income, including realized capital gains, was allocated to operations during 1984 and 1985. While operating ratios were not available for 1986, the data suggest that they will be about 100 percent for general liability and will exceed 100 percent for medical malpractice. Since these are calendar year results, the high ratios in recent years reflect increases in reserves for losses experienced in earlier years.

Errors in Estimating Reserves

As noted, previous errors in estimating loss reserves will affect calendar year financial results in the year in which reserves are restated to reflect the errors. Accident year results, which include losses only for accidents during a given calendar year, provide a better measure of experience during the period in which premiums were earned. However, errors in the reserve estimates as of any given statement date may be substantial, so that calendar year and accident year results and reported surplus may

20. A combined ratio greater than 100 percent indicates a pretax GAAP underwriting loss (exclusive of investment income). As discussed in appendix A, the operating ratio equals the combined ratio minus the ratio of net investment income and realized capital gains to earned premiums. An operating ratio greater than 100 percent indicates a pretax GAAP operating loss exclusive of both unrealized capital gains and the amount of net investment income and realized capital gains that are allocated to surplus.

21. General liability, which is denoted "other" or "miscellaneous" liability on annual statements and in many publications, includes all commercial liability coverage other than auto, workers' compensation and employers' liability, liability coverage provided in commercial multiperil contracts, and medical malpractice.

Table 3-4. *Combined Ratios and Operating Ratios, by Insurance Line, 1977–86*[a]
Percent

Insurance line	1977	1978	1979	1980	1981	1982	1983	1984	1985	1986
General liability										
Combined ratio	100.0	97.3	98.2	107.2	116.0	129.4	138.1	151.8	145.8	120.3
Operating ratio	90.4	87.5	86.0	92.7	96.5	106.4	113.8	125.1	125.8	n.a.
Medical malpractice										
Combined ratio	93.7	104.9	113.9	129.2	137.6	150.9	151.2	162.2	166.9	144.4
Operating ratio	79.6	87.3	92.0	99.8	101.4	109.8	108.9	118.3	129.5	n.a.
Commerical multiperil										
Combined ratio	87.2	84.9	93.3	98.8	107.1	116.4	123.2	134.9	121.3	97.2
Operating ratio	82.8	80.7	88.6	93.4	100.5	109.1	114.8	125.1	112.2	n.a.
Commercial auto liability										
Combined ratio	98.8	99.9	105.0	109.5	118.3	126.4	132.9	143.1	127.1	112.8
Operating ratio	92.7	93.7	97.6	101.1	108.4	115.3	121.3	130.8	116.4	n.a.
Private passenger auto liability										
Combined ratio	99.5	99.8	101.6	103.3	109.6	110.9	112.1	113.6	119.6	119.0
Operating ratio	93.7	93.8	94.8	96.1	101.4	102.1	102.9	103.9	109.5	n.a.
Workers' compensation										
Combined ratio	108.6	105.0	103.0	101.4	102.8	103.9	112.5	121.9	118.8	120.5
Operating ratio	101.2	97.2	93.7	90.7	89.8	88.9	96.3	105.2	103.8	n.a.
All property-liability										
Combined ratio	97.1	97.4	100.6	103.1	106.0	109.6	112.0	118.0	116.3	108.6
Operating ratio	91.8	91.8	94.1	95.9	97.6	100.5	102.3	107.4	106.3	n.a.

Sources: *Best's Aggregates and Averages: Property-Casualty, 1986*; and Wish, "Review and Preview."
n.a. Not available.
a. All ratios are computed after payment of policyholder dividends.

differ greatly from the values that would be reported if future claims were known with certainty.

The problem of errors in estimating reserves always makes interpretation of insurance company financial results tenuous. Large errors in forecasting claims are often highly correlated among firms because of changes in factors that influence losses, such as inflation and the level of economic activity. Reserves also can be deliberately misstated to manage earnings and taxes. Consistent overstatement defers income taxes (or costs associated with tax avoidance, such as lower yields on tax-exempt securities). If shareholders are concerned about net cash flow and if tax deferral reduces costs and hence premiums, neither they nor policyholders would object to overstatement, provided they are aware that reported income and surplus are understated.[22] But deliberate understatement of reserves allows an insurer to show higher income and surplus. Whether shareholders, policyholders interested in security, or regulators would systematically be misled by such a strategy is uncertain.[23]

Errors in estimating reserves eventually can be measured by comparing total claim payments (or total payments plus any remaining reserve) with values initially reported. A number of studies have analyzed errors using historical data from the 1940s through the early 1970s on reserves and claims paid that are reported for third-party lines of business in schedule P of insurance company statutory statements. Almost all empirical studies have analyzed reserve errors for auto liability. Several have analyzed data for general liability and workers' compensation as well. The results, which often differ considerably among companies, indicate overreserving in the 1940s and 1950s for large auto liability insurers and in the 1950s for general liability.[24] The results for the

22. The Internal Revenue Service would object, but it could be difficult to prove deliberate misstatements in reserves, given the possibility of large random errors.

23. Companies that default are almost always grossly underreserved. A number of analysts have considered whether insurers are likely to use reserves to smooth reported income and have provided some evidence to this effect. See, for instance, Barry D. Smith, "An Analysis of Auto Liability Loss Reserves and Underwriting Results," *Journal of Risk and Insurance,* vol. 47 (June 1980), pp. 305–20; and Mary Weiss, "A Multivariate Analysis of Loss Reserving Estimates in Property-Liability Insurers," *Journal of Risk and Insurance,* vol. 52 (June 1985), pp. 199–221.

24. See Stephen Forbes, "Loss Reserving Performance within the Regulatory Framework," *Journal of Risk and Insurance,* vol. 37 (December 1970), pp. 527–38; Dan Robert Anderson, "Effects of Under and Overevaluations in Loss Reserves," *Journal of Risk and Insurance,* vol. 38 (December 1971), pp. 585–600; R. J. Balcarek, "Loss Reserve Deficiencies and Underwriting Results," *Best's Review: Property/Liability Insurance Edition,* vol. 76 (July 1975), pp. 20–23; Craig F. Ansley, "Automobile Liability Insurance Reserve

1960s and early 1970s indicate underreserving both for auto liability and for general liability.[25]

Table 3-5 presents accident year results and evidence on errors in reserve estimates in recent years for schedule P lines of business. The table shows the accident year loss ratios (incurred losses divided by earned premiums) originally reported and accident year loss ratios developed (that is, reflecting all payments and the remaining reserve) through 1985.[26] Results are shown for the industry for accident years 1980–85 using the consolidated schedule P information reported in *Best's Aggregates and Averages: Property-Casualty, 1986,* and for 1976–85 using aggregate information for forty-five large companies supplied by Aetna Life and Casualty.[27]

The data indicate substantial upward development in the loss ratios for malpractice and, especially, general liability in 1981–84. Loss ratios for general liability increased substantially during this time.[28] Substantial upward development occurred for accident years 1976 and 1977 for general liability in the sample data, but developments for malpractice were large and negative. In general, the results for multiperil (aggregated in schedule P and including first-party property losses for homeowners, farmowners, and commercial multiperil business), auto liability (aggregated for private passenger and commercial business), and workers' compensation generally indicate a smaller increase in loss ratios and smaller

---

Adequacy and the Effect on Inflation," *CPCU Journal,* vol. 31 (June 1978), pp. 105–12; Stephen W. Forbes, "The Credibility of the Earnings per Share of Nonlife Insurance Companies," *CPCU Journal,* vol. 31 (March 1978), pp. 30–36; and Smith, "Analysis of Auto Liability Loss Reserves."

25. For auto liability, see Anderson, "Effects of Under and Overevaluations"; Balcarek, "Loss Reserve Deficiencies"; Ansley, "Automobile Liability Insurance Reserve Adequacy"; Forbes, "Credibility of Earnings per Share"; and Smith, "Analysis of Auto Liability Loss Reserves." For general liability, see Anderson, "Effects of Under and Overevaluations"; and Balcarek, "Loss Reserve Deficiencies." See also Forbes, "Credibility of Earnings per Share."

26. Accident year incurred losses include only paid losses and the loss reserve for claims that have occurred (including those incurred but not reported) during the given year. Accident year incurred losses are divided by calendar year earned premiums to obtain the accident year loss ratios.

27. In 1985 these companies represented 69, 34, 76, and 69 percent of net premiums written for general liability, medical malpractice, commercial multiperil, and all property-liability lines, respectively.

28. Developed incurred losses for these years and initial reserves for 1985 still included a sizable reserve for unpaid losses.

Table 3-5. *Accident Year Loss Ratios by Insurance Line: Originally Reported (R) and Developed through 1985 (D), 1976–85*

Sample	General liability		Medical malpractice		Multiperil [a]		Auto liability [b]		Workers' compensation		Schedule P [c]	
	R	D	R	D	R	D	R	D	R	D	R	D
Industry												
1980	0.69	0.73	1.05	1.34	0.69	0.71	0.79	0.78	0.74	0.68	0.74	0.74
1981	0.79	0.86	1.13	1.48	0.69	0.69	0.85	0.85	0.77	0.72	0.78	0.79
1982	0.87	1.02	1.18	1.58	0.75	0.77	0.87	0.88	0.79	0.78	0.82	0.85
1983	0.94	1.09	1.19	1.51	0.75	0.80	0.89	0.91	0.84	0.86	0.85	0.90
1984	0.99	1.10	1.09	1.33	0.77	0.79	0.92	0.96	0.90	0.93	0.88	0.92
1985	0.95	0.95	1.20	1.20	0.77	0.77	0.92	0.92	0.89	0.89	0.88	0.88
45 companies												
1976	0.69	0.86	0.75	0.66	0.63	0.62	0.79	0.78	0.77	0.89	0.73	0.76
1977	0.63	0.66	0.76	0.58	0.59	0.58	0.75	0.73	0.77	0.78	0.69	0.69
1978	0.62	0.59	0.77	0.73	0.58	0.57	0.75	0.75	0.77	0.73	0.69	0.68
1979	0.65	0.64	0.95	0.91	0.65	0.66	0.77	0.78	0.78	0.72	0.73	0.72
1980	0.69	0.71	1.15	1.10	0.69	0.70	0.79	0.79	0.76	0.69	0.75	0.74
1981	0.81	0.85	1.39	1.45	0.70	0.70	0.86	0.86	0.79	0.73	0.80	0.79
1982	0.90	1.05	1.40	1.65	0.75	0.77	0.88	0.87	0.80	0.78	0.83	0.85
1983	0.97	1.08	1.37	1.66	0.76	0.81	0.89	0.91	0.86	0.87	0.86	0.89
1984	1.03	1.12	1.09	1.24	0.78	0.79	0.92	0.95	0.92	0.94	0.89	0.92
1985	0.99	…	1.19	…	0.78	…	0.93	…	0.90	…	0.89	…

Sources: Industry data are from *Best's Aggregates and Averages: Property-Casualty*, 1986. Data for forty-five companies from Aetna Life and Casualty Co.
a. Includes commercial and homeowner's insurance.
b. Includes commercial and private passenger vehicle insurance.
c. Denotes aggregate for schedule P lines—general liability, medical malpractice, multiperil, auto liability, and workers' compensation.

Table 3-6. Estimated Reserve Inadequacy for General Liability Lines, Based on Paid-Loss Development Methods, as of 1985[a]
Percent

Accident year	Industry				45 companies			
	Method A		Method B		Method A		Method B	
	(1)	(2)	(1)	(2)	(1)	(2)	(1)	(2)
1980	−19	0	−17	0	−16	0	−15	0
1981	−28	−14	−26	−12	−22	−10	−21	−10
1982	−39	−27	−34	−23	−23	−14	−20	−12
1983	−36	−27	−34	−25	−26	−18	−26	−20
1984	−38	−31	−38	−31	−22	−16	−24	−18
1985	−12	−6	−15	−10	9	13	3	7
1980–85	−27	−18	−26	−18	−11	−4	−13	−7

Sources: Industry data are from *Best's Aggregates and Averages: Property-Casualty*, 1986. Data for forty-five companies are from Aetna Life and Casualty Co.

a. Values shown are 1985 statement reserve minus projected reserve as a percentage of 1985 statement reserve. Method A uses sum-of-the-year digits to weight loss development factors. Method B uses the most recent factor. Values shown under (2) assume that the ratio of incurred losses to losses paid as of 1985 for accident year 1980 is accurate and applicable to future years. Values shown under (1) are based on paid loss development factors back through 1976. Development factors are shown in appendix B.

absolute development than for general liability. Thus the results generally suggest greater reserve inaccuracy for the longer-tailed liability lines.[29]

Another look at reserve adequacy for general liability is provided by table 3-6, which includes estimates of reserve inadequacy as of 1985 as a percentage of 1985 reported reserves for general liability business. The estimates were calculated using a basic reserve forecasting methodology involving historical data on paid losses. Negative values indicate estimated reserve inadequacy; positive ones indicate estimated redundancy.[30] Results are shown both for the industry and the forty-five-company sample and for two methods of weighting development factors (see appendix B, table 3-16) and two methods of projecting development of claims paid for years six and beyond.[31]

29. Data on cumulative development of statement reserves from 1976 through 1984 for the forty-five-company sample supplied by Aetna Life and Casualty generally had similar implications. The results for general liability and medical malpractice combined indicated especially large underreserving as of 1976 and 1977.

30. For a description of the paid loss development method, see Timothy M. Peterson, *Loss Reserving: Property/Casualty Insurance* (New York: Ernst and Whinney, 1981).

31. With regard to the latter issue, method (1) uses historical paid loss development factors for years six through ten to project future losses, and assumes that development beyond ten years will total 3 percent. Industry data were not available to calculate development factors for all payment years. Factors for the sample were used for method (1) in these instances (see appendix table 3-16). To allow for the possibility that the historical development factors for these years might overstate future development, method (2) uses the ratio of incurred losses to total payments for accident year 1980, as developed

In general, the projections imply that calendar year financial results reported during 1980–85 for the industry as a whole are likely to have overstated surplus and income from operations.[32] With the exception of 1985, reserves reported as of 1985 for the accident years shown in table 3-6 and for years 1980–85 combined were substantially lower than reserves projected using these methods. For 1985 the estimated inadequacy is considerably less for the industry, and projections for accident year 1985 losses for the forty-five-company sample were lower than the reported reserve. Since the sample includes the largest insurers in the industry, the results suggest that small companies may be underreserved to a greater extent than large companies. But the large potential error in projections using paid claims for long-tailed lines should be kept in mind when evaluating the results. In particular, any slowdown (or acceleration) in the rate of claim payment for 1985 accidents could cause projections for 1985 to be far too small (or large).

Disputes about Profitability

The magnitude of profits in the property-liability insurance industry has been debated for at least two decades. In the late 1960s the dispute concerned whether profitability was inadequate compared with that of other industries based on comparisons of accounting returns for assets or net worth. In the 1980s the adequacy of profits was still being questioned based on similar analyses.[33] Recently profitability has been debated by the Insurance Services Office (ISO) and the National Insurance Consumer Organization (NICO).[34] ISO has argued that the indus-

---

through 1985, as the development factor beyond year five for each accident year. This procedure assumes that, as of 1985, reserves for accident year 1980 are accurate and that no development is expected after the sixth year for 1980 and subsequent accident years. This assumption might be considered optimistic, given recent experience and the possibility of continued growth in claims in such areas as liability for environmental hazards (see chapter 5). But changes in tort law might have some downward impact on future development compared with recent years.

32. A firm statement in this regard would require analysis of the impact of errors for each accident year on results in each calendar year.

33. See Emilio C. Venezian, "Are Insurers Under-Earning?" *Journal of Risk and Insurance,* vol. 51 (March 1984), pp. 150–56; and Insurance Services Office, *Insurer Profitability: A Long-Term Perspective* (New York, 1987).

34. See Insurance Services Office, *Insurer Profitability: The Facts* (New York, 1986); ISO, *Insurer Profitability: A Long-Term Perspective;* and National Insurance Consumer

try experienced large losses on operations in 1984 and 1985 and that it is inappropriate to consider capital gains, especially unrealized capital gains, when assessing income from insurance operations. NICO has argued that the industry's emphasis on operating income is deficient in that it fails to consider capital gains, fails to deduct GAAP expenses, inappropriately deducts policyholder dividends, and fails to discount future losses.[35] NICO concluded that the industry's measure of operating income seriously understates profitability and that the robust performance of stock prices for the industry in 1985 illustrates that operations were profitable despite large reported operating losses.

Accounting Results

As table 3-3 shows, the inclusion of either realized or unrealized capital gains substantially improves income relative to premiums and net worth in 1985 and 1986. In contrast to NICO, ISO argued in 1986 that it is inappropriate to include capital gains because they are highly variable and nonrecurring. The variability of unrealized capital gains is pronounced, as can be seen in tables 3-2 and 3-3. In 1987 ISO has shown that unrealized capital gains had little impact on average return on equity for the industry during 1970–86, but that they substantially increased the variability of return on equity. This study also argued that the average return on equity (as defined by ISO) for the property-liability industry was below the average for other industries during 1970–86, regardless of whether unrealized capital gains were included in income.

The theory of competitive insurance prices provides some insight into the appropriate treatment of capital gains.[36] The theory has been developed under the assumption of zero default risk on insurance contracts.

Organization, "And Now the Real Facts: A Response to the Insurance Services Office's 'Insurer Profitability: The Facts' " (Alexandria, Va., undated).

35. NICO frequently cites a General Accounting Office study that argued SAP income was inappropriate for tax purposes; see Natwar M. Gandhi, group director, tax policy, of the General Government Division, U.S. General Accounting Office, speech before the 1985 meeting of the American Risk and Insurance Association, Vancouver.

36. See William B. Fairley, "Investment Income and Profit Margins in Property-Liability Insurance: Theory and Empirical Results," *Bell Journal of Economics*, vol. 10 (Spring 1979), pp. 182–210; also in J. David Cummins and Scott E. Harrington, eds., *Fair Rate of Return in Property-Liability Insurance* (Boston: Kluwer Nijhoff, 1987), pp. 1–26; and Stewart C. Myers and Richard A. Cohn, "A Discounted Cash Flow Approach to Property-Liability Insurance Rate Regulation," in Cummins and Harrington, *Fair Rate of Return*, pp. 55–78.

Since the risk from investing in risky assets is borne completely by shareholders (policyholders are assumed to be unaffected by investment risk), the higher expected return on such investments does not affect the break-even price of insurance paid by policyholders. Instead, the theory suggests that break-even prices will reflect only the risk-free rate of interest on funds supplied by policyholders.[37]

While there is not an exact relationship, most net investment income (interest, dividends, and rents) has a relatively low risk, whereas most realized capital gains and all unrealized capital gains may constitute returns to shareholders for holding risky investments.[38] As a result, the industry's emphasis on a definition of operating income that includes net investment income but excludes capital gains may be reasonable. If so, the magnitude of capital gains may be largely irrelevant to assessing whether income from insurance operations has been inadequate or subject to large increases or decreases.[39]

As noted in appendix A, the failure of SAP income to match revenues and expenses generally produces an income measure that is lower than GAAP income. However, as is shown in tables 3-2 and 3-3, the magnitude of this difference is unlikely to be significant when assessing profitability in recent years.[40] Moreover, common profit measures, such as the combined ratio and the operating ratio, measure income on a GAAP basis by implicitly adjusting for prepaid expenses.

The appropriate treatment of policy dividends depends on how they

37. This result is obtained by solving for the premium level or underwriting profit margin that leaves shareholder wealth unchanged when policies are sold. With default risk, policyholders would be affected by investment risk in the absence of guaranty funds. The theory of break-even prices is not well developed under these conditions, but the existence of guaranty funds suggests that the assumption of zero default risk may be reasonable in this context.

38. Most of the realized capital gains for 1985, the latest year for which data are available, were for stocks rather than bonds.

39. The lack of information concerning unrealized capital gains on bonds may complicate this issue. Depending on insurer investment strategy, changes in the value of the bond portfolio could be anticipated as a source of funds to pay losses. For example, if insurers held immunized portfolios of assets and liabilities, part of a reduction in net investment income due to declining interest rates would be expected to be offset by realized or unrealized capital gains on bonds. Under these conditions, it might be argued that a portion of capital gains on bonds would need to be included in any ex post analysis of profitability.

40. While pretax statutory income generally will be less than GAAP income, statutory surplus generally will be less than GAAP surplus. It is thus not clear that income relative to equity will be understated on a statutory basis relative to GAAP. Data reported in *Insurance Facts* (New York: Insurance Information Institute, annual) suggest that SAP returns on equity or surplus will often exceed similar measures based on GAAP.

affect ex ante prices. If dividends are not anticipated when policies are issued in a given line but instead arise only from favorable deviations of overall losses from those expected, then NICO's suggestion that dividends should not be deducted from income when assessing industry performance and price adequacy may have merit.[41] However, the only line in which dividends accounted for a substantial portion of premiums in 1984–86 was workers' compensation.[42] In this line, regulated premiums often are set well above expected costs so that dividends are anticipated when policies are issued, and it is reasonable to treat dividends as premium refunds. For general liability, medical malpractice, commercial multiperil, and commercial auto liability, the treatment of dividends does not materially affect measures of income relative to premiums or surplus. The fact that aggregate income is higher if a large amount of workers' compensation dividends is added to reported income is irrelevant to the issue of whether income was inadequate on any of these lines.

The failure of reported income to discount future claims payments tends to understate both income and surplus if undiscounted reserves are accurate. As a result, it is not clear that accounting returns to equity are either higher or lower than would be the case if reserves were to be discounted. Moreover, the impact on income and surplus of discounting reserves would depend on reserve adequacy with or without discounting. The evidence that undiscounted reserves probably were inadequate in recent years suggests that the use of discounted but accurate reserves would have much less impact than simply discounting statement reserves.[43] In any case, it is unlikely that discounting reserves would have

41. Claims of inadequate prices and profits in conjunction with large dividends would be incongruous. The GAO has suggested that dividends should not be deducted for tax purposes (Gandhi, address before American Risk and Insurance Association). Also see the statement by Johnny C. Finch, which argues that dividends should not be deducted from income because they are discretionary; statement of Johnny C. Finch, senior associate director, General Government Division, U.S. General Accounting Office, before the Subcommittee on Oversight, House Committee on Ways and Means, on profitability of the property/casualty insurance industry, Washington, D.C., April 28, 1986.

42. For example, according to data reported in *Best's Aggregates and Averages: Property-Casualty, 1986* (Oldwick, N.J.: A. M. Best, 1986), policyholder dividends in 1985 equaled 9.3 percent of earned premiums for workers' compensation but only 0.5, 1.0, 0.7, and 0.1 percent of earned premiums for general liability, medical malpractice, commercial auto liability, and commercial multiperil, respectively.

43. A study in *Best's Insurance Management Reports: Property-Casualty Edition,* June 7, 1986, of loss reserves for the one-hundred largest property-liability groups estimated that reported reserves in 1984 exceeded discounted (at 9 percent) estimates of future claims for ninety of the groups. The results were not disaggregated by line of business.

changed the evidence that operating income *fell* substantially in 1984 and 1985. The level of income would be higher, but the relative reduction in income would probably be similar.

In short, there is some merit to both the industry's position and the views of NICO. It also is not surprising that the magnitude of insurance accounting profits would be vigorously debated given the large premium increases that have occurred since 1984. What is clear is that reported income from operations, whether SAP or GAAP, declined abruptly in 1984, remained relatively low in 1985 and began to increase in 1986. Discounting of reserves, if done consistently over time, would be unlikely to change this picture very much. Omniscient elimination of errors in estimating reserves might well accentuate it. Capital gains contributed substantially to surplus growth in 1985 and 1986, but theory suggests that this may not be relevant to making statements about whether products sold in 1984–86 were priced above or below expected costs.

The debate over profitability has suffered from lack of attention to accident year results and to market values of bonds, the possibility of large errors in estimating reserves, and the lack of a clear standard based on theory against which to judge profitability, however defined. The detailed discussions of calendar year accounting results, especially total dollar income measures, have shed little light on the crucial questions of whether and how much policies in any given year were underpriced or overpriced relative to expected costs. The focus on aggregate results, as opposed to results for commercial liability or general liability alone, involves the implicit assumption that favorable experience in some lines makes unfavorable experience in general liability or other commercial liability lines acceptable. But multiproduct insurance companies cannot be expected to commit capital to a line that does not leave them just as well off as investing the capital in financial assets and not selling coverage in that line, regardless of the experience of other lines. The almost exclusive focus on calendar year results fails to clarify the relationship between premiums and losses for policies in force in a given period. Poor results for earlier years that influence current calendar year results need not imply anything about the adequacy of prices on current business. When evaluating recent performance, greater attention should be given to accident year results for each line, as is done for general liability later in this chapter.

The form of the insurance company annual statement, which is determined by regulators, has probably contributed to the focus on calendar year results. Accident year results are buried in schedule P and are

Table 3-7. *Annual Percentage Changes in A. M. Best and Standard and Poor's Common Stock Indexes, 1981–86*

Year	A. M. Best stock indexes[a]			Standard and Poor's 500	Standard and Poor's over-the-counter 250
	Property-liability	Life-health	Multiple line		
1981	37.8	15.4	25.9	−2.2	12.9
1982	18.3	23.2	−3.6	13.0	50.8
1983	14.7	30.8	13.1	15.2	29.9
1984	0.2	19.2	3.9	−0.4	−5.0
1985	59.4	31.0	48.4	26.9	32.2
1986	14.7	11.8	3.4	19.9	15.4
1981–83[b]	22.4	22.1	10.0	8.4	30.3
1984–86[b]	22.4	20.4	16.8	14.8	13.2
1981–86[b]	22.4	21.3	13.4	11.6	21.4

Sources: Annual percentage changes for the A. M. Best indexes calculated using index values as of the second week of December as reported in the January issues of *Best's Review: Property/Casualty Insurance Edition*. Standard and Poor index values as of the second week of December are from *Standard and Poor's Security Price Index Service*.

a. Indexes reflect returns for about thirty property-liability, twenty life-health, and five multiple-line companies. All returns exclude dividend yield. Stocks of most insurers in the property-liability and life-health indexes are traded on the over-the-counter market.

b. Values are calculated as of December the preceding year. Values for multiyear periods are geometric mean returns.

highly aggregated for such lines as multiperil. Considerable calculation is needed to determine the impact of developments in losses for earlier years on results for the current calendar year. In addition to providing greater detail and emphasis on accident year results in the annual statement, estimates of the market value of bonds should be reported. While many bonds held by insurers are not publicly traded, it still should be possible to develop reasonably accurate estimates for users of financial statements. Accident year and calendar year losses also should be discounted to facilitate comparison of results across lines and to allow more accurate assessment of changes in income over time.

Stock Prices

Table 3-7 shows stock price performance for property and liability, life and health, and multiple-line insurers for 1981–86. Returns on the Standard and Poor's 500 and over-the-counter 250 indexes are also shown. The annual returns illustrate the source of controversy about recent insurance industry performance. Best's property-liability index appreciated by 59 percent in 1985, a year in which large operating losses were reported for the industry. Since the average beta for property-liability stocks during this period probably was less than 1, this performance probably cannot be attributed simply to factors influencing the 32 percent return on the Standard and Poor over-the-counter 250 index during this time.[44]

Rough comparison does not provide strong evidence of unusual performance for the property-liability index. Its average annual return for 1981–83, 1984–86, and 1981–86 was 22 percent in each period, about the same as those for the life-health index. The average return for the property-liability stocks during 1981–86 also is about equal to that for the Standard and Poor over-the-counter 250, although it was much less than that for the Standard and Poor over-the-counter 250 during 1981–83 and much greater during 1984–86. The same general pattern holds for the life-health index.

Stock returns are the ultimate measure of financial performance. In principle it is possible to determine whether returns are abnormally low or high in any given period conditional on some assumed asset-pricing model. However, even if such an analysis could be successfully undertaken for the property-liability insurance industry, the implications for whether business was underpriced or overpriced would be uncertain. Stock prices may reflect all information affecting security returns, but it may be impossible to sort out the impact of various factors that affect prices in a given period. The performance of the property-liability index in 1985 could be consistent with break-even premiums on business written in both 1985 and 1986. It also could be consistent with premiums above expected costs.

To illustrate, let the market value of a firm's equity at time t (the value of its common stock) be

$$(1) \qquad E_t = A_t - L_t + \Pi_t,$$

where A_t is the market value of assets for business written before time t; L_t is the market value of liabilities (that is, the market's assessment of the true value of liabilities) for business written before time t; and Π_t is the market's assessment of the excess of assets over liabilities for busi-

---

44. J. David Cummins and Scott Harrington, "The Relationship between Risk and Return: Evidence for Property-Liability Insurance Stocks," *Journal of Risk and Insurance* (forthcoming). Beta is defined as the covariance of the returns on a security with the returns on a broad portfolio of common stocks. Finance theory suggests that beta is a more appropriate measure of risk than return variance for investors with diversified portfolios. Nelson J. Lacey analyzed returns for life and property-liability insurance stocks for 1982–85. His results suggested that the stocks did less well than the market, but his sample included stocks for only five property-liability insurers. See "Recent Evidence on the Liability Crisis," unpublished manuscript (University of Massachusetts, Department of General Business and Finance, December 1986).

ness written at and after time t (the market value of net cash flows on current and future business). After some manipulation, it can be shown (for Π_{t-1} not equal to zero) that if no new equity is issued, the return on equity in period t ($r_{et} = E_t/E_{t-1} - 1$) is given by

$$(2) \qquad r_{et} = \frac{[r_{At} + (r_{At} - r_{Lt})k_{t-1} + r_{\Pi t}\pi_{t-1}]}{(1 + \pi_{t-1})},$$

where $r_{At} = A_t/A_{t-1} - 1$ (growth in assets), $r_{Lt} = L_t/L_{t-1} - 1$ (growth in liabilities), $r_{\Pi t} = \Pi_t/\Pi_{t-1} - 1$ (growth in Π), $k_t = L_t/(A_t - L_t)$ (market value of liabilities on old business relative to the market value of equity for old business), and π_t equals $\Pi_t/(A_t - L_t)$ (market value of net cash flows on current and future business relative to market value of equity for old business).

If investors believed that business were to be priced to break even, so that $\Pi = 0$ for all t, and if assets and liabilities were immunized against changes in interest rate risk, and forecasts of future claims were accurate, the percentage change in equity during a given period would be approximately equal to the percentage change in the value of assets. In general, property-liability assets have longer duration than liabilities, so that increases (or decreases) in interest rates will tend to produce negative (or positive) growth in the market value of equity for old business.[45] Changes in the value of equity in a given period will also reflect revisions in expectations about future claims on old business as well as changes in the profitability of current and future business. Positive or negative abnormal returns in a period could reflect any of these influences. Total returns in any period could be large and positive even if premiums on current and future business were expected to equal the discounted value of all costs.

As an example, consider a period such as 1985 in which returns on insurance company assets were large because of increasing stock prices and the favorable impact of declining interest rates on bond values. Assume that $r_{At} = 0.20$. Given the longer duration of assets than liabilities, assume that $r_{Lt} = 0.10$ and that there is no revision in expectations about claims on old business. Let $k_{t-1} = 2$. Finally, assume that $\pi_t = 0$ but that $\pi_{t-1} = -0.10$, that is, current and future business are expected to break even, but business written in period $t-1$ was priced below

45. Richard A. Derrig, "The Effect of Federal Taxes on Investment Income in Property-Liability Ratemaking," paper presented at the 1985 meeting of the American Risk and Insurance Association, Vancouver.

expected costs. Based on these assumptions, the value of r_{Et} from equation 2 is 56 percent. While the assumptions are ad hoc, they nonetheless indicate the possibility that stock returns could be expected to be quite large in 1985 without positive profits on business written in 1985 or 1986, especially if business written in 1984 had been underpriced. The market reaction would simply reflect the return to break-even rates and favorable investment performance. The growth in premiums also could be very large, given declining interest rates, rapid growth in expected losses on new business, and a return to break-even pricing.

Growth in Premiums and Losses

Table 3-8 presents annual growth rates in written premiums, earned premiums, and calendar year incurred losses for the major third-party lines and all lines for 1977–86. The growth rates in premiums generally were large in 1977 and 1978, low and even negative during 1979–83, and very large in 1985 and 1986. This pattern is most pronounced for general liability.[46] Calendar year incurred losses, which reflect revisions in reserves on previous years' claims, show a similar pattern, although the growth in losses generally is well above zero even for 1979–83. The 78 percent growth rate in written premiums in 1985 and the estimated 73 percent growth rate in 1986 for general liability, along with smaller but still large growth rates for medical malpractice, commercial multi-peril, and commercial auto liability, clearly indicate what the debate is about, especially since the amount of coverage provided for general liability and perhaps other lines may have been declining during these years.[47]

Casual observation suggests the cyclical pattern of large but declining increases in premiums written following the adverse financial experience of 1974 and 1975 and dramatic increases following the adverse results of 1984. Without cyclical influences, growth rates would primarily re-

46. J. David Cummins and David J. Nye note that general liability (including medical malpractice) had the highest annual growth rate in net premiums written for all major property-liability lines from 1952 to 1980; see "Inflation and Property-Liability Insurance," in John D. Long and Everett D. Randall, eds., *Issues in Insurance,* 3d ed., vol. 1 (Malvern, Pa.: American Institute for Property and Liability Underwriters, 1984), p. 200.

47. Since there is no standard unit of exposure for most property-liability lines, and coverage levels are not reported, statements about reductions in coverage are anecdotal. It should also be noted that the growth figures for medical malpractice could be influenced by changes in the proportion of business written by insurers that report to A. M. Best Co.

Table 8

Table 3-8. *Growth Rates for Net Premiums Written, Net Premiums Earned, and Incurred Losses, by Line of Insurance, 1977–86*
Percent

Item	General liability	Medical malpractice	Commercial multiperil	Commercial auto liability	Private passenger auto liability	Workers' compensation	All property-liability
Net premiums written							
1976–77	37.5	10.2	22.7	23.5	20.3	24.2	19.8
1977–78	11.0	–2.6	17.3	11.4	9.7	20.8	12.8
1978–79	1.9	–0.9	14.4	8.8	13.0	16.5	10.3
1979–80	–3.0	5.9	3.3	0.3	9.9	8.2	6.0
1980–81	–5.7	4.9	–0.2	0.3	7.2	2.7	3.9
1981–82	–6.2	11.4	2.0	–0.1	9.4	–4.6	4.7
1982–83	0.2	5.2	4.0	–0.1	8.6	0.4	4.8
1983–84	14.1	13.2	13.6	14.2	6.3	7.9	8.4
1984–85	78.2	56.0	46.0	45.0	13.8	12.8	22.0
1985–86	73.1	29.3	32.5	n.a.	n.a.	14.7	22.3
Net premiums earned							
1976–77	36.7	8.2	22.9	23.6	22.2	24.7	20.5
1977–78	15.2	–0.4	17.3	13.2	12.9	18.7	14.3

1978–79	5.8	−1.3	15.7	11.1	11.1	17.5	10.4
1979–80	0.8	1.6	6.7	1.6	11.4	9.8	7.8
1980–81	−7.5	5.6	−0.2	1.9	7.3	3.7	4.0
1981–82	−6.3	7.3	3.0	−0.8	8.5	−3.4	4.7
1982–83	0.2	11.1	4.0	0.1	9.2	1.3	4.9
1983–84	9.1	13.2	9.4	9.5	7.3	7.5	7.2
1984–85	49.1	41.6	30.9	33.1	10.2	11.3	15.7
1985–86	77.2	35.7	38.8	n.a.	n.a.	13.9	24.0
Incurred losses (calendar year)							
1976–77	27.4	−9.4	9.6	17.0	3.6	25.1	13.0
1977–78	9.1	9.7	10.7	13.6	18.1	13.4	13.4
1978–79	5.1	10.9	33.0	16.7	18.1	12.7	15.1
1979–80	11.5	17.2	13.2	5.8	6.0	5.0	10.5
1980–81	1.0	11.7	10.8	10.9	9.5	2.3	6.6
1981–82	7.6	18.8	14.2	6.5	9.5	−5.6	8.7
1982–83	8.6	11.2	12.6	6.3	10.4	10.3	7.1
1983–84	25.4	22.6	26.3	22.2	9.7	22.2	16.0
1984–85	49.9	49.3	20.5	18.9	18.7	10.9	16.4
1985–86	44.0	16.6	3.6	n.a.	n.a.	18.8	15.4

Sources: Data for 1976–85 are from *Best's Aggregates and Averages: Property-Casualty, 1986*. For 1986, estimated net premiums written are from Wish, "Review and Preview." Estimated net premiums earned and incurred losses for 1986 were calculated using data reported in Wish.
n.a. Not available.

flect growth in demand, expected losses, expenses, and changes in interest rates. As interest rates increase (or decrease), break-even premiums decline (or increase), other things being equal, since the discount rate for future losses increases (or decreases). The low and even negative growth rates in general liability premiums for 1979–82 were influenced by the sharp increases in interest rates through 1981 and their continued high level in 1982 (see appendix B, table 3-15). Whether the declines in premiums also reflected excessive competition is discussed later, as is whether decreases in interest rates after 1982 and growth in losses can explain the large growth in premiums in 1985 and 1986.

Table 3-9 shows geometric mean annual growth rates for premiums and incurred losses relative to growth in nominal GNP in 1976–86.[48] Both premiums and losses grew more slowly than GNP from 1976 to 1981, when interest rates were rising and the 11.4 percent growth rate in nominal GNP reflected a CPI growth rate of almost 10 percent. Since 1981, when interest rates were falling and the growth in GNP was slower, largely because of lower inflation, the growth of both premiums and losses significantly exceeded that for GNP. These rates contributed to substantial growth relative to GNP for the entire 1976–86 period. This pattern is most pronounced for general liability and for medical malpractice.

Growth rates for calendar year losses reflect revisions in reserves on losses incurred in earlier periods. An alternative measure of growth is provided by accident year data, which give losses incurred only for accidents (including claims not reported) during a given year. Nominal growth rates for accident year losses and rates relative to GNP growth are shown for the entire industry and for the forty-five company sample in table 3-10. Two sets of growth rates were calculated: accident year

48. The geometric mean growth rate for GNP was 11.4 percent for 1976–81, 6.6 percent for 1981–86, and 9.0 percent for 1976–86. Comparisons of real growth rates per capita would show values in all periods larger than those based on GNP, and the difference would be greatest for subperiods in the 1980s. Some of the increase in growth rates for losses relative to GNP after 1981 that are shown in table 3-9 and subsequent tables could be due to inflation in medical care costs. Norton E. Masterson has periodically reported claim cost indexes for various property-liability lines that are weighted averages of wage and price indexes that should be highly correlated with factors associated with loss costs for each line; see "Economic Factors in Liability and Property Insurance Claims Costs," *Best's Review: Property/Casualty Edition*, vol. 81 (June 1980), p. 74. Comparison of his index for "other bodily injury liability" through 1980 with the GNP implicit price deflator (Cummins and Nye, "Inflation and Property-Liability Insurance," pp. 211–15) provided little motivation for construction of a more elaborate index to analyze growth in premiums and losses in this study.

Table 3-9. *Growth Rates for Net Premiums Written, Net Premiums Earned, and Incurred Losses Relative to GNP, by Line of Insurance, Selected Periods, 1976–86*
Percent

Item	General liability	Medical malpractice	Commercial multiperil	Commercial auto liability	Private passenger auto liability	Workers' compensation	All property-liability
Net premiums written							
1976–81	-3.6	-7.2	-0.2	-2.5	0.5	2.5	-0.8
1981–85	9.9	12.1	7.7	6.0	3.6	-2.9	2.6
1976–85	2.1	1.0	3.2	1.2	1.9	0.1	0.7
1981–86[a]	19.1	14.2	11.1	n.a.	n.a.	-0.6	5.2
1976–86[a]	7.1	3.0	5.3	n.a.	n.a.	1.0	2.1
Net premiums earned							
1976–81	-1.9	-7.8	0.7	-1.2	1.4	3.0	-0.1
1981–85	3.9	9.9	4.0	2.5	2.9	-2.8	1.0
1976–85	0.6	-0.3	2.2	0.4	2.0	0.4	0.4
1981–86[a]	14.4	13.4	9.1	n.a.	n.a.	-0.7	4.1
1976–86[a]	5.9	2.3	4.8	n.a.	n.a.	1.1	2.0
Incurred losses (calendar year)							
1976–81	-0.8	-3.4	3.4	1.2	-0.4	0.1	0.3
1981–85	13.8	16.5	10.5	5.8	3.2	1.9	4.7
1976–85	5.4	5.0	6.5	3.3	1.2	0.9	2.2
1981–86[a]	18.1	15.4	8.0	n.a.	n.a.	4.0	5.6
1976–86[a]	8.2	5.6	5.7	n.a.	n.a.	2.0	2.9

Sources: Premium and loss data are from Best's Aggregates and Averages: Property-Casualty, 1986; and Wish, "Review and Preview." Growth rates are annual geometric means. GNP data are from the *Economic Report of the President*, January 1987.
n.a. Not available.
a. Estimated.

Table 3-10. *Growth Rates for Accident Year Incurred Losses, by Line of Insurance, Selected Periods, 1976–85*
Percent

Sample	Period	General liability	Medical malpractice	General liability and medical malpractice	Multiperil	Auto liability	Workers' compensation	Schedule P[a]	Schedule O[a]
Initially reported									
Industry	1981–85	17.3	19.2	17.7	11.6	11.5	8.2	11.7	n.a.
	1976–81	11.5	3.1	10.0	14.9	11.8	14.4	12.9	10.9
45 companies	1981–85	16.8	12.2	16.2	11.1	10.9	8.2	11.0	8.2
	1976–85	13.9	7.0	12.7	13.2	11.4	11.6	12.0	9.7
Ratio of initially reported/GNP									
Industry	1981–85	9.6	11.4	10.1	4.3	4.3	1.2	4.4	n.a.
	1976–81	0.1	−7.4	−1.3	3.2	0.4	2.7	1.4	−0.4
45 companies	1981–85	9.2	4.9	8.6	3.9	3.7	1.1	3.7	1.2
	1976–85	4.1	−2.1	3.0	3.5	1.8	2.0	2.4	0.3
Developed through 1985									
Industry	1976–81	10.9	17.1	12.4	15.2	11.9	10.7	12.5	12.3
	1981–85	14.7	11.4	13.8	11.5	11.5	10.3	11.6	8.5
	1976–85	12.6	14.5	13.0	13.5	11.8	10.5	12.1	10.6
45 companies	1976–81	7.9	6.8	7.7	15.1	11.8	9.3	11.5	10.7
	1981–85	15.4	11.0	14.8	11.1	11.0	10.6	11.4	9.3
	1976–85	11.2	8.7	10.8	13.3	11.5	9.8	11.5	10.1
Ratio of developed through 1985/GNP									
Industry	1976–81	−0.4	5.2	0.9	3.4	0.5	−0.6	1.1	0.8
	1981–85	7.2	4.2	6.4	4.2	4.2	3.1	4.3	1.4
	1976–85	2.9	4.7	3.3	3.8	2.2	1.0	2.5	1.1
45 companies	1976–81	−3.1	−4.1	−3.3	3.3	0.4	−1.9	0.1	−0.5
	1981–85	7.9	3.8	7.3	3.9	3.8	3.4	4.1	2.2
	1976–85	1.6	−0.7	1.3	3.6	1.9	0.4	1.9	0.7

Souces: Industry data are from *Best's Aggregates and Averages: Property-Casualty, 1986*; data for forty-five companies provided by Aetna Life and Casualty Company. Growth rates are annual geometric means.

n.a. Not available.

a. Schedule P includes aggregate experience for the groupings of third-party lines. Schedule O includes aggregate experience for first-party coverages.

losses initially reported and losses for the accident year developed through 1985.[49]

The results have much the same pattern as those for the calendar year losses shown in table 3-9. For general liability and the forty-five company sample, losses grew at about the same rate as GNP during 1976–81, but grew 9.2 percent faster than GNP during 1981–85, which is much faster than the rates for the other lines shown. The results using developed losses provide some evidence of errors in estimated reserves but have the same general implication as those based on initially reported losses and calendar year losses. The results for medical malpractice are a possible exception, since they indicate a decline in the growth relative to GNP in 1981–85 compared with 1976–81. However, the possibility exists that changes in the market share of malpractice insurers that do not report data to A. M. Best could distort these rates.

Table 3-11 shows growth rates for total losses paid for the forty-five company sample and for accident year losses paid through three years for the industry and for the sample.[50] While the rates for total paid losses are shown separately for general liability and for medical malpractice, these results could be distorted by changes in reporting methods following 1975. Calculation of total paid losses uses the change in the total loss reserve during a given year. Before 1975, separate reserves were not reported for medical malpractice and general liability. After separate results began to be reported, some companies segregated reserves for the two lines for accidents before the change, others did not. Since the separate results for total losses paid may be distorted by these differences, it is better to focus on the combined results for the two lines.[51]

49. It is not clear which procedure is better. If loss development is similar over time, use of initially reported losses would provide a more accurate measure of the underlying growth in losses. If reserve accuracy improved, the use of developed losses as of 1985 would tend to be more accurate. The source for the industry data, *Best's Aggregates and Averages,* provided initially reported losses beginning with the 1979 accident year, so that growth rates for 1976–81 could not be calculated for the industry.

50. Total paid losses for a given year were calculated as calendar year incurred losses less the change in the loss reserve for the year. Since the loss reserve data began in 1976, the paid loss figures begin in 1977. Total paid losses could not be calculated for the industry using information provided in *Best's Aggregates and Averages.* Using other A. M. Best data, both Insurance Services Office and Carole Banfield provide graphs showing large growth in paid losses relative to GNP for general liability and medical malpractice since the late 1970s. See ISO, *Insurer Profitability: The Facts;* and Banfield, "P/C Insurer Profitability: ISO Paid Claims Data," *Journal of Insurance Regulation,* vol. 5 (December 1986), pp. 268–76.

51. The much higher rates shown for medical malpractice than for general liability probably are due to this effect.

Table 3-11. *Growth Rates for Paid Losses, by Line of Insurance, Selected Periods, 1976–85*
Percent

Sample	Period	General liability[a]	Medical malpractice[a]	General liability and medical malpractice	Multiperil	Auto liability	Workers' compensation	Schedule P[b]	Schedule O[b]
Total paid									
45 companies	1981–82	12.8	24.6	14.2	13.9	11.9	9.8	12.3	3.5
	1982–83	10.0	43.2	14.2	5.3	8.1	6.5	7.6	–11.7
	1983–84	17.6	–11.9	12.9	17.9	12.4	13.6	14.2	29.3
	1984–85	–2.9	30.6	13.8	7.7	12.6	13.0	11.4	12.4
	1977–81	11.9	33.0	13.6	17.6	12.1	12.5	13.8	11.7
	1981–85	9.1	38.0	13.8	11.1	11.2	10.7	11.4	9.9
	1977–85	10.5	35.5	13.7	14.3	11.7	11.6	12.6	10.8
Ratio of total paid/GNP									
45 companies	1977–81	0.6	19.5	2.1	5.7	0.7	1.1	2.2	0.4
	1981–85	2.0	29.0	6.4	3.8	4.0	3.5	4.1	2.7
	1977–85	1.3	24.2	4.2	4.7	2.3	2.3	3.2	1.5
Accident year losses paid through three years									
Industry	1979–83	15.3	29.6	17.3	12.4	11.0	9.1	11.5	n.a.
45 companies	1976–79	11.1	14.6	11.4	18.4	13.0	12.7	14.4	11.9
	1979–83	13.8	30.9	15.6	12.5	10.5	8.1	10.9	8.5
	1976–83	12.6	23.6	13.8	15.0	11.6	10.0	12.4	10.0
Ratio of accident year losses paid through three years/GNP									
Industry	1979–83	6.8	20.0	8.6	4.1	2.8	1.0	3.3	n.a.
45 companies	1976–79	–0.9	2.3	–0.6	5.7	0.9	0.6	2.1	–0.1
	1979–83	5.4	21.2	7.1	4.2	2.4	0.1	2.8	0.5
	1976–83	2.7	12.7	3.7	4.8	1.7	0.3	2.5	0.2

Sources: Industry data are from *Best's Aggregates and Averages: Property-Casualty, 1986*; data for forty-five companies provided by Aetna Life and Casualty Company. Growth rates are annual geometric means.
n.a. Not available.
a. Separate rates for general liability and medical malpractice distorted because of reserve reporting practices.
b. Schedule P includes aggregate experience for the groupings of third-party lines. Schedule O includes aggregate experience for first-party coverages.

Apart from this problem, the value of looking at growth rates for losses paid is that they will not be distorted by reserve errors. They will, however, be affected by changes in the speed at which claims are paid. A slowdown in the rate at which claims are settled will tend to reduce the growth rate in paid losses; more rapid payment will tend to increase it. For general liability, the paid loss development factors shown in appendix B, table 3-16, suggest some slowdown in claims payment during 1976–84, especially during 1976–80. Thus growth rates for this line would tend to be depressed.[52]

The nominal growth rates in total paid losses for general liability and medical malpractice combined were just under 14 percent for 1977–81, 1981–85, and 1977–85. As a result, the growth rate relative to GNP was 4.3 percent higher during 1981–85 than during 1977–81. The results for auto liability and workers' compensation are comparable. The results for multiperil show a decline relative to GNP during the two periods, although growth in total paid losses still exceeded the GNP growth rate by 3.8 percent during 1981–85. The decline in this line could reflect an increase in the proportion of third-party business with slower claims payment. The results for accident year paid losses through three years have implications similar to those for total paid losses.

Table 3-12 gives per capita growth rates in real written premiums and paid losses on direct business during 1976–84 for the ten most populous states in the 1980 census.[53] Based on the ten-state average for medical malpractice and general liability combined, the mean annual growth rate for real written premiums per capita was −0.6, 1.7, and 0.2 percent for 1976–81, 1981–84, and 1976–84, respectively. These periods precede the large premium increases in 1985 and 1986. The corresponding rates for real paid losses per capita were 6.6, 15.7 and 9.8 percent. While not directly comparable with the results for total paid claims net of reinsurance shown in table 3-11, these rates suggest that the growth of losses may have been considerably higher in large states than in the remainder of the country.

The overall results in tables 3-9 through 3-12 suggest that commercial

52. Comparable analysis was not conducted for the remaining lines.
53. GNP data are not available by state. These premium and loss data were reported by National Insurance Consumer Organization, "Property/Casualty Insurance Industry Income and Payouts" (Alexandria, Va., 1986); data were from *Best's Executive Data Service*. While NICO reported data for 1975–84, 1975 was excluded to make the first subperiod comparable to that used in the previous tables. The essence of the report was that insurers took in far more in written premiums than they paid in losses during the period.

Table 3-12. *Growth Rates for Direct Premiums Written and Losses Paid per Capita, by Line of Insurance, for Ten Largest States, Selected Periods, 1976–84*

Percent

Line	Period	California	New York	Texas	Pennsylvania	Illinois	Ohio	Florida	Michigan	New Jersey	North Carolina	Average
Real premiums written												
General liability	1976–81	-3.0	2.4	1.0	-0.5	-2.6	0.3	-2.3	1.2	1.0	1.4	-0.1
	1981–84	-1.8	0.1	-2.0	-0.9	-2.0	-4.9	0.2	9.0	-0.3	2.4	0.0
	1976–84	-2.6	1.6	-0.1	-0.6	-2.4	-1.7	-1.4	4.0	0.5	1.8	-0.1
Medical malpractice	1976–81	-11.8	4.9	-5.9	-6.2	-3.8	-5.3	10.8	-3.0	-2.9	0.6	-2.3
	1981–84	4.9	-3.7	0.7	10.6	9.3	4.7	14.1	7.6	28.6	15.7	9.3
	1976–84	-5.8	1.6	-3.5	-0.2	0.9	-1.7	12.0	0.8	7.9	6.0	1.8
General liability and medical malpractice	1976–81	-5.3	3.0	0.2	-1.5	-2.8	-1.0	-0.6	0.5	0.4	1.2	-0.6
	1981–84	-0.3	-0.8	-1.7	1.1	0.1	-2.9	2.9	8.8	4.5	5.1	1.7
	1976–84	-3.5	1.6	-0.5	-0.5	-1.7	-1.7	0.7	3.5	1.9	2.7	0.2
Real losses paid												
General liability	1976–81	5.0	8.4	9.4	12.7	1.3	6.6	0.3	13.1	3.5	-7.4	5.3
	1981–84	11.1	16.0	14.3	9.0	16.7	24.1	13.2	14.6	14.1	19.8	15.3
	1976–84	7.3	11.2	11.2	11.3	6.8	12.8	5.0	13.7	7.4	2.0	8.9
Medical malpractice	1976–81	8.1	19.3	5.1	17.0	8.8	11.6	9.5	24.1	19.1	18.7	14.1
	1981–84	13.4	16.4	20.2	6.2	12.9	35.1	-6.0	15.5	16.4	44.2	17.4
	1976–84	10.1	18.2	10.5	12.8	10.3	19.9	3.4	20.8	18.1	27.7	15.2
General liability and medical malpractice	1976–81	5.5	10.6	9.1	13.3	2.4	7.2	1.7	14.7	6.2	-0.5	6.6
	1981–84	11.5	16.1	14.7	8.6	16.0	25.9	10.0	14.7	14.6	24.6	15.7
	1976–84	7.7	12.6	11.2	11.5	7.3	13.9	4.8	14.7	9.3	5.2	9.8

Sources: Loss and premium data are from A. M. Best's Executive Data Service: Experience by State, as reproduced in National Insurance Consumer Organization, "Property/Casualty Insurance Industry Income and Payouts" (Alexandria, Va., 1986). Growth rates are annual geometric means. State rankings are based on the 1980 census, and real values are calculated using CPI; see U.S. Bureau of the Census, *Statistical Abstract of the United States*, various years.

liability losses have grown rapidly relative to GNP in recent years. While the 1981 cutoff was largely arbitrary, the results indicate that when inflation slowed in the early 1980s, the growth rate in losses did not.

Causes of Underwriting Cycles

Most observers believe that the property-liability market is characterized by underwriting cycles: soft markets with readily available coverage at falling prices followed by hard markets with difficulty in obtaining coverage and rapidly rising prices. Insurer profits (both accounting and economic), premiums written, and surplus vary accordingly. Theoretical work does not, however, provide a clear explanation for underwriting cycles. Empirical work also leaves something to be desired, perhaps because of the difficulty of using time series data for several decades to estimate structural relationships that are likely to alter because of changes in types of coverage, regulation, and other factors. Until the most recent cycle, the accepted wisdom was that the underwriting cycle had a period of about six years.[54] A number of authors have tried to explain why the most recent hard market began almost a decade after the hard market of 1975 and 1976.[55]

The traditional explanation of underwriting cycles is that competition

54. See, for example, Barbara D. Stewart, "Profit Cycles in Property-Liability Insurance," in John D. Long, ed., *Issues in Insurance,* 2d ed., vol. 2 (Malvern, Pa.: American Institute for Property and Liability Underwriters, 1981), pp. 79-140; and Milton E. Smith and Fikry S. Gahin, "The Underwriting Cycle in Property and Liability Insurance," unpublished manuscript (Brigham Young University, 1983). Some of this work has looked at combined ratios without considering the likely impact of changes in interest rates. Nonetheless, a casual look at premiums, accounting profits including investment income, and return on equity suggests cyclical patterns. The results of several studies indicate that such underwriting profit measures as the combined ratio follow a second-order autoregressive process that is consistent with a cycle; see Emilio C. Venezian, "Ratemaking Methods and Profit Cycles in Property and Liability Insurance," *Journal of Risk and Insurance,* vol. 52 (September 1985), pp. 477–500; and J. David Cummins and J. François Outreville, "An International Analysis of Underwriting Cycles in Property-Liability Insurance," *Journal of Risk and Insurance,* vol. 54 (June 1987), pp. 246–62. See also David Oakden, "Discussion," of Kaye D. James, "Underwriting Cycles in the Property-Casualty Insurance Industry," in Casualty Actuarial Society, *Inflation Implications for Property-Casualty Insurance* (New York, 1981). Some studies have suggested that the timing, amplitude, and frequency of cycles may vary by insurance line; see Stewart, "Profit Cycles in Property-Liability Insurance"; and Venezian, "Ratemaking Methods and Profit Cycles."

55. See, for example, Barry D. Smith, "The Property and Liability Underwriting Cycle: What Lies Ahead?" *CPCU Journal,* vol. 35 (September 1982), pp. 138–42; and

leads to excessive price cutting and that the resultant underwriting losses and reductions in surplus lead to a substantial reduction in aggregate supply so that prices, profits, and surplus increase until price cutting begins once again.[56] Two interesting questions arise in view of this explanation. Do prices on new business rise above costs? And why would rational, profit-maximizing firms have a persistent tendency in the first place to price business below cost so that retrenchment en masse is eventually needed to avoid financial collapse?

Empirical work has been silent about the extent to which prices exceed costs on a cycle's upswing. With free entry and perfectly informed buyers, existing insurers would not be able to raise prices above expected costs for new business to recoup past losses. Based on the current state of theory, it is unclear why existing insurers would not have incentives to issue new equity and to expand supply to prevent overpricing. This may have happened. The data in table 3-2 indicate an infusion of new capital into the industry in 1985 and 1986, which, along with the favorable capital gains experience, may have been expected to increase supply. Moreover, anecdotal evidence suggests that many specialty insurers entered the market in 1985 and 1986, often as association captives. Nonetheless, entry could have been slow enough to allow prices to exceed costs in the short run, provided that the previous deterioration in insurers' financial condition actually caused a substantial upward shift in supply.[57] Moreover, if competition periodically caused inadequate prices, recoupment of the attendant losses through subsequent price increases would be necessary for individual insurers to break even over the long run.

What about the pervasive tendency to price below cost? In a comprehensive review of regulation in other industries, Stephen Breyer has referred to the scenario of destructive competition as an "empty box."[58] Such competition has often been alleged to justify price and entry regulation, but there is little evidence it has existed in any industry. The

---

Robert T. McGee, "The Cycle in Property/Casualty Insurance," *Federal Reserve Bank of New York Quarterly Review* (Autumn 1986), pp. 22–30. Reasons discussed include increased capacity in the late 1970s and early 1980s because of entry by captives and numerous foreign reinsurers.

56. Stewart, "Profit Cycles in Property-Liability Insurance"; and Smith and Gahin, "Underwriting Cycle in Property and Liability Insurance."

57. The traditional view and theory currently do not provide a rigorous or concise explanation of why losses would actually lead to such a shift.

58. Stephen Breyer, *Regulation and Its Reform* (Harvard University Press, 1982).

possibility remains that prices may tend to go below expected costs in insurance because of difficulty in forecasting future claims. However, if forecasts were unbiased over the long run, errors would contribute to variability in cash flows and accounting profits, but they would not be expected to produce cycles, as opposed to random, although perhaps large, variation.

Cash-flow underwriting has been alleged to have aggravated the recent downturn in profits because high interest rates led insurers to sell coverage at inadequate prices to obtain funds for investment.[59] Since break-even premiums equal the discounted value of losses and other costs, premiums will tend to decline as interest rates increase.[60] But these suppositions shed little light on why this relationship should allow prices to fall too low. For example, if future claims were known with certainty, increases in interest rates would not be expected to cause insurers to sell coverage below cost in order to invest money at rates insufficient to pay future claims.

Emilio Venezian has argued that forecasting methods used by insurance rating bureaus may lead to profit cycles. While he presents some evidence consistent with his conjecture, it raises the difficult question of why forecasting techniques would be both widely used and relied on if they produced large fluctuations in premiums. In an alternative view Robert McGee has suggested that companies with optimistic expectations about the magnitude of future claims may cause prices to decline below average expectations of future costs. If so, companies that believe prices to be temporarily inadequate may maximize profits (minimize losses) by maintaining coverage to avoid substantial losses in volume in the presence of fixed costs.[61] In a world in which all economic agents are making accurate forecasts on the basis of all available information, expectations would be homogeneous. Since such a world does not exist, further development of this heterogeneous expectations argument that considers expectations of buyers as well as sellers might help explain cycles. As it is, this view would imply that insurers with unfavorable expectations about future claims would start to show large losses before those with favorable expectations, provided that loss reserves reflected

59. This view has often been expressed in the trade press and by NICO.

60. Michael L. Smith, "Investment Yields and Insurance Underwriting," unpublished manuscript (Ohio State University, February 26, 1987), provides evidence that premiums are negatively related to interest rates.

61. Venezian, "Ratemaking Methods and Profit Cycles"; and McGee, "Cycle in Property/Casualty Insurance."

expectations. However, incentives could exist for sellers with unfavorable expectations to underreserve, perhaps to avoid reaction by regulators, shareholders, or buyers that might be sensitive to the probability of default. Further work is needed to explore these issues.

The theory of insurance company capital structure raises the possibility that the supply functions of individual firms could differ, with the result that prices could fall below costs even with homogeneous expectations. If customer demand is inelastic with respect to default probability, the theory suggests that insurers with little to lose in the event of default would be willing to sell more coverage relative to capital at a given premium rate than insurers with a lot to lose.[62] The possibility exists under these conditions that high-risk insurers could cause prices to fall below costs. Again, other insurers might find it best to maintain volume at below-cost prices.

Both the hypotheses of heterogeneous expectations and of excessive risk taking could be consistent with a tendency toward large losses and increases in the number of insurance company failures. In contrast to these hypotheses and the traditional view, others suggest that cycles in reported prices and profits may arise even if decisions of all companies are based on unbiased estimates of expected future claims.[63] J. David Cummins and J. François Outreville argue that cycles in reported profits may arise despite rational expectations because of the reporting procedures and adjustment lags associated with data collection, regulation, and periodic renewal of contracts. Neil Doherty and Han Bin Kang argue that any apparent cyclicality in prices or profits could be caused by lagged adjustment of demand and supply to optimal levels based on break-even prices. It is unclear whether either approach is capable of explaining the large price increases that have occurred since 1984.

Another possibility consistent with unbiased forecasts of future claims is that insurers periodically make large errors. Future losses for long-tailed occurrence contracts are very difficult to predict, given possible changes in accident risk, legal rules and standards, medical care costs, and other factors. For a line in which many claims may be unpaid ten

62. See Munch and Smallwood, "Theory of Solvency Regulation"; and Finsinger and Pauly, "Reserve Levels and Reserve Requirements." The papers focus on fixed and sunk costs that may be borne by shareholders in the event of default.

63. Cummins and Outreville, "International Analysis of Underwriting Cycles"; and Neil A. Doherty and Han Bin Kang, "Price Instability for a Financial Intermediary: Interest Rates and Insurance Price Cycles," working paper 87–1 (University of Pennsylvania, Center for Research on Risk and Insurance, January 1987).

years after policies were sold, the rate-making process may use data on how much was paid the previous year for losses arising out of policies issued ten or more years before to forecast how much may be paid ten or more years after new policies are issued.[64] If substantial forecast errors arise, they may become apparent only slowly, and revisions in expectations and ultimate changes in supply might occur only after it is too late to avoid large losses and large premium increases to catch up with expected costs.

For the sake of argument, consider the following. Data indicate that percentage increases in paid and incurred losses were commensurate with increases in GNP during 1978–81. If this relationship were expected to persist, much of the apparently large increase in paid claims and incurred losses relative to GNP since 1981 may not have been anticipated. Evidence may have begun to become available in 1982 that claim costs were not declining with inflation, but it might have taken two years of additional information before expectations were substantially modified. If so, this lag would appear capable of explaining the deteriorating financial position of the industry through 1984 and into 1985 and the evident underreserving on business written between 1982 and 1984—without relying on any pervasive tendency to underprice.

A number of observers have also pointed to changes in reinsurance capacity as major factors that have affected recent financial results for the primary market.[65] Many new reinsurers entered the U.S. market in the 1970s and early 1980s, and a significant number withdrew from the market in 1984 and 1985. Financial results for the reinsurance market deteriorated in 1984 and 1985, a decline that may have been worse than for the primary market. As was the case for the primary market, a significant amount of new capital entered the reinsurance market in 1985 and 1986. Such expansions and contractions undoubtedly affect the primary market, especially the sale of excess coverage. However, the similarity in the performance of reinsurance and primary markets suggests that reinsurance problems are unlikely to be a major cause of primary-market problems. In periods of unanticipated growth in losses,

64. The difficulty in forecasting claims on long-tailed third-party lines may be reduced in the future if claims-made coverage that provides for claims presented to the insurer only during the policy period becomes more common.

65. See, for example, Smith, "Property and Liability Underwriting Cycle"; and McGee, "Cycle in Property/Casualty Insurance." For a detailed discussion of recent experience in the U.S. reinsurance market, see Gottheimer, "Crisis of Confidence."

reinsurers can be expected to experience worse results than primary insurers because of the nature of excess-of-loss contracts.[66] Subsequent price adjustments also could be expected to be greater than for primary limits of coverage considering that growth in losses would have greater effects on costs for excess coverage. Price fluctuations in the reinsurance market are probably subject to the same underlying causes as those in the primary market, although the effects could be greater, given the greater difficulty of forecasting claims for excess layers of coverage than for primary layers. Questions thus remain concerning the extent to which entry into the reinsurance market was associated with underpricing and, if so, whether this reflected excessive risk taking or heterogeneous expectations. These questions are essentially the same as those that remain unanswered for the primary market.

All of the factors discussed—heterogeneous expectations, excessive risk taking, lags in adjustment, and random but large forecast errors—could have contributed to the most recent round of deteriorating financial results and subsequent rate increases in both the primary and reinsurance markets. Little is known about the magnitude of each influence, which makes it difficult to evaluate appropriate public policy responses.

Premium Increases for General Liability Insurance

Have premium increases for general liability, the line with the largest increases, been commensurate with changes in discounted expected costs during recent years? According to financial theory, break-even insurance premiums equal the total of the present value of expected future claims, taxes, and other costs using discount rates that reflect the risk of future cash flows.[67] While in principle the theory is simple, a number of difficult problems arise when applying it to estimate break-even premiums, especially with regard to the choice of discount rates and the treatment of taxes. Moreover, applying the model requires estimates of the timing of future claim payments, and any comparison of estimated break-even premiums with actual premiums in a given period must use estimates of incurred losses for the period, which may be subject to significant errors.

66. Excess-of-loss contracts require the reinsurer to pay losses in excess of a specified retention limit for the primary company. Unanticipated growth in losses increases the reinsurer's obligation for losses that would have exceeded the retention limit without such growth, and it causes more claims to exceed the limit.

67. See Myers and Cohn, "Discounted Cash Flow Approach."

As a result, any analysis that attempts to assess the relationship between premiums and expected costs cannot support firm conclusions.

These caveats notwithstanding, two methods are employed to compare premium increases for general liability insurance with growth in the discounted value of expected losses. The first projects earned premium increases that would have occurred in 1982–86 had the ratio of earned premiums to the estimated present value of expected accident year incurred losses in 1981 continued during 1982–86.[68] This method uses 1981 as a benchmark. As can be seen in table 3-4, the operating ratio for general liability was greater in 1981 than it had been in the preceding few years, but it was still less than 100. A sharp jump in both the combined ratio and operating ratio occurred in 1982. As table 3-5 shows, the accident year loss ratio initially reported for general liability in 1981 was 0.1 greater than the value for 1980 but much lower than the values for 1982–85.

The second method applies a variant of the Myers-Cohn model to derive estimates of break-even prices for 1981–86, which are then compared with actual prices. This method is used to try to control for changes in costs other than losses (underwriting expenses and taxes) that could cause changes in the relationship between premiums and the discounted value of expected losses. Since the calculations must be based on assumptions for which theory provides only rough guidance, the discussion focuses on the relationship between actual prices and predicted prices over time, again using 1981 as a benchmark, as opposed to absolute differences in a given year.

Consider first the simple case in which break-even premiums in time t are a constant multiple of the present value of expected future losses:

$$(3) \qquad P_t = \lambda \gamma_t L_t,$$

where λ is a constant loading factor, L_t is the undiscounted value of expected future claims, and γ_t is the present value of $1.00 of expected future claims, which will depend on the discount rate and the proportion of claims expected to be paid in each future year on business sold in year t.[69] If λ were constant over time, equation 3 could be used to project break-even premiums using λ and estimates of L_t and γ_t.

68. Finch's statement before the House Ways and Means Committee contains some crude calculations to illustrate premium increases that would have been needed for insurers to break even on calendar year operating results for general liability and medical malpractice in 1984.

69. Factors influencing the choice of a discount rate are discussed briefly in appendix B.

Based on equation 3, the first method uses an estimate of γ and reported accident year incurred losses for 1981 to calculate λ. The estimate of λ is then used with estimates of γ_t and reported losses for 1982–85 to project premiums for 1982–85. For 1986, in which accident year losses were not available, projections were made assuming two ratios of accident year losses to earned premiums: 70 and 80 percent. A loss ratio of 70 percent would have occurred if 1985 accident year losses were to increase by 10 percent during 1986 (which is commensurate with the one-year development in reported losses for 1984 and the two-year development for 1983) and if the growth rate for developed incurred losses for 1981–85 (17 percent a year) had continued for 1986. The estimated calendar year loss ratio reported by Paul Wish for general liability in 1986 was 99 percent.[70] The assumed loss ratios are substantially lower in view of the likelihood that increases in reserves on losses before 1986 contributed significantly to the 99 percent calendar year result.

The payout pattern for future losses was estimated using the average loss development factors shown for the industry in appendix B through year ten and assuming development factors of 1.02 and 1.01 in years eleven and twelve, at which time all claims are assumed to be paid.[71] Specifically, the proportion of losses assumed to be paid in years one through twelve is 0.083, 0.114, 0.130, 0.138, 0.134, 0.114, 0.095, 0.067, 0.054, 0.042, 0.019, and 0.010. It was assumed that each year's increment of losses would be paid at midyear. For 1981–85, average yields on five-year U.S. government bonds for years t and $t-1$ were used along with this payout schedule to calculate γ_t.[72] For 1986 the average yield on January issues was employed since data for later months were not yet available in the source used.[73]

Table 3-13 shows the results of the projections, along with the inter-

70. Paul E. Wish, "Review and Preview: Up from the Ashes," *Best's Review: Property/Casualty Insurance Edition*, vol. 87 (January 1987), p. 91. Editor's note: The 1986 accident year loss ratio for general liability, which became available after this book was in press, was 80.8 percent. See *Best's Aggregates and Averages: Property-Casualty, 1987*.

71. Development factors for years seven through ten were based on data for the forty-five company sample.

72. The two-year average was used because earned premiums in year t primarily will reflect business written in years t and $t-1$.

73. See Salomon Brothers, *An Analytical Record of Yields and Yield Spreads* (New York: Salomon Brothers, 1986). Similar results would have been obtained with one- and ten-year yields. See appendix B.

Table 3-13. *Actual and Projected Earned Premiums for General Liability Using 1981 Ratio of Earned Premiums to Discounted Accident Year Losses, 1981–86*
Millions of dollars unless otherwise specified

Item	1981	1982	1983	1984	1985	1986[a]	1986[b]
Actual net premiums earned	6,023	5,638	5,688	6,291	9,472	16,506	16,506
Initial loss ratio (percent)	79	87	94	99	95	70	80
Initial incurred losses	4,733	4,919	5,364	6,238	8,985	11,554	13,205
Projected net premiums earned	6,023	6,063	6,969	8,247	11,936	16,935	19,355
Actual/projected (percent)	100	93	82	76	79	97	85
Developed loss ratio (percent)[c]	86	102	109	110	n.a.	n.a.	n.a.
Developed incurred losses[c]	5,180	5,762	6,222	6,901	n.a.	n.a.	n.a.
Projected net premiums earned	6,023	6,522	7,423	8,381	n.a.	n.a.	n.a.
Actual/projected (percent)	100	86	77	75	n.a.	n.a.	n.a.
Interest rate[d]	12.8	13.6	12.0	11.5	11.3	8.6	8.6
Present value of $1.00 of incurred loss (dollars)	0.608	0.592	0.624	0.635	0.640	0.704	0.704

Sources: Net premiums earned and losses incurred for 1981–85 are from schedule P, *Best's Aggregates and Averages: Property-Liability, 1986.* Earned premiums for 1986 calculated using estimates in Wish, "Review and Preview."
n.a. Not available.
a. Assumes accident year loss ratio of 70 percent.
b. Assumes accident year loss ratio of 80 percent.
c. Losses developed through 1985.
d. Rate for 1981–85 is two-year average of rate on five-year U.S. government bonds. Rate for 1986 is rate for January issues. See appendix B.

est rate used for discounting and the present value of $1.00 of estimated incurred loss for each year. Results are shown using both initially reported losses and losses developed through 1985. As can be seen, actual premiums earned for 1982–86 are less than projected premiums. The shortfall is greatest for 1984, when the ratio of actual to projected premiums is 76 percent for the initial loss comparison and 75 percent using developed losses. For a 1986 loss ratio of 70 percent, actual premiums are 3 percentage points lower than projected premiums; for a loss ratio of 80 percent, the shortfall is 15 percentage points. The present value factors indicate that projected premiums for 1986 would have been 16 percent $(0.704/0.608 - 1)$ higher than 1981 premiums because of the decline in interest rates if the value of claims had not grown during the period.

The Myers and Cohn model of break-even prices provided some control for the possibility that changes in non-loss costs such as underwriting expenses or taxes could have led to the deterioration in the ratios shown above. The original model was modified to allow for underwriting expenses, and different assumptions were used to obtain the present value of costs resulting from income taxes. Myers and Cohn developed the model under the assumption that underwriting losses would be deductible from taxable income as paid, and their model did not consider the impact of investments in tax-exempt securities on the implicit tax rate for returns on the investment of premiums and surplus.[74] The formulation used here assumes that insurers would pay no income tax in any year (which would appear to be consistent with long-run experience before tax reform) and that the only impact of taxes on costs would be the return foregone from investing in tax-exempt securities. Yields on five-year U.S. government bonds and five-year prime municipal bonds (see appendix B) were used to calculate the implicit tax with the assumption that tax-exempt bonds represent half the investment portfolio.

The five-year U.S. government yields were used to discount the future implicit tax liability. The appropriate rate for discounting future losses is a risk-adjusted rate that compensates shareholders for bearing the risk of underwriting. To date, adjustments based on the capital asset pricing model have been used.[75] Betas for uncertain losses are very difficult to estimate and may be unstable. A downward adjustment (denoted u) in the risk-free rate of 2 percent would correspond to a beta of 0.2 if the expected excess return on the market portfolio were 10 percent. Previous analysis of the break-even pricing issue commonly has assumed a beta of 0.2.[76] Comparisons are shown under the assumption that the

74. Derrig, "Effect of Federal Taxes on Investment Income," discusses modification of the tax rate to reflect investment in tax-exempt securities.

75. For example, in Myers and Cohn, "Discounted Cash Flow Approach."

76. See Raymond D. Hill and Franco Modigliani, "The Massachusetts Model of Profit Regulation in Nonlife Insurance: An Appraisal and Extensions," in Cummins and Harrington, *Fair Rate of Return,* pp. 27–54; and Fairley, "Investment Income and Profit Margins." Evidence of considerable instability in underwriting betas and that beta estimates may have been negative in the late 1970s is provided in J. David Cummins and Scott Harrington, "Property-Liability Insurance Rate Regulation: Estimation of Underwriting Betas Using Quarterly Profit Data," *Journal of Risk and Insurance,* vol. 52 (March 1985), pp. 16–43. To date, beta estimates have been for all lines combined. The appropriate beta to use in the calculations for general liability is very uncertain.

Table 3-14. *Actual and Predicted Prices for General Liability, 1981–86*[a]
Percent

Category	u[b]	1981	1982	1983	1984	1985	1986[c]	1986[d]
Initial losses								
Actual price	...	208	194	170	159	165	203	178
Actual/predicted	0	114	109	100	96	104	132	120
	2	109	104	96	92	99	126	114
	4	104	99	91	87	93	119	108
Developed losses[e]								
Actual price	...	191	166	147	143	n.a.	n.a.	n.a.
Actual/predicted	0	108	98	91	90	n.a.	n.a.	n.a.
	2	103	93	86	85	n.a.	n.a.	n.a.
	4	98	89	82	81	n.a.	n.a.	n.a.

Source: Author's calculations.
n.a. Not available.
a. Actual price is the ratio of earned premiums to discounted accident year losses. Predicted price is calculated using a variant of the Myers-Cohn model.
b. Variable denotes assumed risk-adjustment factor (percent).
c. Assumes loss ratio of 70 percent.
d. Assumes loss ratio of 80 percent.
e. Losses developed through 1985.

adjustment in the risk-free discount rate equals 0 percent (no underwriting risk), 2 percent, and 4 percent. Further details concerning application of the model and the assumptions used are provided in appendix B.

Table 3-14 presents actual prices for general liability and the ratios of actual to predicted prices. Prices are defined as the ratio of premiums to the discounted value of expected future losses using the assumed payout schedule and previously employed U.S. government bond rates.[77] The decline in actual prices during the period corresponds to the excess of projected over actual premiums in table 3-13. The ratios of actual to predicted prices decline through 1984, and while they increase in 1985, they are still 10 percentage points below the 1981 levels. The differences are smaller than those for actual prices and the premium projections because of declining underwriting expense ratios (whether relative to premiums, undiscounted losses, or discounted losses) and declining implicit tax rates on investment income during the period.

The ratios of actual to predicted prices for 1986 are larger than those for 1981 for both the 70 and 80 percent assumed-loss ratios. For the 70 percent loss ratio, the results imply that the ratio of premiums to the present value of expected costs for initial reported losses was about 15 percent higher in 1986 than in 1981 (132/114 − 1, and so forth).

77. The actual prices shown equal λ_t. See equation 3.

While this result may provide evidence that premiums rose above the present value of expected costs in 1986, the use of assumed-loss ratios and at least four other factors could have contributed to the increase in the ratios of actual to predicted prices for 1986.[78]

First, the accounting data on underwriting expenses used to calculate prices may include outlays for product and distribution network development that from an economic perspective constitute investment expenditures. If a decline in such expenditures occurred during 1981–86, which may not be unlikely given changes in market conditions, then the ratios of actual to predicted prices for 1986 could be overstated relative to those for 1981. Second, the assumed implicit tax on investment income, which equals one-half of the difference between the yield on five-year U.S. government bonds and that on prime municipal bonds, declined from 2.65 percent in 1981 to 2.00 percent in 1985 and to just 1.05 percent in 1986. If some of this decline actually reflects greater risk in the prime municipal bond market caused by, say, uncertainty about the treatment of tax-exempt interest under tax reform, the ratios for 1986 would again be overstated relative to those for 1981. Third, the predicted price calculations make no allowance for the possible increase in tax costs (because of tax reform) on business written late in 1986. Finally, if the risk of writing general liability increased from 1981 to 1986 so that greater capital per dollar of premiums was needed in 1986, the assumption of a constant premium-to-surplus ratio could cause the predicted price for 1986 to be understated relative to 1981.[79]

To illustrate the potential magnitude of the first two effects, assume that the expense ratio for 1986 would need to be 0.255 rather than the value used of 0.225 to be comparable with the 0.300 value used for 1981. Also assume that the implicit tax rate for 1986 would need to be 2 percent (the 1985 value). If u equals 0 percent, the ratio of actual to predicted price would decline to 121 percent for a loss ratio of 70 percent and to 111 percent for a loss ratio of 80 percent.[80]

The comparisons of actual and projected premiums using both projection methods thus suggest that most of the recent increase in pre-

78. If the accident year loss ratio for 1986 were available (see note 70), the possibility of large reserve errors would still prevent solid conclusions. The possibility also exists that rates were too low in 1981 relative to the initially reported losses.

79. See Department of Justice, Antitrust Division, "Crisis in Property-Casualty Insurance," and the sources cited there for further discussion of the possible impact on prices of increases in risk.

80. Similar changes would occur if u equals 2 or 4 percent. The changes in the expense ratio and implicit tax rate contribute about equally to the declines.

miums reflected increases in reported losses. Without further developments in the theory of break-even prices and without waiting a number of years for reasonably accurate estimates of developed losses for 1985 and 1986 business, a stronger statement cannot be made. If, for example, it turns out that the fully developed accident year loss ratio for 1986 is much less than 70 percent, then this conclusion could be wrong. But given the competitive structure of the industry, the favorable impact of realized capital gains on surplus, and the inflow of new funds in 1985 and 1986, a reasonable expectation is that short-run prices would be unlikely to rise far above expected future costs.

Policy Implications

Because of theoretical and empirical problems in measuring present value of expected future costs for liability insurance contracts, it is difficult to assess the extent to which prices may have deviated from costs in a cyclical manner. If there is a systematic tendency for prices to fall below costs, then a certain degree of recoupment would be expected so that individual insurers could break even over the long run. Otherwise the supply of capital to the industry would be likely to contract to the point at which a competitive structure would no longer exist.

Based on what is known, the case for relying on regulations requiring prior approval of rates to dampen price variability, whether in the form of flexible rating or more traditional modes, is very weak. If market problems are largely the result of unanticipated changes in claim costs as opposed to a systematic tendency to underprice, there is no case for rate regulation. If an unpredictable cycle of inadequate prices followed by recoupment of past losses does exist, it is far from clear that rate regulation would provide benefits in excess of its costs.[81] Risk-averse insurance buyers conceivably could benefit if regulation reduced the variance of prices. However, if inadequate prices were largely due to excessive risk taking by some insurers, other methods of regulation, such as improved monitoring of insurers' financial conditions, might be preferable to rate regulation.[82] Moreover, if inadequate prices were

81. If the cycle were predictable and capital markets were perfect, there could be no advantage to using regulation to smooth prices, since consumers could borrow and lend to achieve their optimal consumption pattern despite fluctuations in insurance prices.

82. Rate regulation also could reduce the attention paid to insolvency problems, given limited budgets for state insurance departments.

caused largely by heterogeneous expectations, limiting rate reductions for insurers with favorable expectations about future costs might not be of much use. Given the uncertainty about future costs that may result in heterogeneous expectations, regulators would probably not be able to identify firms seeking approval of inadequate prices.

Regulators could also have difficulty enforcing rate limits effectively.[83] And political pressure could lead to asymmetry in rate regulation, in that price reductions would be much easier to obtain than price increases.[84] Would regulators really be likely to keep prices above market levels for several years following the most recent round of price increases and availability problems? If rate regulation were used mostly to limit rate increases following periods of potentially large losses, the scope and duration of availability problems would likely become much worse. If so, the increased use of mandated markets involving cross-subsidization, such as reinsurance plans and joint underwriting associations, could be expected. The net result could be higher injury rates and a large efficiency loss. For all of these reasons, increased regulation of commercial liability insurance rates is unwarranted.

Two other issues have received considerable attention in conjunction with recent experience: whether it would be desirable to repeal the McCarran-Ferguson Act and whether some form of federal regulation should replace or augment state regulation. Both issues are complex and have been subject to extensive debate for many years, but a few observations can be made about their relationship to recent market problems. First, there is no evidence that the limited antitrust exemption under the McCarran-Ferguson Act has contributed to or aggravated these problems. Furthermore, if repeal of the act increased the difficulty in forecasting losses by making it either more costly or illegal for firms to pool data for analysis of expected losses, any tendency for firms to underprice could be made worse. Second, while the defects of state regulation have been subject to almost continuous study, there is little evidence that they have led to recent market problems or that some form of federal regulation would have prevented these problems. Again, not nearly enough

83. Stewart, *Remembering a Stable Future.*

84. The evidence of the depressing impact of rate regulation on auto insurance prices in the past decade is suggestive in this regard. Stewart, *Remembering a Stable Future,* shows that from 1972 to 1985 commercial liability insurance combined ratios were roughly equal in states with and without prior approval regulation, suggesting little impact of regulation on rates. However, given the recent interest of regulators in the affordability of commercial liability coverage, the possibility exists that any impact of regulation in the future would be in the direction of reducing rates.

is known about the causes of the problems to justify fundamental changes in the type or form of regulation. Moreover, the uncertainty associated with significant changes in regulations suggests extreme caution unless traditional mechanisms and institutions are clearly inadequate to prevent large welfare losses and a new system could be expected to reduce such losses significantly. While pressure exists for changing insurance regulation, deficiencies in state regulation do not clearly justify replacing all or part of a system that has survived for more than a century.

What does the future hold concerning the possible recurrence of deteriorating financial results followed by large price increases and availability problems? Will another crisis occur in five or ten years? The traditional view of underwriting cycles suggests the answer is yes, although the crisis might not be as severe. Other views that involve systematic underpricing also suggest that problems will eventually recur. If recent problems were largely caused by unexpected growth in losses, the possible recurrence of a crisis would be tied to factors that may lead to large unanticipated growth in claims, such as new sources of injury, changes in legal rules, and increased demand by the public for broader and greater compensation for injury. Increased regulation of the market may not be able to prevent a recurrence and could make things worse.

We need a greater understanding of the causes of market problems. Theoretical and empirical work on the possible impact of excessive risk taking and heterogeneous expectations on prices should be undertaken. Research also is needed using available data that focuses on the extent to which the growth in expected claims in recent years could have been anticipated. Although it is unlikely to be conclusive, work in these areas should provide greater insight into whether prior approval of rate changes or other forms of regulation would be likely to have a beneficial impact on prices and availability.

Appendix A: Profit Measurement

Some knowledge of insurance accounting rules and alternative income measures is needed to interpret financial results and to understand the dispute about insurance industry profitability. If a few simplifying assumptions are used and arcane factors such as deferred income taxes are ignored, the major measures of profitability can be made fairly clear.

Insurance company annual statements that must be filed with regulators are prepared using statutory accounting principles (SAP). These principles tend to be more conservative than generally accepted accounting principles (GAAP) in that income and net worth (surplus) tend to be less than income and net worth calculated using GAAP. A major difference between SAP and GAAP is the treatment of acquisition expenses, those incurred in selling and issuing insurance contracts. SAP requires that acquisition expenses be charged against income and surplus when incurred. GAAP requires that revenues and expenses be matched, which means expenses generally are deferred compared with SAP.

Two important concepts in both SAP and GAAP accounting are earned premiums, EP, and incurred losses, IL. Premiums are said to be written when the policy is issued and the premium becomes payable. Premiums are earned evenly over the duration of the policy period. A principal liability of property and liability insurers is their unearned premium reserve, UPR, which reflects the amount of written premiums, WP, that have yet to be earned as of the statement date. The relationship between these items in a given year is given by $EP = WP - \Delta UPR$. If earned and written premiums are equal during a year, UPR does not change.

Incurred losses are defined as losses paid, LP, plus the change in the insurer's second major liability, the loss reserve, LR: $IL = LP + \Delta LR$. The loss reserve is the estimated liability for all unpaid claims that have occurred as of the statement date. Since future claim payments traditionally have not been discounted, the book value of the liability, if accurately estimated, overstates its market value. Moreover, incurred losses for a given calendar year will be affected by revisions in reserves for previous years' claims to reflect new information about expected total claims. That is, increases in the loss reserve in year t for claims that occurred in year $t - n$ will affect reported incurred losses in year t.

SAP surplus, S, is given by the basic accounting identity

(A-1) $$S = A - LR - UPR,$$

where A is the SAP value of assets, which reflects bonds at amortized (book) value and common stocks at market value.[85] The change in surplus during a given period can be written

(A-2) $$\Delta S = \Delta A - \Delta LR - \Delta UPR.$$

The change in SAP assets equals premiums written less losses paid,

---

85. For simplicity the presentation assumes only two types of assets and two liabilities.

underwriting expenses, E, policyholder dividends, D, and income taxes, T, plus total investment gains, IG.[86] Substituting for ΔA in equation A-2 and using $\Delta UPR = WP - EP$ and $\Delta LR = IL - LP$ gives

(A-3) $$\Delta S = (EP - IL - E - D) - T + IG.$$

The first four terms total SAP underwriting income. IG has three components: net investment income, I, which consists of interest (including changes in the book value of bonds due to amortization), dividends, and rents, less investment expenses; realized capital gains or losses on stocks and bonds, RCG; and unrealized capital gains or losses on common stocks, $URCG$. A popular measure of income in industry publications and the trade press is pretax operating income, which is defined as SAP underwriting income plus I; after-tax operating income deducts T.

The principal modification of SAP surplus to obtain GAAP surplus involves creating an asset account to reflect prepaid acquisition expenses. Assuming that all underwriting expenses are acquisition expenses gives the following definition of surplus adjusted for prepaid expenses (S_A):

(A-4) $$S_A = A + (E/WP)UPR - LR - UPR,$$

where E/WP, the underwriting expense ratio, is assumed to be constant from year to year. This treatment essentially adds to SAP surplus the amount of the unearned premium reserve being held for acquisition expenses associated with the remainder of the policy period that have already been paid. Using the definitions of ΔA, ΔLR, and ΔUPR gives the following expression for the change in adjusted surplus:

(A-5) $$\Delta S_A = [EP - IL - (E/WP)EP - D] - T + IG.$$

Pretax GAAP underwriting income is given by the first four terms of this expression. As noted, the difference between GAAP and SAP underwriting income is that GAAP automatically matches expenses with revenues as premiums are earned.[87]

The most common summary measure of underwriting profit (excluding investment income) is the combined ratio, CR, either before or after

86. Again for simplicity, stockholder dividends, new capital, nonadmitted assets, and other minor items are ignored.

87. In the absence of such matching, differences in premium growth rates may have a significant effect on reported income. When written premiums exceed earned premiums, SAP income is lower than GAAP income, which reduced taxable income before the tax reform in 1986.

policyholder dividends. If after dividends it is defined as the sum of the ratio of incurred losses and dividends to earned premiums plus the ratio of underwriting expenses to written premiums:

$$(A\text{-}6) \qquad CR = (IL + D)/EP + E/WP.$$

One minus the combined ratio gives the pretax GAAP underwriting margin relative to earned premiums: $(1 - CR)EP = [EP - IL - (E/WP)EP - D]$.[88] The pretax GAAP operating margin including net investment income is given by $(1 - CR) + I/EP$.

Another measure of income that analysts have looked to in recent years is the operating ratio, which is defined as

$$(A\text{-}7) \qquad OR = CR - \alpha(I + RCG)/EP,$$

where α is the amount of net investment income plus realized capital gains that is allocated to insurance operations (or, for results by line, to a given line of business) as opposed to surplus. Thus the operating ratio equals the combined ratio minus the ratio of investment income allocated to a line to earned premiums for the line.[89] The operating ratio differs from the pretax GAAP operating margin in that it reflects realized capital gains, and only net investment income and realized capital gains allocated to operations are included. If the operating ratio for all lines of business were equal to 1, the pretax increase in adjusted surplus would equal all unrealized capital gains plus the share of net investment income and realized capital gains allocated to surplus. A ratio greater than 1 indicates that the increase in adjusted surplus would be less than this amount.

The operating ratio essentially measures profit from insurance operations under the assumption that net investment income and realized capital gains on surplus plus all unrealized capital gains should be credited to owners. Critics have, however, argued that all capital gains should be included when assessing the profitability of insurance operations. Does the operating ratio provide a good measure of whether insurance operations were profitable in any year or over time even if

88. In practice, $1 - CR$ only approximates the GAAP margin, since some underwriting expenses are not acquisition expenses and should be deducted when incurred under GAAP, and since the acquisition expense ratio is not constant over time.

89. Insurers are required to allocate $I + RCG$ to lines of business and to surplus in the insurance expense exhibit. Allocations essentially are in proportion to liabilities for each line.

one assumes that the underlying assumption about investment gains is appropriate? The answer generally will be no.

Theory suggests that break-even premiums would equal the risk-adjusted present value of expected future claim payments plus the present value of all other costs of writing the business, including income taxes or foregone investment returns resulting from cost-reducing tax avoidance.[90] Even if all policies were priced to break even, loss forecasts were perfectly accurate, and investment returns including capital gains were equal to the rate used to discount future costs, the operating ratio generally would not equal 1. The principal reason is the failure to discount losses in insurance accounting (both SAP and GAAP). Lack of discounting is one major reason that accounting profits may differ greatly from economic profits. Another factor is the use of book values rather than market values for bonds.

To illustrate economic profit measurement, let the market value of an insurer's surplus for all business written (old and new) before the statement date, S_M, be defined as

(A-8) $$S_M = A + B - PVL,$$

where A is the SAP value of assets, B is the market value of bonds less book value, and PVL is the market value of unpaid claims, that is, the present value of unpaid claims discounted at a market-determined rate of interest.[91] The change in S_M is given by

(A-9) $$\Delta S_M = [WP - (LP + \Delta PVL) - E - D] - T + IG',$$

where $IG' = IG + \Delta B$, that is, net investment income plus realized and unrealized capital gains on bonds (in excess of bond amortization) and on stocks.

An expression for ΔS_M that is more comparable to equations A-3 and A-5 can be obtained by defining PVL' as the present value of unpaid claims only for accidents that have occurred by the statement date and by noting that the unearned premium reserve less the adjustment for prepaid acquisition expenses would approximately equal the present

90. See, for example, Myers and Cohn, "Discounted Cash Flow Approach"; and appendix B.

91. *PVL* includes losses that have already occurred as of the statement date and the value of claims expected to occur after that date for business written before the date. If all expenses were not assumed to be acquisition expenses, the present value of unpaid expenses also would be deducted.

value of unpaid losses for claims that are expected to occur after the statement date for policies written as of the statement date. Using these results gives

$$(A\text{-}10) \quad \Delta S_M = [EP - (LP + \Delta PVL') - (E/WP)EP - D]$$
$$- T + IG'.$$

The quantity in brackets equals GAAP underwriting profit using discounted losses.

Appendix B: Calculation of Break-Even Prices

According to the Myers-Cohn model, the break-even premium equals the present value of expected future losses discounted at a risk-adjusted rate plus the present value of income taxes discounted at the risk-free rate. In illustrating their model, Myers and Cohn ignored underwriting expenses, assumed that funds backing policies were invested in taxable risk-free securities, and assumed that tax deductions for losses were taken as the losses were paid. The modification used here considers underwriting expenses. The appropriate treatment of taxes is complex, given that they can be reduced by holding tax-exempt securities.[92] While value-maximizing portfolio decisions may involve tax minimization,[93] questions concerning the allocation of tax costs across business lines and years for multiperiod contracts have barely been raised, let alone answered.

For this reason, it is assumed in this analysis that investment decisions eliminate income taxes over time and that break-even premiums reflect the implicit tax cost that results from holding tax-exempt securities to eliminate taxes. To illustrate the model, assume that break-even premiums, P, and underwriting expenses, E, for a group of contracts are paid at the beginning of the period of coverage and that the amount of loss paid at time $t = 1, 2, \ldots, n$ equals $\beta_t L$, where L is total expected losses. If no income taxes are paid and all investments are risk-free, break-even premiums are given by

92. See Derrig, "Effect of Federal Taxes on Investment Income."
93. Patric H. Hendershott and Timothy W. Koch, "The Demand for Tax-Exempt Securities by Financial Institutions," *Journal of Finance,* vol. 35 (June 1980), pp. 717–27; and Smith, "Investment Yields and Insurance Underwriting."

(B-1) $P = E + \gamma_1 L + (r_f - r_p)(P - E + S)(\gamma_2 - \gamma_3),$

where S is the initial surplus supporting the contracts, r_f is the rate of interest on taxable risk-free securities; r_p is the rate of interest earned on the investment of $P - E + S$; γ_1 is $\Sigma[\beta_t/(1 + r_f - u)^t]$; u is the adjustment factor for the risk of future losses; γ_2 is $\Sigma[1/(1 + r_f)^t]$; γ_3 is $\Sigma[\partial_{t-1}/(1 + r_f)^t]$; and ∂_t is the cumulative proportion of total losses paid through time t.[94]

The first two terms in equation B-1 give the discounted values of expenses and losses, respectively. The third term gives the implicit tax on insurance operations in the form of foregone return from holding tax-exempt securities to eliminate taxes. Following Myers and Cohn, the formula assumes that funds invested to back the contracts, and thus implicit taxes, decline in proportion to claims paid.

As discussed in the text, let the break-even price of the contracts be defined as $\lambda = P/(\gamma L)$, where γ equals $\Sigma[\beta_t/(1 + r_f)^t]$, that is, the ratio of break-even premiums to the present value of expected future losses discounted at the risk-free rate. Using this definition and equation B-1 gives

(B-2) $$\lambda = \frac{(e/k)(1 - \tau) + \gamma_1}{\gamma[1 - (1 + s)]\tau},$$

where $e = E/P$, $k = L/P$, $s = S/P$, and $\tau = (r_f - r_p)(\gamma_2 - \gamma_3)$.

The accident year loss ratio for general liability for 1981–85 and assumed loss ratios of 70 and 80 percent for 1986 were used for k. The remaining variables used to calculate λ for each year follow.

Since the accident year loss ratio in year t reflects business primarily written in years t and $t-1$, the average ratio of underwriting expenses to written premiums for years t and $t-1$ was used to obtain a GAAP expense ratio and then substituted for e in equation B-2. The values were 0.300, 0.312, 0.318, 0.311, 0.271, and 0.225 for the years 1981–86, respectively. Data were obtained from *Best's Aggregates and Averages: Property-Casualty, 1986.*

Yields on U.S. government and prime municipal bonds of various maturities for 1977–86 are shown in table 3-15, along with the ratios of tax-exempt to taxable yields. As can be seen, the implicit tax from holding tax-exempt bonds declines with maturity. Property-liability insurance companies invested heavily in long-term taxable and tax-exempt

94. All summations are from $t = 1$ through $t = n$.

Table 3-15. *U.S. Government and Prime Municipal Bond Yields, 1977–86*
Percent unless otherwise specified

Year	U.S. government bonds				Prime municipal bonds				Ratio of municipal to U.S. government			
	one-year	five-year	ten-year	twenty-year	one-year	five-year	ten-year	twenty-year	one-year	five-year	ten-year	twenty-year
1977	5.9	6.9	7.4	7.6	2.9	3.9	4.4	5.2	0.49	0.56	0.59	0.68
1978	8.2	8.2	8.3	8.4	4.2	4.7	4.9	5.5	0.51	0.57	0.59	0.65
1979	10.5	9.4	9.3	9.2	5.3	5.4	5.5	6.0	0.50	0.57	0.58	0.64
1980	12.1	11.4	11.4	11.3	6.1	6.4	6.8	7.8	0.51	0.56	0.60	0.69
1981	14.7	14.2	13.7	13.7	7.9	8.5	9.4	10.6	0.54	0.60	0.69	0.77
1982	12.4	13.1	13.2	13.1	7.1	8.7	9.9	11.1	0.58	0.66	0.75	0.85
1983	9.5	10.8	11.0	11.3	5.3	6.8	7.9	8.9	0.55	0.63	0.72	0.79
1984	10.9	12.3	12.4	12.5	6.1	7.6	8.7	9.7	0.56	0.62	0.70	0.78
1985	8.5	10.3	10.7	11.0	5.1	6.9	8.0	8.9	0.60	0.67	0.75	0.80
1986	7.6	8.6	9.0	9.5	5.4	6.5	7.4	8.1	0.71	0.76	0.82	0.86

Source: Salomon Brothers, *An Analytical Record of Yields and Yield Spreads* (New York: Salomon Brothers, 1986), pt. 1, table 1, and pt. 3, table 3. Values for 1977–85 are average values for the year; values for 1986 are for January issues.

Table 3-16. Paid-Loss Development Factors, 1976–84[a]

Accident year (t)	P_{2t}/P_{1t}	P_{3t}/P_{2t}	P_{4t}/P_{3t}	P_{5t}/P_{4t}	P_{6t}/P_{5t}	P_{7t}/P_{6t}	P_{8t}/P_{7t}	P_{9t}/P_{8t}	P_{10t}/P_{9t}
1976	2.215	1.544	1.404	1.301	1.207	1.157	1.089	1.062	1.045
1977	2.063	1.550	1.461	1.303	1.200	1.124	1.075	1.060	...
1978	2.175	1.610	1.460	1.281	1.179	1.128	1.086	...	...
1979	2.214	1.616	1.441	1.289	1.185	1.121	...	...	...
	(2.234)	(1.646)	(1.393)	(1.301)					
1980	2.437	1.649	1.428	1.293	1.189	...	...	...	...
	(2.354)	(1.632)	(1.432)	(1.290)	(1.183)				
1981	2.510	1.736	1.431	1.273	...	...	...	...	...
	(2.387)	(1.730)	(1.421)	(1.271)					
1982	2.351	1.634	1.472	...	...	...	...	...	...
	(2.292)	(1.620)	(1.435)						
1983	2.511	1.695	...	...	...	...	...	...	...
	(2.362)	(1.685)							
1984	2.615	...	...	...	...	...	...	...	...
	(2.441)								
Average	2.485	1.666	1.446	1.288	1.192	1.133	1.083	1.061	1.045
	(2.367)	(1.663)	(1.420)	(1.289)	(1.191)				
Sum-of-the-years digits	2.509	1.676	1.447	1.285	1.189	1.127	1.083	1.061	1.045
	(2.377)	(1.667)	(1.426)	(1.286)	(1.187)				
Most recent year	2.615	1.695	1.472	1.273	1.189	1.121	1.086	1.060	1.045
	(2.441)	(1.685)	(1.435)	(1.271)	(1.183)				

Sources: Data for industry calculations are from Best's *Aggregates and Averages: Property-Casualty*, 1986; data for the forty-five-company sample are from Aetna Life and Casualty Company.

a. P_{jt} equals cumulative losses paid through year j for accident year t. Values in parentheses reflect industry data; remaining values are for the forty-five-company sample. Average and sum-of-the-years digits values are for the industry when industry data are not available (or the number available for the forty-five-company sample, if smaller), except for P_{4t}/P_{3t} for the industry, for which only four years were used.

bonds during this period. Derrig argues that the implicit tax in the Myers-Cohn model should be based on yields available on a portfolio of taxables and tax exempts that matches the duration of assets and liabilities. His argument assumes that all risk of holding long-term investments is borne by shareholders rather than policyholders.[95] This argument may be reasonable, given the existence of guaranty funds.

For simplicity, yields on five-year U.S. government and prime municipal bonds were used to calculate r_p. For each year from 1981 to 1985, average yields on issues during years t and $t-1$ were used, since accident year loss ratios reflect business written in years t and $t-1$. The variable, r_p, was calculated assuming equal investments in taxable and tax-exempt bonds. For 1986 the yield on January 1986 issues was used. This was the last month for which yields were available in Salomon Brothers, *An Analytical Record of Yields and Yield Spreads*. The values were 0.0265, 0.0250, 0.0215, 0.0215, 0.0200, and 0.0105 for 1981 to 1986, respectively.

For 1981–85, average yields on five-year U.S. government bonds in years t and $t-1$ were used to discount future values. It was assumed that expenses were paid at the beginning of the year and that all loss payments were made at the middle of the year of payment. As described in the text, β_t was calculated using the average industry loss development factors shown in table B-2 and assuming development of 1.02 and 1.01 in years eleven and twelve. The resultant β_t for years one through twelve was 0.083, 0.114, 0.130, 0.138, 0.134, 0.114, 0.095, 0.067, 0.054, 0.042, 0.019, and 0.010.

A value of 0.5 was used for s. This value corresponds to a premium-to-surplus ratio of 2, a common industry benchmark.

95. Derrig, "Effect of Federal Taxes on Investment Income."

CHAPTER FOUR

Medical Malpractice Liability

Patricia M. Danzon

Pʜʏsɪcɪᴀɴs have been liable for medical malpractice since the eighteenth century, but malpractice claims were rare until the late 1960s, when both the frequency of claims and size of awards began to increase at rapid rates. The failure of malpractice insurance premiums to keep pace with rising claim costs led to inevitable attempts to catch up—premiums increased more than 300 percent in some states in 1974–75. Where their increases were denied, insurance carriers withdrew from the market. This malpractice crisis prompted legislatures in virtually every state to enact tort reforms designed to curb the increases in claims and awards. In addition, measures were taken to make certain that insurance would be available. In many states, physicians established their own mutual insurance companies, which now write more than 50 percent of malpractice insurance. Several states established joint underwriting associations or mandatory risk pools, in which all insurers are required to participate as a condition of writing other lines of property and liability insurance.

During the second half of the 1970s the system functioned relatively smoothly. Insurance once more became widely available except in a few states (New York, Massachusetts, and Rhode Island, for example) where rates were heavily regulated and joint underwriting associations remained a major source or the sole source of coverage. Premium rates stabilized, implying a reduction in real costs. The respite, however, was incomplete and short-lived. Claim severity, the average amount paid per paid claim, continued to rise more rapidly than the general inflation rate, although the rate of increase was somewhat slower in states that enacted caps on awards and collateral source offsets.[1] After 1978 the frequency of claims also began to increase once more.

In the 1980s, as in the early 1970s, insurance rates initially lagged behind rising claim costs. But since 1984 most states have experienced sharp rate increases, although the average increase in any single year has been less dramatic than in the crisis of the mid-1970s. Lack of availability has generally not been caused by the withdrawal of carriers from entire states and does not appear to be directly attributable to rate regulation, as was common in the 1970s.[2] However, the major commercial insurers are writing only renewal business, and for many providers, higher limits of coverage are available, if at all, only at sharply increased rates.

Once again, a crisis in insurance markets has generated demands for reform of the tort system or for more radical alternatives. The purpose of this chapter is to review the evidence on the operation of the tort system for medical malpractice and the performance of malpractice insurance markets, to outline the components of a complete cost-benefit analysis, which ideally should precede adoption of changes in the current system, and to review proposed changes. Because of the widespread perception that this crisis has been more extreme for obstetricians and gynecologists than for other physicians, evidence on the experience of OBG specialists is reported separately where data permit.

Trends in Claims and Premiums

Claim Frequency

After rising rapidly in the early 1970s the frequency of claims filed stabilized and actually fell in some states between 1975 and 1978. After 1978 the upward trend resumed. From 1975 to 1984 claims per physician rose at an average rate of 10 percent a year; between 1982 and 1986 claim

1. Under traditional tort rules of damages, evidence that the plaintiff may be eligible for compensation through private or public insurance is not admissible in court. Several states have changed this rule to permit evidence of collateral sources of compensation. Some permit offset at the discretion of the court; others mandate offset of at least some sources, possibly with credit to the plaintiff for any premium paid.

2. One exception is Florida, where availability of coverage has been in jeopardy because of the state insurance department's denial of rate increases. See St. Paul Fire and Marine Insurance Company, "Physicians' and Surgeons' Update" (July 1987). The effects of statutory ceilings on rates charged by the Florida patient compensation fund are described in Patricia M. Danzon and Charles E. Phelps, "Florida Insurance Practices: Law and Economics," in Henry G. Manne, ed., *Medical Malpractice Policy Guidebook* (Jacksonville: Florida Medical Association, 1985), pp. 149–68.

Table 4-1. *Claims Filed per 100 Physicians, Selected States, 1980, 1984*

	All specialties			Obstetrics and gynecology			Neurosurgery		
State	1980	1984	Percent change	1980	1984	Percent change	1980	1984	Percent change
Arkansas	6.6	8.6	30	20.3	28.4	40	15.6	12.3	−21[a]
California	20.4	26.0	27	33.9	51.1	51	40.2	53.5	33
Florida	20.8	26.1	25	51.6	44.0[b]	−15	48.2	88.6	84
Indiana	5.3	10.2	92	9.5	33.3	251	23.7	24.5	3
New York	27.1	35.7	32	n.a.	n.a.	n.a.	n.a.	n.a.	n.a.
North Carolina	7.5[c]	8.9	19	10.8[c]	29.3	171	12.8	24.5	91
Countrywide	10.6	16.5	56	n.a.	n.a.	n.a.	n.a.	n.a.	n.a.

Sources: U.S. General Accounting Office, *Medical Malpractice Case Studies* (GAO, 1986); countrywide data from St. Paul Fire and Marine Insurance Company.
n.a. Not available.
a. Approximately 6.5 in 1981 and 1983 but 39.7 in 1982.
b. Roughly constant from 1980 to 1983.
c. 1981.

frequency per 100 physicians rose from 13.5 to 17.2 a year.[3] There remain large differences among states and among specialties within states in both the overall level of claims and the rate of increase. For example, of six states recently surveyed by the General Accounting Office, claim frequency per 100 physicians in 1984 ranged from 8.6 in Arkansas to 35.7 in New York (table 4-1). The rate of increase appears to have been greater for obstetricians and gynecologists than for physicians as a whole, but not necessarily greater than for other high-risk surgical specialties. The current level of claims against OBG specialists and high-risk surgical specialties is two to three times the average level for all specialties. By contrast, anesthesiology, which was one of the specialties hardest hit in the mid-1970s, has had very stable claim experience in the 1980s. How much this reflects changes in technology and how much improved risk management is unclear.

The differences in claim rates among states can in part be explained by medical, demographic, and legal factors. Claim frequency is higher in states with high rates of surgical procedures per capita and in states with

3. The 10 percent figure is based on the experience of the St. Paul Fire and Marine Insurance, combining its claims made and occurrence coverages; Patricia M. Danzon, *New Evidence on the Frequency and Severity of Medical Malpractice Claims* (Rand Corporation, Institute for Civil Justice, 1986). As the largest malpractice insurer, St. Paul writes coverage for physicians in forty-two states and insures roughly 20 percent of physicians nationwide. Estimates of trends in claim frequency based on the experience of the physician-owned companies formed after the 1975 crisis are inherently biased for the first few years of operation. Such data will tend to show an acceleration of claim frequency as their experience matures.

a large percentage of the population in urban areas. After controlling for these factors, average per capita income is not a significant factor nor is the number of attorneys per capita. Although there is a strong simple correlation between number of attorneys and claim frequency, statistical analysis suggests that attorneys tend to locate in areas with high rates of litigation rather than that they create the high rates.[4]

Interstate differences in common-law doctrines and statutory laws have also been important. Early modification of the doctrines of respondeat superior, informed consent, and the locality rule contributed to the increased number of claims in the early 1970s. States that enacted shorter statutes of limitations and provided for the offset of collateral benefits against tort awards have had slower growth in claims filed since the mid-1970s. Statistical analysis suggests that reducing the statute of limitations for adults by one year from the date of injury reduces claim frequency by 8 percent. Collateral source offset reduces claim frequency by 14 percent.[5]

It would be of great interest to know how much of the growth in claims reflects an increase in the number of injuries caused by medical negligence as opposed to an increase in the proportion of potential claims that are actually filed. Unfortunately, there are no data on the total number of medically caused injuries or on the number caused by negligence. In-hospital mortality rates for a wide variety of case types, however, did decline between 1972 and 1981.[6] Thus by this admittedly crude measure, quality of hospital care has improved. Much of the decline is attributable to a decrease in mortality risk from anesthesia in the past three decades, from about 1 in 3,000 to 1 in 10,000.[7]

Claim frequency does not appear to have been affected by any major explicit changes in liability doctrine since the mid-1970s. The standard is still nominally one based on negligence as defined by customary practice. It is possible—and widely alleged—that the standard has de facto increasingly become one of strict liability, or no-fault, but such allegations are very hard to document. It is also possible that a higher proportion of potential claims under a negligence standard are being filed. Evidence from

4. Patricia M. Danzon, "The Frequency and Severity of Medical Malpractice Claims," *Journal of Law and Economics,* vol. 27 (April 1984), pp. 115–48; and Danzon, *New Evidence.*

5. Danzon, *New Evidence,* p. 20. These are average annual percentage reductions between 1975 and 1984.

6. Frank A. Sloan, "Economic Issues in Medical Malpractice," in Manne, ed., *Medical Malpractice Policy Guidebook,* p. 23.

7. "Deaths during General Anesthesia," *Journal of Health Care Technology,* vol. 1 (Winter 1985), p. 157.

the mid-1970s suggests that at most one in ten victims injured as a result of negligence actually filed a claim.[8] Thus as the expected payoff from filing has grown, a greater number of potential claimants may be finding it worthwhile to file.

Several factors could contribute to the especially rapid increase in claims against OBG specialists, although so far the hypotheses remain untested. Technological advance now permits the survival of neurologically impaired infants who once would have died. However, it remains very difficult to determine whether a particular impairment is "caused" by genetic factors or by inappropriate medical care before or during birth. Technological advance may have interacted with the long statute of limitations for minors to produce a transitory surge in claims. Most states have adopted statutes of limitation for adults of two to five years from date of injury, but for minors the time allowed to file a claim is typically at least ten years. The longer the statute of limitations, the greater the backlog of potential claims that become worth filing when a new cause of action, a liberalization of standards of evidence, or an increase in expected net recovery occurs. Longer statutes of limitations therefore tend to increase volatility as well as mean claim frequency.

Claim Severity

Claim severity is measured by averaging the indemnity paid on all claims that are closed with a payment, including court awards and out-of-court settlements (which account for over 90 percent of paid claims).[9] In 1984 the median and mean claim payments were $18,000 and $80,741, respectively.[10] Severity had increased at roughly twice the rate of the consumer price index from 1975 to 1984. The increase cannot be explained by the more rapid growth in the medical price index, since medical expenses account for less than one-quarter of the reported economic loss in malpractice cases closed with payment.[11]

8. Patricia M. Danzon, *Medical Malpractice: Theory, Evidence, and Public Policy* (Harvard University Press, 1985). A claim is as defined in National Association of Insurance Commissioners, *Malpractice Claims Final Compilation: Medical Malpractice Closed Claims, 1975–78* (Brookfield, Wisc.: NAIC, 1980). It includes all claims filed with an insurance company by a patient or patient's attorney, including claims that are settled or dropped without filing a legal suit. It does not include cases in which a hospital might provide remedial medical care without a patient's filing a formal claim.

9. Some insurers also include claim adjustment expense in reported severity.

10. U.S. General Accounting Office, *Medical Malpractice: Characteristics of Claims Closed in 1984,* GAO/HRD-87-55 (GAO, 1987), p. 2.

11. National Association of Insurance Commissioners, *Malpractice Claims,* p. 51.

Table 4-2. *Average Indemnity per Paid Claim, Selected States,*
1980, 1984
Current dollars unless otherwise specified

	All specialties			Obstetrics and gynecology			Neurosurgery		
State	*1980*	*1984*	*Percent change*	*1980*	*1984*	*Percent change*	*1980*	*1984*	*Percent change*
Arkansas	31,619	51,685	63	n.a.	81,370	n.a.	n.a.	20,000	n.a.
California	32,963	61,774	87	50,973	92,628	82	41,667	91,619	120
Florida	80,556	140,594	75	65,081	86,465	33	3,000	98,250	3,175
New York	46,789	104,810	124	n.a.	n.a.	n.a.	n.a.	n.a.	n.a.
North Carolina	36,064[a]	62,043	72	22,438	97,483	334	n.a.	20,000	n.a.
Country-wide[b]	28,059	56,739	102	n.a.	n.a.	n.a.	n.a.	n.a.	n.a.

Sources: See table 4-1.
n.a. Not available.
a. 1981.
b. Maximum amount per claim: $1,000,000.

There are significant differences among states in both the level of claim severity and its rate of increase (table 4-2). There are also differences among specialties, although these tend to be very erratic because of the small number of paid claims and the huge range of awards.

Trends and interstate differences in observed severity may understate differences in potential severity (the expected jury verdict for a particular category of injury), which can be called jury generosity. An increase in jury generosity not only increases the amounts awarded in verdicts and settlements on claims that would have been filed anyway, but also encourages the filing of claims that would not be brought if juries were less generous. Specifically, if higher generosity encourages the filing of marginal claims for small injuries or claims with low probabilities of winning, these marginal claims will tend to pull down the average paid severity. Thus upward trends in observed severity and differences among states generally understate true trends and differences in generosity.

There is some evidence that the largest jury awards have grown more rapidly than the median.[12] Compensation for noneconomic loss (pain and suffering) may account for an increasing proportion of these awards. Data on jury verdicts in Cook County show that medical malpractice cases increased from 2.0 percent of all liability cases in 1959–79 to 4.6 percent in 1980–84. Malpractice plaintiffs increased their share of total dollar

12. Mark A. Peterson, *Civil Juries in the 1980's: Trends in Jury Trials and Verdicts in California and Cook County, Illinois* (Rand Corporation, Institute for Civil Justice, 1987).

indemnity fourfold, from 3.7 percent to 16.4 percent, and their share of total payment for pain and suffering more than sevenfold, from 3.4 percent to 29.0 percent. Payments in excess of $100,000 for pain and suffering in malpractice cases increased from 1.8 percent to 12.8 percent of total payments to plaintiffs in all tort litigations.[13] Even allowing for possible errors in using jury verdicts to estimate levels and trends in compensation for pain and suffering, these data strongly suggest that if Cook County is typical of other jurisdictions, payments for pain and suffering in excess of $100,000 in medical malpractice cases are increasing disproportionately relative to payments for economic loss.

Malpractice Insurance Costs

The conceptually correct measure of trends in the cost of malpractice insurance is the cost of covering a constant percentage of the expected loss distribution. Thus the cost of coverage has risen both because of increasing rates for given levels of coverage and because the levels of coverage necessary to provide a given measure of financial protection have risen.

RATES. Table 4-3 shows that premium rates for basic limits of coverage ($100,000 per claim and up to $300,000 aggregate) increased very little from 1976 through 1979, on average, which implies decreasing cost in constant dollars. But from 1980 to 1984 the increases averaged between 10 and 30 percent a year. For 1985 to 1987, data are not available disaggregated by state and by specialty. The St. Paul Fire and Marine Insurance Company reports average rate increases of 25 to 35 percent, and the physician-owned companies report increases averaging 30 to 40 percent.[14] For 1976–84 as a whole, the increase is 109 percent for the

---

13. Based on data provided by George Priest and reported in Patricia M. Danzon, "Florida Malpractice Awards for Pain and Suffering," in Manne, ed., *Medical Malpractice Policy Guidebook*, p. 139. There are several possible sources of error in generalizing from such data. Payment for pain and suffering is estimated as the difference between the total award and reported economic loss (wages lost and medical and other tangible expenses). These data do not correct for awards reduced on appeal. The sample of cases litigated to verdict tends to be unrepresentative of cases settled out of court because they are more likely to involve atypical issues and very large stakes; Patricia M. Danzon and Lee A. Lillard, "Settlement Out of Court: The Disposition of Medical Malpractice Claims," *Journal of Legal Studies*, vol. 12 (June 1983), pp. 345–77. Estimates of trends may be biased by changes in caseload composition; see Peterson, *Civil Juries in the 1980's*. In particular, estimates of trends in the mean may be biased upward if cases tried to verdict represent an increasingly small percentage of the largest cases.

14. American Medical Association, *The Continuing Need for Legislative Reform of the Medical Liability System: A Response by the Medical Profession to Opponents of Tort*

Table 4-3. *Premium Rates for a $100,000–$300,000 Policy, Mean Percentage Change Nationwide from Previous Year, 1978–84*[a]

	Specialty		
Year	Low-risk	High-risk	Obstetrics and gynecology
1978	−1.0	−2.0	−1.3
1979	5.9	8.4	5.8
1980	11.3	13.9	15.8
1981	22.7	32.7	26.6
1982	9.2	17.9	11.4
1983	15.6	19.1	29.5
1984	16.2	18.3	19.5
1977–84	109.0	189.0	179.9

Source: U.S. Department of Health and Human Services, Health Care Financing Administration, annual malpractice insurers' surveys.

a. Coverage of $100,000 per claim and up to $300,000 aggregate. Mean of state-specific rates of change. Unweighted average. Companies included in sample vary from year to year.

lowest-risk specialists, such as general practitioners who do no surgery, and 189 percent for high-risk specialists. The average rate of increase among the states for OBG specialists does not appear significantly greater than for other high-risk surgical specialties, although this may not be true in specific states. During the same period, the consumer price index increased 82.5 percent and its medical care component increased 125.1 percent. Thus for low-risk specialties, premium costs for basic limits between 1976 and 1984 have not increased more rapidly than other components of medical care. This is not true, however, for the latter half of the period alone, and for the entire period it is not true for high-risk specialties.

INCREASED LIMITS OF COVERAGE. More than 75 percent of physicians purchase limits of coverage higher than the basic $100,000–$300,000, so that increases in rates for basic limits understate the total increase in premium rates. The percentage of physicians carrying at least $1 million in coverage increased from 21 percent in 1976 to 41 percent in 1983.[15] The cost of higher levels of coverage relative to the cost of basic coverage fell in the late 1970s, but increased in the early and mid-1980s, more for surgeons than for other physicians.[16]

Reform (AMA, 1987), p. 17; and St. Paul Fire and Marine Insurance Company, "Physicians' and Surgeons' Update" (July 1987).

15. Benson L. Dutton, Jr., "Trends in Medical Malpractice," working paper 86-18 (Health Care Financing Administration, September 1986), p. 6.

16. The cost of higher limits of coverage is expressed as a multiple of the cost of basic

Table 4-4. *Malpractice Premiums and Losses, Percentage Change Nationwide from Previous Year, 1977–85*

Year	Net premiums written	Losses incurred	Loss plus adjustment expense[a]
1977	10.15	−14.64	−9.38
1978	−2.57	15.25	9.68
1979	0.94	8.39	10.90
1980	5.92	21.12	17.22
1981	4.92	16.54	11.78
1982	11.36	19.34	18.82
1983	5.22	6.32	11.07
1984	13.19	28.81	22.57
1985	56.03	45.22	49.27
1976–85	144.46	257.23	248.77
1977–85	121.93	318.50	284.85

Source: A. M. Best and Company, *Aggregates and Averages: Property-Liability* (various years).
a. Loss adjustment expense comprises 30 to 40 percent of loss incurred.

Premiums and Claims Costs

Table 4-4 shows trends over the past decade in net premiums written nationwide, losses incurred by insurance companies, and loss adjustment expense.[17] Losses and loss adjustment expense have risen steadily since 1978, accelerating in 1984. However, net premiums written barely increased until 1980 then increased sharply, particularly in 1985.[18] The increase from 1976 to 1985 was 257 percent for losses incurred, 249 percent for loss plus loss adjustment expense, and 144 percent for net premiums written. The change in losses incurred in any year reflects losses anticipated on new business written during the year plus revisions in loss reserves for policies written in previous years. In competitive markets, earlier errors in anticipating losses cannot be recouped by overcharging on current rates without inviting the entry of new companies into the market.

---

coverage. For example, the St. Paul Fire and Marine Insurance Company increased-limits factor for $1 million–$1million coverage for surgeons was 2.0 in 1977, fell to 1.7 in 1980, and rose to 2.08 in 1984 and 2.26 in 1986; St. Paul Fire and Marine, private communication.

17. These data, from A. M. Best and Company, *Aggregates and Averages: Property-Liability* (various years), include all the major commercial insurers, most of the physician-owned companies, and some of the hospital-owned companies.

18. The percentage change in premium volume is not a pure measure of the percentage change in premium rates for a given level of coverage if demand is not perfectly inelastic or if there has been an exogenous shift in demand, for example because physicians perceive a higher expected loss.

Thus increases in premiums that do not fully reflect losses are consistent with the hypothesis that malpractice insurance markets are sufficiently competitive to prevent insurers from recouping underestimates of losses for earlier years. Indeed the widespread entry of physician-owned and hospital-owned companies that now write more than 50 percent of premium volume nationwide is compelling evidence that lack of competition has not caused the recent sharp increases in malpractice rates.

Costs and Benefits of the Tort System

The increases in the frequency and severity of malpractice claims are not necessarily evidence that the tort system is malfunctioning. Similarly, that the cost of delivering compensation through the tort system is two or three times the cost of delivering it through private and public insurance systems is not in itself grounds for inferring that the system is not cost-effective and should be reformed or abandoned. The tort system can potentially perform two functions: compensation and deterrence.[19] An evaluation should ideally weigh the benefits for both against the costs of the system. Because the data necessary for such a complete evaluation are unavailable, this section outlines the information required and presents the evidence that is available on the costs and benefits of the malpractice system.

Costs

The costs of the malpractice system may be divided into the direct costs associated with malpractice litigation and the indirect costs associated with changes in the practice of medical care.

DIRECT COSTS. The largest and most visible component of direct costs is liability insurance premiums paid by medical service providers and the equivalent costs to self-insured providers. Malpractice insurance costs for physicians and hospitals have been estimated at $4.7 billion in 1985, or just over 1 percent of total health care spending that year.[20]

In addition, there are uninsured costs of litigation to both plaintiff and defense, including out-of-pocket indemnity payments and legal costs,

19. Retribution or equity is sometimes listed as a third potential function of the civil liability system but is ignored here.
20. U.S. General Accounting Office, *Medical Malpractice: A Framework for Action,* GAO-HRD 87-73 (1987), p. 2.

time and "embarrassment" costs of litigation, and the loss in utility to physicians of living with the risk of suit.[21] Finally, there are public costs of litigation not borne by the parties.

INDIRECT COSTS. The major component of indirect costs is prevention, that is, the real resource cost of measures taken by physicians and hospitals to reduce the risk of injury or risk of suit.[22] There is strong evidence that in the past decade hospitals have adopted extensive risk management programs. A substantial fraction of physicians also report changing their patterns of practice in response to the liability threat. For example, in a 1984 survey 41 percent reported ordering extra tests, 36 percent spent more time with patients, 57 percent kept more detailed records, and 45 percent referred more cases.[23]

There are no reliable estimates of how much these responses cost. It is difficult to determine the extent to which patterns of medical practice reportedly induced by the liability threat would have developed anyway in response to the incentives created by extensive insurance for health care. With full fee-for-service insurance the patient has the incentive to demand and the physician has the incentive to provide any test or procedure that potentially provides any benefit to the patient, no matter how small. Thus traditional forms of insurance alone could account for much of the low- or zero-benefit medical practice that is often called defensive medicine. But traditional coverage is increasingly being replaced by insurance plans that create stronger incentives for patients or providers to eliminate low-benefit care, either because patients bear part of the cost or because the various forms of prospective reimbursement encourage providers to keep costs down.[24] It remains to be seen whether this trend toward forms of health insurance that create incentives for physicians to control costs in general will also reduce the incidence of so-called defensive medicine.

Some physicians also report withdrawing entirely from practice or

21. In other words, if physicians are risk-averse, the utility cost exceeds the expected value of these uninsured costs.

22. I use the term *prevention costs* rather than *defensive medicine* because defensive medicine tends to imply that such measures have no benefit other than possibly to reduce a physician's risk of being sued.

23. Stephen Zuckerman, "Medical Malpractice: Claims, Legal Costs, and the Practice of Defensive Medicine," *Health Affairs,* vol. 3 (Fall 1984), pp. 128–33.

24. In a health maintenance organization the physician receives a fixed monthly payment for each patient enrolled and so has strong incentives to minimize the cost of care. In a preferred provider organization the physician is paid a fee for service according to a fixed fee schedule and so has an incentive to minimize the cost per billable procedure. Most PPOs also employ utilization review to control frequency of use.

ceasing to perform certain procedures. In a 1985 survey of OBG specialists, 12 percent reported dropping obstetrics and 23 percent reported that they had stopped performing certain high-risk procedures. The social costs of such changes in practice are hard to measure. Individual physicians may lose income. The costs to patients depend on the inconvenience and disutility of transferring to other physicians.[25] Again, it is difficult to distinguish changes in practices caused by the threat of malpractice suits from those that might have occurred anyway in response to underlying changes in the health care sector. In particular, the increasing supply of physicians and the declining birthrate are surely factors contributing to early retirements and changes in practice.[26]

INCIDENCE OF COSTS. The costs of malpractice insurance and litigation fall in the first instance on medical providers. In the longer run, however, some part of them is borne by taxpayers because of the tax deductibility of physicians' liability insurance costs and the tax-exempt status of most of first-party health insurance premiums. Some part is also borne by patients through higher prices for medical care. The ultimate incidence depends on the relative elasticities of demand for and supply of medical care.

Physicians are likely to bear a greater share of the burden in the short run but to shift an increasing share onto patients as time goes by. In the short run, fees for medical services tend to be fixed, given the norms of reimbursement by public and private third-party payers. For example, in principle medicare adjusts its "reasonable charge" (the maximum it will pay for specific procedures) annually according to an index of medical care component costs that includes the cost of malpractice insurance. In practice, medicare fees for physicians were frozen from 1983 through 1986. Medicaid fees are even lower in most states.[27] Private insurers also typically set fee levels for a year at a time. Under some insurance plans the physician is precluded from billing the patient for more than the amount the insurer will pay. When such balance billing is permitted, demand is likely to be elastic because the patient bears the full amount of the excess. Thus as a rough approximation,

25. There may be a long-run gain from the concentration of high-risk procedures among fewer physicians and in fewer facilities if volume leads to greater skill or lower cost.

26. Among physicians that reported giving up obstetrics, 50 percent were between the ages of thirty-five and fifty-four. This suggests that some withdrawals do not simply represent early retirement.

27. Controls on medicaid fees may particularly affect the ability of OBG specialists to pass on higher costs for deliveries.

Table 4-5. *Percentage Changes in Median Premiums, Net Income, and Fees, by Speciality, 1983–86*

Specialty	Premiums	Net income	Ratio of premium to premium plus net income	Initial office visit fee
General practice	109.8	3.7	51.6	18.2
Obstetrics and gynecology	97.0	12.1	45.5	25.0
Orthopedics	83.2	21.0	26.8	25.0
Neurosurgery	99.5	35.2	22.8	19.7
All surgical	102.3	15.4	33.2	28.6
All nonsurgical	72.0	10.2	14.9	17.1

Source: *Medical Economics* (various issues).

any increase in premium costs must be borne by the physician in the short run. Traditional insurance plans make it easier to pass on the cost of preventive practices that involve additional intensity of services per visit. To the extent this is more true for tests than for additional time that a physician may spend with a patient, incentives for providing the most efficient mix of preventive services are distorted.[28]

PREMIUMS RELATIVE TO PHYSICIAN INCOME. The ratio of malpractice premiums to physicians' incomes is often cited as evidence of the impact of the malpractice system on physicians or on consumers and of the changes in this impact over time and among specialties. In fact, any such inferences should be tentative and depend on several assumptions. For example, that premiums represent a larger percentage of net income for surgical than for nonsurgical specialties does not necessarily imply that net income differentials among specialties would be any different in the absence of premiums or that prices to consumers are higher as a consequence of the premiums. However, changes in the ratio of premiums to net income at least suggest the incidence of premium costs over time.

Table 4-5 shows the percentage change from 1983 through 1986 for median premium payments and median net income for four specialty categories. During this period, premium increases averaged 72.0 percent for nonsurgical specialties and 102.3 percent for surgical specialties. The 97 percent increase for OBG specialists is not out of line with other high-risk specialties. The changes in median net income are 10.2 percent for nonsurgical specialties, 15.4 percent for surgical specialties, and 12.1 percent for OBG specialists. Table 4-5 also shows the change in

28. Patricia M. Danzon, "Liability and Liability Insurance for Medical Malpractice," *Journal of Health Economics,* vol. 4 (December 1985), pp. 309–31.

the ratio of median premium to the sum of median premium plus median net income. This ratio increased by 33.2 percent for surgical specialties and 14.9 percent for nonsurgical specialties. The increase was much greater for OBG specialists (45.5 percent) and even greater for general practitioners (51.6 percent), this despite the fact that GPs and OBG specialists do not report below-average increases in median fees charged for a first office visit or for specialty-specific procedures.[29]

It appears, then, that although premiums paid by OBG specialists have not increased more quickly than premiums paid by other specialists, net incomes have increased more slowly, if more quickly than those of nonsurgical specialists. The percentage increase in median fees charged by OBG specialists appears comparable to the increase for other specialties. Given the limitations of the data used here, inferences on whether premium increases have had a proportionately greater effect on OBG net incomes are necessarily tentative. The slower increase in net income may be attributable at least in part to a shrinking patient base rather than atypical premium increases or more limited ability to raise fees. There are, however, several caveats to this conclusion. First, the data on premiums paid may understate the increase in the cost of coverage if policies purchased have lower limits of coverage or more exclusions or limitations on practice. Second, reimbursement actually received may be less than the fee charged, particularly for medicaid patients. Third, the figures may mask increased dispersion, with a few physicians facing atypically large premium increases.

Benefits

Any system of third-party liability can potentially deliver at least three types of benefits: compensation to injured parties (risk spreading or insurance), injury prevention through deterrence of excessive risk taking, and justice or retribution. Retribution is ignored here, since its intrinsic value is more controversial and is even harder to measure than compensation and deterrence.

COMPENSATION. Observers often argue that the tort system is being expanded to provide compensation for losses not covered by other sources of insurance. They also contend that the system provides excessive levels of compensation in particular cases and possibly on average.

29. For specialty-specific procedures, the average increase in fees for OBGs was higher than the average for all physicians in each year and ranked in the top four in three of the four years.

To address the first issue requires information on the losses incurred by malpractice victims and the compensation provided through litigation and other sources.[30] The limited evidence available on this point is reviewed here. To address the second requires a benchmark of the optimal level of compensation and information on the extent to which, if at all, private insurance markets fail to provide this level of insurance. This complex question is briefly discussed later in this chapter.

Estimates of the relationship between indemnity paid (including jury awards and out-of-court settlements) and economic loss are necessarily rough. The largest available survey of malpractice claims encompassed almost all claims closed between July 1975 and December 1978. For 39 percent of paid claims, economic loss was reported as zero (25 percent) or the data were missing. If economic loss was truly zero for all 39 percent, then total economic loss represented only 54.6 percent of total indemnity paid. But if one assumes that claims with zero or missing data are no different, on average, from claims with reported data, then economic loss was 208 percent of indemnity. Consistency checks tend to reject both extremes. Under intermediate assumptions, economic loss averaged 81.1 percent of total indemnity, of which medical expense accounted for 30.4 percentage points, wage loss for 47.4 percentage points, and other expense for the remaining 3.3 percentage points.[31]

However, claim file data usually underestimate the extent of compensation relative to actual economic loss because most indemnities are paid in a single lump sum and so represent discounted present values of future expenses, whereas economic loss reported in claim files is probably not discounted. If the concern is with rules for damage awards, further downward bias is introduced by the fact that 95 percent of paid claims are settled. On average, cases that settle out of court receive 74 percent of their potential court award.[32] Assuming, then, that the mean potential award is 1.3 times the mean indemnity reported, tort awards yielded compensation roughly 60 percent higher than undiscounted economic loss from 1975 to 1978. Because awards have since risen twice as fast as the consumer price index, current awards probably pay twice the undiscounted economic loss. Even allowing for legal expenses of one-third of the award, net compensation to the plaintiff would exceed economic loss by at least one-third.

30. Such information would also permit an estimate of the potential savings in claim costs from collateral source offsets.
31. For details see Danzon, *Medical Malpractice.*
32. Danzon and Lillard, "Settlement Out of Court."

These averages may mask great discrepancies among cases, with some plaintiffs receiving much more and others much less than enough to cover economic loss. Further, although 60 percent of economic loss would on average be covered by other sources of public and private insurance,[33] the tort award may be the only source of compensation for some patients (for example, those without private or public health insurance, who now constitute 17 percent of the nonelderly population) and for some types of expenses such as those for private nursing care and rehabilitation.

DETERRENCE. In response to the increased threat of liability, hospitals have adopted more extensive risk management programs, and some physicians have changed their practices in ways that probably reduce the risk of injury—spending more time with patients, referring difficult cases, keeping better records, ordering extra diagnostic tests. Unfortunately, the benefits of these measures—the number of injuries prevented—have also eluded measurement.

Although there are no current comprehensive data on the incidence of injuries caused by medical negligence, several studies have suggested it is not trivial. The most comprehensive data base on treatment-induced injury used a representative sample of California hospitals surveyed in 1974. That study found that one in twenty hospital admissions resulted in an adverse outcome due to medical care; of these, 17 percent were probably caused by negligence.[34] Assuming that California hospitals are representative of hospitals nationwide, these data suggest that 1 in 126 patients admitted to hospitals in 1974 incurred an injury caused by negligence.[35] The proportion of the injured patients who filed a claim is not known. However, a comparison of the number of claims filed in the subsequent years with the number of injuries implies that at most 1 in 10 of the patients who suffered an injury because of negligence filed a claim, and at most 1 in 25 received compensation through the tort system.

Since then the number of claims has more than doubled, but there is no current estimate of the number of injuries caused by negligence.[36]

33. Danzon, *Medical Malpractice.*
34. California Medical Association, *Report on the Medical Insurance Feasibility Study* (San Francisco: Sutter Publications, 1977). For several reasons these are probably lower-bound estimates of the number of negligent injuries; see Danzon, *Medical Malpractice.*
35. A study is currently under way in New York to update these estimates. See Harvard Medical Practice Study Group, "Medical Care and Medical Injuries in the State of New York: A Pilot Study" (April 1987).
36. If there has been some increase in the number of defendants named in each claim, the percentage increase in claims per physician slightly overstates the increase in the

Assuming that number is unchanged, injuries caused by negligence would still outnumber claims five to one. Concern over creating incentives for injury prevention is therefore not redundant.

Weighing Costs and Benefits

Although the number of injuries actually prevented is unknown, the benefits from deterrence necessary to justify the costs of operating the liability system as it applies to malpractice can be estimated. Assume that the only net social costs of the system are litigation and insurance overhead costs, that is, that the portion of liability insurance premiums representing indemnity paid to plaintiffs provides compensation valued at cost and that indirect costs of the tort system are negligible. These litigation and overhead costs absorb sixty cents of the malpractice premium dollar. Thus only forty cents reaches the victim as compensation, compared with eighty cents of every first-party insurance dollar. The additional forty cents incurred to provide compensation through the tort system may be viewed as an investment in loss prevention under the assumption that the system sends signals about appropriate levels of care and penalties for failing to meet standards. This litigation expense (or, viewed alternatively, regulation expense) is worth incurring only if it yields at least equivalent net benefits. Thus as a first approximation the tort system would pay for itself if at least one injury of comparable severity were deterred for every injury compensated. To the extent that efforts to prevent injuries entail resource costs and the tort system entails costs such as embarrassment and loss of time for the litigating parties, the deterrence benefits would have to be higher. To the extent that awards received by victims understate their willingness to pay for injury prevention, however, the level of deterrence necessary to justify the system is lower.

To convert these estimates into the required reduction in the rate of injuries caused by negligence, we need an estimate of the percentage of victims currently compensated. Using the 1974 estimate that one in twenty-five patients injured through negligence receives compensation,[37]

---

proportion of incidents that give rise to a claim. Since the mid-1970s, exposure to risk of iatrogenic injury has increased because of greater use of medical care. The rate of injury, however, may have decreased if more rigorous loss-prevention measures have had an effect. The assumption that the number of injuries is unchanged would imply that these two effects offset one another.

37. For sources of this estimate see Danzon, *Medical Malpractice*.

only a 4 percent reduction in the rate of negligent injuries would be required to justify the litigation costs of the tort system. If compensation per injury is currently twice as high as in 1974, then an 8 percent reduction in the injury rate would be required. If the tort system entails other costs equal to, for example, twice the litigation costs (or $4 billion), then a 24 percent reduction in the injury rate would be required to justify the costs. The required reduction would be less, however, if willingness to pay for injury prevention exceeds compensation actually received or if there are other benefits of the tort system, such as providing compensation for certain losses that are not covered by other private or social insurance programs and ideally should be.

Conclusions on the Current System

Continued increases in the frequency and severity of malpractice claims and recent rapid increases in insurance rates and restrictions on availability have once again focused attention on the malpractice system. The costs of the system are substantial. The benefits, in terms of improved quality of care, are impossible to quantify. Thus whether the benefits outweigh the costs remains in doubt.

Unfortunately, there are no obviously superior alternatives. Given the inevitable asymmetry of information between medical providers and patients, reliance on market forces with a rule of no liability would probably lead to deteriorating levels of care. There is thus a strong prima facie case for a rule of third-party liability based either on a standard of negligence or strict liability.[38]

However, the negligence standard does not appear to be operating as it should. In theory, under a negligence standard in long-run equilibrium, there should be no claims because there should be no negligence: if the due care standard is efficiently defined, it is always cheaper to prevent injuries than to be negligent and insure against the resulting claims. Under an efficient negligence system, claims can only be explained if standards of due care are continually changing because of new technologies and if patterns of practice tend to lag behind. This explanation, however, does not fit well for professional liability, where due

38. Under a negligence rule the level of care per encounter should be optimal, although if patients systematically underestimate risk, their use of care would exceed the amount they would choose if they correctly perceived the risks; Steven Shavell, "Strict Liability vs. Negligence," *Journal of Legal Studies,* vol. 9 (January 1980), pp. 1–25.

care is in principle defined as the customary practice of the profession at the time of the allegedly wrongful act.

The high and continually rising number of claims per physician and the probably equal or larger number of injuries caused by negligence suggest that in operation the system does not closely resemble the theoretical model. There are several possible reasons for this discrepancy. First, deterrence incentives may be too weak because some patients injured through negligence do not sue. This failure of deterrence may be offset to the extent that awards paid exceed levels necessary for optimal deterrence.

Second, deterrence incentives may be too weak because malpractice insurance protection is too extensive: copayments and premium rating based on physicians' individual records are uncommon.[39] However, such a conclusion remains tentative because it presupposes that competitive insurance markets fail to provide the optimal structure of insurance policies. Moreover, the actual level of uninsured risk carried by the average physician may be greater than it appears, depending on whether there are uninsured time and embarrassment costs of suit, selective underwriting by insurers who offer lower rates to better risks, nonlinear pricing for higher limits of coverage, and incomplete coverage of the upper tail of the loss distribution. Finally, the optimal level of physicians' copayments (including experience rating of premiums) decreases as the frequency of error by plaintiffs and courts in filing and permitting claims for injuries not caused by negligence increases; it also decreases as the insurer's need to control moral hazard in providing legal defense increases.[40]

Third, the negligence rule may not have eliminated claims because the standards applied by the courts may be too high, defining injuries caused by negligence to include some that could not be prevented at a cost less than damages incurred or less than willingness to pay for prevention. This is implied by the widely held perception that courts adopt a de facto strict liability standard when they perceive a need for compensation. Whether such deviations from a fault-based rule are

---

39. Some companies do add a surcharge for physicians who have multiple claims or multiple paid claims. St. Paul Fire and Marine recently introduced policy options with a flat deductible or a participating deductible (copayment). In most states the minimum deductible is $5,000. See St. Paul Fire and Marine Insurance Company, "Physicians' and Surgeons' Update."

40. See Danzon, "Liability and Liability Insurance," for development of these arguments.

common is an important question, but it cannot be determined with the data available.[41]

In addition to the issue of whether it is generally set at an efficient level, the liability standard appears to vary considerably, thus creating uncertainty, which is necessarily inefficient because it encourages expenditure on litigation. Uncertainty also puts physicians at risk because they cannot determine the standard of appropriate care or be sure they will not be sued if they do determine it and adhere to it. The expected responses to such risk are to purchase too much or too little insurance and to spend too much or too little on prevention.[42]

Turning from liability standards to standards for awards, one can make a strong case that by attempting to provide full compensation for all economic and noneconomic losses, damage rules are inefficient. People do not voluntarily insure against noneconomic losses, partly because money cannot restore the irreplaceable faculties lost and partly because problems of moral hazard and adverse selection would raise the cost of such insurance coverage far above actuarially fair levels. No other social insurance program provides such compensation, which suggests that even when the problem of adverse selection is eliminated through compulsory insurance, we do not collectively choose to compensate for noneconomic damages when the choice is explicit. The tort system is unique in compensating for pain and suffering, perhaps because it is the only social insurance program in which the level of compensation is determined on a case-by-case basis in the presence of the injured party. This appears to be another instance of the tendency to place higher values on identified lives than on "statistical" lives. Determining compensation in this way certainly leads to inequity between victims whose injuries happen to be compensable through litigation and those who must rely on social insurance programs in which benefit levels are determined by statute. It is also likely to lead to higher levels of compensation

41. Even if the standard were optimally set for the average physician, it might be higher than appropriate for less competent physicians. If physicians could be ranked by quality of care and if customary practice were defined as the median of the distribution, then 50 percent of physicians would be practicing negligently. However, if lower-quality physicians charged lower fees, some patients might prefer them, and it would not be efficient to find such physicians negligent.

42. Richard Craswell and John E. Calfee, "Deterrence and Uncertain Legal Standards," *Journal of Law, Economics and Organization,* vol. 2 (Fall 1986), pp. 279–303, show that under a negligence rule operated with error, defendants may face incentives to undercomply or overcomply.

than we would collectively choose to pay for ex ante if faced with the choice and the bill.

Alternative Institutional Arrangements

Unfortunately, decisions to retain or reform the tort system cannot wait until the costs and benefits of all alternatives have been precisely measured. To require such an evaluation is to settle indefinitely for the status quo. The discussion that follows therefore draws on theory and the limited empirical evidence available to evaluate alternatives to the current system. The discussion assumes that the objective is to minimize the social cost of injuries, defined as the sum of the costs of injuries, prevention, litigation and other overhead, and uninsured risk. This objective is consistent with equity between all parties before individual victims and defendants have been identified, conditional on the distribution of income. The goal of retributive justice is ignored.

Reform of the Tort System

Among other defects the tort system is perceived as depending on erratically defined and therefore unpredictable standards of liability, with a possible trend away from using a fault-based rule toward using a standard of strict liability. The system has been criticized for awarding unpredictable and potentially excessive levels of compensation and for high costs of litigation, which in part result from the unpredictability of standards for liability and damages and their susceptibility to influence by the litigants.[43] The cost and the volatility in price and availability of insurance, again in part a result of unpredictability, have also been noted. Thus any reform that would increase predictability without significant loss of deterrence or of optimal compensation would improve the cost-effectiveness of the tort system.

STANDARDS OF LIABILITY. Generally there appears to be no practical alternative to the standard of customary or usual practice of either the

43. Utility-maximization models of litigation show that if the outcome at verdict were perfectly predictable, both parties could gain by settling out of court. Litigation expense is incurred to influence the outcome. Therefore the incentive to invest in litigation is directly related to the susceptibility of verdicts to influence by the litigants.

majority or a substantial minority of medical professionals.[44] The relevant standard should be that prevailing at the time of the allegedly wrongful conduct.[45] No useful deterrent function is served by retroactive application of newer medical or legal standards.

There is some concern that liability for malpractice will become an obstacle to the evolution of more cost-effective patterns of medical care and will slow the elimination of practices yielding few benefits. To provide some bulwark against this, costs must be an admissible defense against any claim alleging failure to take additional precautions or prolong hospitalization. In such a defense the relevant measure is the full social cost of taking the additional precautions relative to expected benefits for the class of patients in a situation similar to that of the plaintiff.

RULES OF DAMAGES. To attempt full compensation for noneconomic loss is almost certainly not efficient. Further, determining compensation on a case-by-case basis using very imprecise guidelines creates uncertainty, which is not efficient insurance for the potential plaintiff and encourages expenditure on litigation. These inefficiencies could be reduced for both economic and noneconomic loss by creating a schedule of compensation based on the age of the plaintiff and the severity of the injury. The more generous the payment for quasi-medical expenses such as rehabilitation and nursing care, which may significantly improve the quality of life of a severely disabled plaintiff, the less generous the compensation, if any, for pain and suffering.[46]

In general, a schedule related to age and severity of injury is more efficient and equitable than the simple caps on awards that many states have enacted.[47] Caps that do not adjust for age and severity of injury imply that the young, severely injured plaintiff, who may often have little coverage from such collateral sources as workers' compensation or

44. Using a cost-benefit test for medical care is difficult because the measure of cost is ambiguous. The efficient standard requires a weighing of social costs and benefits, but because most patients are insured, the private cost at point of purchase is often minimal or nothing. See Danzon, *Medical Malpractice*.

45. This is the standard currently required by the letter of the law; whether it is applied in practice is very hard to document.

46. Ideally compensation should equalize the marginal utility of income before and after the injury. This could require compensation in excess of economic loss for injuries that raise the marginal utility of income.

47. Washington state recently enacted a schedule for noneconomic damages. For each year of life expectancy the plaintiff would receive about 50 percent of the average annual wage in the state.

medicaid, will receive the largest proportionate reduction in compensation. The schedule should be indexed to the relevant measures (medical costs, wages) to prevent either erosion or inflation of standards of compensation relative to real incomes.[48]

In instances of severe personal injury under the current tort system, optimal compensation to the plaintiff may be less than the amount he or she would have been willing to pay for prevention, which would be the appropriate penalty for purposes of deterrence. In principle, appropriate deterrence incentives could be obtained by levying a fine to be paid the state in addition to the compensation paid the plaintiff. The optimal level of such a fine is reduced to the extent that patients' willingness to pay for safety is conveyed to physicians through market forces (but in that case why have any system of liability?). The optimal level of the fine is also reduced to the extent that the defendant faces substantial uninsured costs of suit (lost time, embarrassment) in addition to the damage payment. A large award that is either fully insured or exceeds the defendant's assets obviously serves no deterrent purpose. A reasonable compromise might be a modest but uninsurable fine that would replace punitive damages in cases of gross negligence. However, there are serious practical difficulties in implementing such a system.[49]

Another useful reform is to permit periodic payment of damages. Many states have allowed defendants to pay damages by purchasing an annuity for the plaintiff. If the plaintiff dies prematurely, the residual reverts to the defendant, net of a reasonable payment to the decedent's estate. This practice permits the defendant to take advantage of market interest rates and, through the market for annuities, of risk-pooling with respect to life expectancy. Any desired level of compensation can thereby be achieved at lower cost than if the jury bases the award on the maximum possible life of the plaintiff and uses a below-market rate of discount. To reduce moral hazard, the amount to be paid must be fixed, not contingent on the actual losses incurred by the plaintiff.

Another widely adopted reform is to subtract collateral sources of compensation from the tort award to prevent double recovery. A more efficient way of achieving the same result is to give all private and public insurers rights of subrogation against the tort award. This eliminates

---

48. Schedules are commonly used for workers' compensation. The proposal here is to use a schedule in conjunction with a fault-based rule of liability.

49. This is discussed at length in Patricia M. Danzon, "Tort Reform and the Role of Government in Private Insurance Markets," *Journal of Legal Studies,* vol. 13 (August 1984), pp. 517–49.

double recovery on the part of the plaintiff while still making the defendant responsible for the costs of injury. The alternative of offsetting collateral compensation may seriously undermine deterrence because a substantial number of small injuries, which are relatively well insured through first-party sources, may not be worth litigation. Evidence shows that states adopting some form of collateral source offset have experienced a reduction in claim severity of roughly 18 percent and in claim frequency of 14 percent.[50]

STATUTES OF LIMITATIONS. Statutes that run from the time an injury is discovered instead of from the time it occurs in effect provide no limit on the duration of liability. While this lack of limitation ensures maximum compensation, it also creates the risk of retroactive application of new standards of liability, which is of no deterrent value. Such retroactiveness tends to create a nondiversifiable sociolegal risk that increases the cost of liability insurance and may make it less available.[51] Given incomplete insurance, some physicians may take excessive care or avoid performing procedures that expose them to risk. The ideal statute therefore would require a trade-off between more complete compensation on the one hand and cost and volatility of insurance, overdeterrence, and a nonoptimal supply of services on the other. If the perception is accurate that OBG specialists and nurse-midwives have experienced much higher premiums or less availability than other specialties in buying insurance, the difficulty could plausibly be attributed to the long statute of limitations for minors, together with the larger and more uncertain awards for severely injured infants.

Alternative Systems of Deterrence

In addition to the tort system, physicians are subject to quality control through state medical licensing boards, credential committees that review applications for hospital staff privileges, and other peer review processes. Hospitals must also meet certain requirements for accreditation; many have voluntarily adopted more extensive risk management programs.

These alternatives have severe limitations. Serious disciplinary actions (defined as probation, suspension, or revocation of license) by state boards are relatively rare: according to one report there were only 563

50. Danzon, *New Evidence,* p. 20.
51. Danzon, "Tort Reform."

of them in 1983.[52] This may reflect a general reluctance of professions to discipline their own members, particularly when the sanctions available tend to threaten the livelihood of the disciplined member. By contrast, the economic and noneconomic penalties that flow from the tort system can be more finely graded to match the magnitude of the damages caused in a given case.

The incentives for enforcing discipline are also greater under the tort system. Plaintiffs have more incentive to bring an action when compensation is contingent on proving their case. Insurers that operate in competitive markets must pass on these penalties through higher insurance premiums, which get built into the cost of medical care. Thus the tort system is, at least in theory, more likely than regulatory proceedings to provide optimal incentives for preventing injuries, even if the tailoring of sanctions to damages caused by any given physician is crude.

Finally, quality controls outside the tort system would probably not be as actively pursued if the system were abolished or significantly modified. Credentialing and peer review, for example, have surely been strengthened by the increasing liability of hospitals for injuries caused by physicians on their staffs.[53]

Alternative Systems of Compensation

There are undoubtedly gaps in existing systems of private and public health and disability insurance, particularly insurance for permanently disabling injuries. Seventeen percent of the population has no health insurance. And because health insurance is usually obtained as an employment fringe benefit, even those currently insured may lose coverage if a severe disability makes them unemployable. Private coverage of long-term wage loss is far less extensive. Although most people are eligible for social security disability insurance (SSDI), coverage is less complete than for the old age component of social security (OASI) because spouses and dependents who have not qualified in their own right are not covered under SSDI. Private coverage of long-term nursing care or rehabilitation services is virtually nonexistent.

Most public and private insurance programs have lower overhead

52. Sidney M. Wolfe, Henry Bergman, and George Silver, *Medical Malpractice: The Need for Disciplinary Reform, Not Tort Reform* (Washington, D.C.: Health Research Group, 1985).

53. See, for example, *Darling v. Charleston Community Memorial Hospital,* 2111 N.E. 2d 253 (1965).

costs (roughly twenty cents on the dollar, compared with sixty cents) than the tort system, in part because determination of fault or cause of the injury is not required. This has led to proposals for a no-fault system of compensation for treatment-related injuries similar to the workers' compensation system for work-related injuries, which has an overhead rate of about forty cents on the dollar.

But a no-fault system for iatrogenic injury has serious disadvantages. First, it would be necessary to show that the injury arose "out of or in the course of medical care," as opposed to being the unavoidable outcome of the underlying condition for which treatment was sought. Litigating over cause could be as costly as litigating over fault because it would be necessary to show some defect in treatment.

Second, if the system were financed through liability insurance purchased by individual physicians, premiums would account for a much larger fraction of physicians' gross incomes than under the present system. Fluctuations in premiums would therefore introduce greater variability into physicians' net incomes, with associated utility costs.

Third, to the extent premiums were experience-rated, inefficient preventive practices by physicians might be greater than under the present system. In particular, physicians would have an incentive to avoid difficult cases with a risk of a bad outcome unless they could charge fees commensurate with the higher liability risk. But fine-tuning fees and reimbursement for medical care on the basis of the severity of the patient's condition or expected liability risk is probably not feasible— how would the health insurer verify the accuracy of the physician's perception? Charging sicker patients a higher fee for a given procedure may also be distributionally undesirable.

These problems could be avoided if the no-fault system were financed by either a tax on medical care or a general tax, but it would be at the cost of eliminating efficient as well as inefficient deterrence incentives.

Conclusion

The liability system as it relates to malpractice is costly to operate and its benefits remain unproven, but there is no obviously superior alternative. The two extreme alternatives—no liability or physician liability without regard to fault—would probably cost even more than the present system relative to benefits. The search for cost-effective reforms should focus on modifications of the tort system to reduce uncertainty and eliminate inappropriate levels of compensation while retaining a fault-based rule of liability. The main candidates for reform are the rules determining damages and the long or unrestricted statutes of limitations. By reducing nondiversifiable risk, such changes should also reduce the volatility of insurance premiums.

CHAPTER FIVE

Environmental Hazards and Liability Law

Peter Huber

L ITIGATION stemming from the presence of possibly hazardous substances in the environment represents the liability system's latest and largest frontier, one that the courts have only begun to explore. In recent years rapid scientific advances have permitted litigants to make plausible claims for personal injury on the basis of very diffuse exposures to suspected hazards. Early lawsuits involved individuals or small groups of claimants; one of the most recent involved several million. But as the suits have grown more inclusive, they have grown factually thinner and more circumstantial. Today's large environmental liability cases are built on knowledge that admits à host of possibles but answers with very few probables. Despite more sophisticated scientific measurements and testing, the diffuse, low-level hazards addressed by modern environmental litigation present unresolvable questions of cause and effect.

As a result, courts have repeatedly accepted compromise verdicts or settlements built on ignorance and distrust of the liability system itself. Such compromises resolve one controversy but invite yet more litigation of similar character. Private insurers have correctly concluded that in suits arising from potential hazards in the environment the liability system operates without rigorous standards of proof. They have largely abandoned attempts to provide coverage against these hazards and are unlikely to try again.

Demands for regulation of suspected environmental hazards are nevertheless growing, as are demands for compensation for those who can vigorously and plausibly claim to have suffered injury from them. Attempting to meet these demands through a capricious liability system will force a steady erosion of industrial activity on many fronts without concomitant improvement in environmental quality or benefit to the true victims of diffuse pollution.

Regulatory agencies such as the Environmental Protection Agency and the Occupational Safety and Health Administration must, of course, grapple with equally intractable questions of cause and effect, but they can provide more orderly and rational regulation of environmental hazards. Providing compensation for injuries suspected to have been caused by diffuse environmental pollutants, however, is a very much more difficult issue and will remain so no matter how much science and toxicology may advance. The only rational possibilities lie at poles that may be socially unacceptable. One is that there be no compensation without rigorous proof of cause and effect, a rule that would mean no compensation in all but a few cases. The other is a steady drift toward a broad-ranging socialized insurance system funded by mandatory taxes and making payments according to rules of entitlement largely divorced from the issue of causation.

Origins of Environmental Liability Law

Liability law has historically dealt with diffuse hazards—smoke, water pollution, the noise of a howling dog next door, vibration, radiation, and other so-called environmental torts—under the umbrella of the nuisance doctrine. Nuisance cases typically involved small insults, and until recently courts were reluctant to award damages. A plaintiff bringing a nuisance action generally had to show that, in light of both the costs of the challenged activity—say, stream pollution from a papermill—and benefits— the mill's contribution to area prosperity—the environmental disturbance was serious, continuing, and unreasonable. Nor could the injury result from the plaintiff's hypersensitivity. The procedural obstacles to nuisance actions were larger still. Groups of people suffering from the same source of pollution could not readily consolidate their claims under a single litigation action. Both substantive and procedural rules thus prevented most suits directed against diffuse environmental pollutants.

Focused injuries were another matter, however. The classic example is the situation in *Rylands* v. *Fletcher,* an 1868 decision in England in which water from an artificial reservoir maintained near the defendant's mill broke into an unused mine shaft and flooded the plaintiff's adjoining mine.[1] There was no negligence, but the defendant was nonetheless held liable: "the person who for his own purposes brings on his land and collects and keeps there anything likely to do mischief if it escapes," the court declared, "must keep it at his peril, and if he does not do so is prima facie answerable for all the damage which is the natural consequence of its escape."[2] The ruling was carefully limited, however, to "non-natural" uses of land—in this instance an artificial reservoir in coal mining country.

U.S. courts gradually adopted the *Rylands* rule to complement the existing body of nuisance law. In time a rule of strict liability came to be applied consistently against a landowner who used dynamite, accumulated water in an unnatural reservoir, stored flammable liquids in quantity, or kept dangerous wild animals, and who did any of these things in a residential area or other place clearly unsuited for such activities. The logic ran something like this: the risks are both obvious and difficult to contain, the conduct is abnormal for its place and time, and victims do not consent to the activity that gives rise to the accident. These circumstances, it was argued, justify an unusually strict rule of liability when accidents do happen. Even if the defendant is engaged in something socially necessary or desirable, and even if he acts with all possible care, the defendant rather than the unintended and unwilling victim should bear the full costs of any accident.

Application of the *Rylands* rule was traditionally reserved for cases in which cause and effect—the origin of the accident and its consequences—were clearly, simply, and immediately linked. A dynamite blast, a flood from a reservoir, or an attack from a wild animal that has escaped from its pen is neither subtle nor uncertain in its effects; injury, if it occurs at all, is direct and easy to ascertain. The accidents in question are well defined in space and time. Their taxonomy is not very different from that of a two-car accident at an intersection. The liability suits that resulted were correspondingly narrow and self-contained. *Rylands* thus addressed primarily *sudden* environmental accidents. A separate and much more parsimonious set of rules covered gradual, ongoing environmental nuisances.

1. *Fletcher* v. *Rylands,* 1865, 3 H. & C. 774, 159 Eng. Rep. 737, *rev'd, Fletcher* v. *Rylands,* 1866, L.R. 1 Ex. 265, *aff'd, Rylands* v. *Fletcher,* 1868, L.R. 3 H.L. 330.

2. *Fletcher* v. *Rylands,* 1866, L.R. 1 Ex. 265, 279–80. "What emerges from the English decisions as the 'rule' of *Rylands* v. *Fletcher* is that the defendant will be liable when he damages another by a thing or activity unduly dangerous and inappropriate to the place where it is maintained, in the light of the character of that place and its surroundings." W. Page Keeton, ed., *Prosser and Keeton on the Law of Torts* (St. Paul: West Publishing, 1984), pp. 547–48.

New Science, New Sociology, and the Legal System

In the 1950s, epidemiologists established the first solid links between the incidence of cancer in humans and exposure to chemicals in tobacco, alcohol, and the workplace. Tests with animals also suggested—though available human epidemiological evidence could not confirm—that many other chemicals common in drugs, workplaces, food, air, and water might cause disease at sufficiently high levels of exposure. Some scientists came to believe that damage to the molecules of cell chromosomes caused by even a "single hit" from the wrong chemical might suffice to trigger fatal disease, though the hypothesis eluded direct confirmation. Scientists could now sketch many possible ways—though few probable ones—by which the trivial might be transformed into the tragic. At the same time, they grew increasingly skilled at detecting minute traces of chemicals in air, food, and water.

Social perceptions about environmental hazards evolved apace. Rachel Carson's *Silent Spring,* published in 1962, was followed by a cascade of similar books, culminating with Samuel Epstein's *The Politics of Cancer,* revised in 1979. The common message was that hidden, insidious, widely dispersed, man-made poisons were corrupting the environment, undermining human health, perhaps even threatening the human gene pool. As Edith Efron chronicled in *The Apocalyptics: Cancer and the Big Lie* in 1984, dozens of regulatory agencies, much of the press, and others who shape public opinion were quickly convinced. The growing perception was that most cancers and many chronic or degenerative diseases were caused by diffuse, man-made pollutants.

The scientific community did not for the most part share in this view. Regulatory agencies vacillated. Although some, such as the Occupational Safety and Health Administration, briefly embraced an apocalyptic reading of the situation before returning to more sober estimates, for the most part the agencies moved cautiously. But the new science of environmental causation triggered increasingly large and complex liability actions. This uneasy marriage between science and modern liability jurisprudence has lasted.

Science's new insights blur the old, intuitive lines between minor nuisances and grave hazards and offer a direct, intellectual bridge between two once-separate strands of tort law. A diffuse, low-level hazardous substance in the air can now be analogized to a dangerous wild animal escaped from its enclosure or the directly harmful shock from a blasting operation.[3]

3. Indeed, in the congressional debate that led to the outlawing of polychlorinated

Hazards that a few years ago could not have been targeted under any liability theory are now not only labeled as "nuisances" but also "trespasses" and even deliberate "assaults and batteries." An entirely new liability jurisprudence of environmental risks has begun to take shape.

And science now suggests that even molecular-level exposures at the lowest conceivable concentrations may cause grave injury, at least to some unfortunate individuals. Exposures may be vanishingly small and the actual likelihood of injury correspondingly slight, but the gravity of the injury if it materializes is serious. Millions of people, moreover, may be exposed to the same diffuse hazard. Science now offers plausible tools for multiplying out zero risk and infinite exposure to arrive at finite possibilities for injury, possibilities made all the more concrete because they appear to have been quantified.

The Diffusion of Environmental Liability

The science and sociology of causation have made liability for environmental hazards virtually limitless. Diffusion and dispersion mix inexorably, guaranteeing that every activity flows into every other at some level or another. There are no boundaries to the environment or to the environmental lawsuit. The history of the so-called toxic tort lawsuit in the past two decades is that of an ever-widening circle.[4]

The first generation of cases involved products liability, mostly pharmaceutical drugs. The key variables in a toxic tort action—exposure to the substance, its toxicity, and its harmful effects—were comparatively easy to ascertain in cases involving thalidomide (teratogenesis), DES (adenocarcinoma), medical X-rays, birth control pills, arthritis medicines, and other drugs. Relatively few people were swept into these cases, since most drugs and pharmaceutical devices affect small and discrete populations.

The second generation of toxic torts involved occupational hazards. The workplace offers the best laboratory, except for an actual laboratory, for studying chemically induced disease. Exposure levels can be as high as

---

biphenyls, Congressman Gilbert Gude characterized this class of chemicals as "the mad dog of the environment." See Philip Shabecoff, "PCB's, Long Banned, Prove Hard to Banish," *New York Times,* March 22, 1987.

4. See Peter W. Huber, "The Bhopalization of U.S. Tort Law," *Issues in Science and Technology,* vol. 2 (Fall 1985), pp. 73–82.

they are with drugs because exposure may occur over many years. Work-places also generally contain more or less well defined populations of workers. For these reasons some of the first links between chemicals and cancer involved occupational hazards: cancer of the scrotum in Victorian-era children working as chimney sweeps; bladder cancer among dye work-ers; lung disease from stone, coal, asbestos, and textile operations; liver cancer from working with vinyl chloride; and leukemia from working with radiation. Until the early 1960s most liability suits involving work-place disease were precluded by workers' compensation laws (see chap-ter 6). But new legal theories have since been adopted by the courts to bypass the statutory immunities. The most successful litigations have been products liability actions directed not against employers but against man-ufacturers of the substances later implicated in workplace disease. Al-though these second generation environmental cases were bounded by the walls of a factory, boiler room, or foundry, they signaled a quantum expansion in the scope of the problems being litigated. Plaintiffs began to be counted in the thousands.

The third generation cases, which began to unfold in the early 1980s, promise to reach much further. Again many of the substances encountered earlier in the workplace cases—asbestos, formaldehyde, benzene, radia-tion, dioxin—are involved. But the chemicals are now spread much more widely and thinly, exposing much larger and less well defined groups of people at much lower concentrations. The toxic tort once circumscribed by the human body in drug cases or the factory walls in occupational cases now encompasses rivers, municipal water supplies, outdoor air, and entire communities, cities, or watersheds.

Hazardous chemical waste, a by-product of the synthetic organic chem-ical revolution of post–World War II America, brought the issue to na-tional attention. One of the first incidents, and certainly the most publicized, involved the Love Canal area of Niagara Falls, New York, where Hooker Chemical Company had dumped 21,000 tons of hazardous substances into a landfill from 1942 to 1953. In 1978 residents of the area were alerted to alarming concentrations of chemicals in the soil and groundwater. In May 1980 President Jimmy Carter declared a state of emergency and ordered the relocation of 710 families who lived in the area. Lawsuits were subsequently filed against Hooker and the city of Niagara Falls, which had acquired the dump site decades before the prob-lems were discovered. These actions sought billions of dollars in damages on behalf of thousands of claimants. In 1984 more than 1,300 current and former residents of Love Canal settled their suit against Hooker for $20 million.[5]

A torrent of liability suits involving other hazardous waste sites has followed. The cases are now cataloged not by the name of a plaintiff but by a town or community—Kellogg, Idaho; Jackson Township, New Jersey; Hardeman County, Tennessee; Triana, Alabama; Woburn, Massachusetts; Times Beach, Missouri; Three Mile Island, Pennsylvania.[6] Some

5. Lindsey Gruson, "Ex-Love Canal Families Get Payments," *New York Times,* February 20, 1985; and BNA *Environment Reporter,* January 4, 1985, p. 1445.

6. In Kellogg, Idaho, thirty-three children and four young adults sued Gulf Resources and Chemical Corp., alleging that emissions from its smelter had caused high levels of lead in their bloodstreams. The company settled for $23 million. BNA *Environment Reporter,* April 15, 1983, p. 2321.

Ninety-seven families in Jackson Township, New Jersey, sued the municipal government, charging that pollutants from the township's landfill had leached into their well water. See *Ayers* v. *Township of Jackson,* 461 A.2d 184 (N.J. Super. Ct. Law Div. 1983). A jury awarded the families $16 million. An appellate court reversed most of the decision, reducing the award to $5.6 million. *Ayers* v. *Township of Jackson,* 493 A.2d 1314 (N.J. Super. Ct. App. Div. 1985). The case is under review by the Supreme Court of New Jersey.

One-hundred residents of Hardeman County, Tennessee, sued the Velsicol Chemical Co., which owned a hazardous waste landfill in the county. The residents claimed that carbon tetrachloride, chloroform, and benzene had leached into and contaminated their groundwater. A federal judge awarded the residents $12.7 million; the case is on appeal. BNA *Environment Reporter,* August 8, 1986, p. 535.

Dioxin-contaminated waste oil was sprayed in the area of Times Beach and other Missouri towns in the 1970s. The Environmental Protection Agency bought the entire city for $33.1 million in 1983 after residential property was contaminated during flooding; 2,400 families were relocated. See BNA *Environment Reporter,* February 25, 1983, p. 1886. Local residents filed suits alleging personal injury and property damage. The first of these involved 4 people from Lincoln, Missouri, who sought damages for increased risk of cancer and pregnancy complications; they settled with one of the defendant corporations in October 1983 for $2.68 million; BNA *Environment Reporter,* October 21, 1983, p. 1050. In 1986, 150 residents agreed to a $19 million settlement with four chemical companies linked to the incident. The settlement must still be reviewed by state courts and a federal bankruptcy court where two of the companies have filed for bankruptcy. See *Drinkard* v. *Independent Petrochemical Corp.,* No. 832-05206A (Mo. Cir. Ct.). Claims by the Justice Department under the federal Superfund law (the Comprehensive Environmental Response, Compensation, and Liability Act) seeking reimbursement for the government's cost of responding to the contamination are still pending. See *U.S.* v. *Bliss,* No. 84-0200-C(1) (E.D. Mo.); and BNA *Environment Reporter,* November 28, 1986, p. 1266.

Litigation following the accident at the Three Mile Island nuclear power plant involved a class action brought by 67 named plaintiffs representing three classes. The first two comprised all businesses and individuals who lived within twenty-five miles of the plant and who claimed to have suffered ordinary economic losses as a result of the turmoil and partial evacuation of residents immediately after the accident. The trial court also approved a third class, embracing all who claimed to have already "suffered personal injury, incurred medical expenses, [or] . . . suffered emotional distress," as well as those "threatened with medical expenses and/or illness" or who might "require medical detection services, including inde-

of the more important decisions are summarized in table 5-1. Eight prominent families in Woburn, Massachusetts, for example, claimed that W. R. Grace and Company had contaminated city water wells with two probable carcinogens, trichloroethylene and tetrachloroethylene, which caused the deaths of six children from leukemia. Grace eventually settled for a reported $8 million.[7] The Triana, Alabama, litigation started when local residents and fishermen sued Olin Corporation, a manufacturer of DDT, for polluting a waterway a few miles upriver from the town. This first round of cases was settled in December 1982 for $24 million to be paid over five years; a second round was tentatively settled for $15 million three-and-a-half years later.[8] Other similar if less publicized lawsuits have proliferated.[9]

The challenge for plaintiffs' lawyers in many of these cases is to collect into a single claim the dispersed, low-probability, attenuated injuries that a large group might suffer from toxic micropollution. Only a massed attack of this type can take full advantage of the economies of using only one litigating team and can justify the often huge initial outlays required from the plaintiffs' lawyers.[10] In 1966 the rules that govern procedure in

---

pendent inspections and surveys, for a reasonable number of years in the future," but only to address damages for future medical monitoring; *In re Three Mile Island Litigation,* 87 F.R.D. 433 (M.D. Pa. 1980). About $25 million was paid to 280 claimants, with $20 million covering economic losses and $5 million provided for a research-oriented public health fund. The settlement of claims by Three Mile Island residents provided for a fund for monitoring their health. See *In re Three Mile Island Litigation,* 557 F. Supp. 96 (M.D. Pa. 1982).

7. *BNA Environment Reporter,* September 26, 1986, p. 774.

8. Olin also agreed to pay cleanup costs of the area; *Wall Street Journal,* April 22, 1983. For second-round cases, see *BNA Environment Reporter,* June 13, 1986, p. 177.

9. A jury in West Chester, Pennsylvania, awarded $788,867 to a family of five that charged its water supply was polluted by carcinogenic wastes including tce and pce that were dumped on an adjoining farm; *BNA Environment Reporter,* March 23, 1984, p. 2103. The defendant corporations, Gray Brothers, Inc., and MOS Technology, Inc., have filed for a new trial.

Links between vinyl chloride and a rare form of liver cancer, which had given rise to an earlier phase of litigation involving injured workers, were now at the center of lawsuits by people residing near factories where the chemical was used. See, for example, *Grasso v. B. F. Goodrich Co.,* No. 78-1562 (D.N.J. 1981). Grasso alleged that his angiosarcoma had been caused by vinyl chloride from a factory located near his home. A jury returned a verdict for the plaintiff, which was appealed. The case was settled before the appellate argument.

After the Consumer Product Safety Commission banned the use of formaldehyde foam in home insulation, damage suits based on formaldehyde exposure have become more common. An estimated 400 to 700 formaldehyde lawsuits were filed almost immediately; David Ranii, "Formaldehyde Suits Erupt," *National Law Journal,* May 10, 1982, p. 30.

10. See David Rosenberg, "The Causal Connection in Mass Exposure Cases: A 'Public

Table 5-1. *Summary of Selected Toxic Tort Cases, 1983–86*

Location	Plaintiffs	Defendants	Issue	Settlement or verdict
Three Mile Island, Pa.	280 residents	General Public Utilities Corp.	Radioactive emission from nuclear power plant	$25 million (February 1982)
Triana, Ala. (round 1)	1,100 residents and fishermen	Olin Corp.	DDT pollution of waterway	$24 million (December 1982)
Kellogg, Idaho	33 children and 4 adults	Gulf Resources and Chemical Corp.	Lead poisoning from smelter emissions	$23 million (April 1983)
Jackson Township, N.J.	97 families	Jackson Township	Well water contamination by pollutants from municipal landfill	$16 million (April 1983; under appeal)
Lincoln, Mo.	4 residents	Independent Petrochemical Corp.	Contamination by dioxin-contaminated waste oil	$2.7 million (October 1983)
West Chester, Pa.	5 residents	Gray Brothers Inc. and MOS Technology	pce and tce contamination of water supply	$788,867 (February 1984)
Nevada atomic bomb test site	10 residents	U.S. Government	Radioactive fallout	$2.6 million (May 1984; reversed April 1987)
Love Canal, N.Y.	1,300 former and current residents	Hooker Chemical Co.	Chemical contamination of the soil and water	$20 million (December 1984)
Vietnam	2.4 million veterans and relatives	Dow Chemical Co. and others	Exposure to Agent Orange	$180 million (January 1985)
Three Mile Island, Pa.	280 residents	General Public Utilities Corp.	Radioactive emission from nuclear power plant	$25 million (February 1982)
Triana, Ala. (round 2)	9,000 residents	Olin Corp.	DDT pollution	$15 million (June 1986)
Hardeman County, Tenn.	100 residents	Velsicol Chemical Co.	Groundwater contamination by carbon tetrachloride, chloroform, and benzene	$13 million (August 1986, under appeal)
Woburn, Mass.	8 families	W. R. Grace and Co.	Contamination of city water wells by tce and pce	$8 million (September 1986)
Times Beach, Mo.	150 residents	Syntex Corp., Charter Co., Independent Petrochemical Corp., and Northeastern Pharmaceutical	Contamination of residential property by waste oil containing dioxin	$19 million (November 1986)

federal courts were amended to permit consolidations of just this type under the umbrella of the "common question class action." Many states adopted similar class action rules. Though not intended for personal injury litigation, the class action suit is tailor-made for the ultimate environmental lawsuit. Today, a short complaint filed with a court clerk can trigger a titanic clash of interests.

The cases usually do not start large, but they often end that way. Once a hazardous substance has been identified and successfully attacked in a first case involving high levels of exposure, subsequent suits involving lower levels of exposure and more people follow almost automatically. The first generation radiation cases, for instance, involved medically administered X-rays; the second, occupational exposures in uranium mines and fuel reprocessing facilities. The third generation may involve the entire planet. In 1984 a jury awarded $2.6 million to ten plaintiffs who claimed that fallout from above-ground atomic bomb tests in the 1950s caused at least nine cancer deaths in Utah and Arizona.[11] Other suits have been filed by servicemen and their families based on exposure to radiation from testing at Bikini and Eniwetok atolls and in the Nevada desert.[12] Lawsuits stemming from dioxin exposure also initially involved small groups of individuals exposed in factories or after accidental spills. The Agent Orange suit later embraced more than 2 million plaintiffs, 7 major corporate defendants, and the U.S. government.[13]

Again, following a 1983 settlement involving 1,100 claimants in Triana, Alabama, a second round of litigation engaged 9,000 more who lived somewhat further from the source of the DDT pollution but otherwise had identical claims.[14] The first asbestos cases involved insulation work-

---

Law' Vision of the Tort System," *Harvard Law Review*, vol. 97 (February 1984), pp. 851–929.

11. *Allen* v. *United States*, 588 F. Supp. 247 (D. Utah 1984). On April 20, 1987, a federal court of appeals reversed the judgment on the grounds that the U.S. government was legally immune from such suits; 816 F.2d 1417 (10th Cir. 1987).

12. See, for example, *Mondelli* v. *United States*, 711 F.2d 567 (3d Cir. 1983), *cert. denied*, 465 U.S. 1021 (1984).

13. Peter H. Schuck, *Agent Orange on Trial: Mass Toxic Disasters in the Courts* (Cambridge, Mass.: Belknap, 1986), pp. 4–5; and Barry Meier, "Agent Orange Settlement Is Approved; Cash Awards Are Likely to Be Limited," *Wall Street Journal*, January 8, 1985. No payments have yet been made, and none will be until the ongoing appeals are resolved. See Ralph Blumenthal, "Agent Orange Payments Plan Limits the Number of Awards," *New York Times*, February 28, 1985; and Joseph P. Fried, "Judge Rules on Allocation of the Agent Orange Fund," *New York Times*, May 29, 1985.

14. Rich Arthurs, "Students Give DDT Discovery a Boost," *Legal Times*, August 13,

ers; later rounds swept in school districts, building contractors, and municipalities across the country.[15] In the later phases of litigation over formaldehyde foam, a class action suit was filed on behalf of 70,000 to 130,000 New York homeowners with foam insulation.[16]

There is in fact no apparent outer limit to the size of the environmental lawsuit. Indoor radon has recently been identified as a major health hazard, and radiation-related environmental claims may soon include millions of homeowners, building contractors, municipal inspectors, real estate agents, and others. Every one of the several thousand major toxic chemical dump sites scattered across the country can be counted as a potential center of liability litigation, with the pool of claimants spreading outward indefinitely from the epicenter. Third generation asbestos suits may look to car brakes, hair dryers, home furnaces, and countless other mass-market products that have used and continue to use the insulator in various applications. Traces of dioxin, the contaminant at the center of the Agent Orange litigation, are also found in power transformers and cooling fluids. Minute traces are indeed now detectable in nearly every living person. And another environmental contaminant, the AIDS virus, is also beginning to figure in litigation. The Creator of this particular chemical cannot be sued directly, but those who transport and distribute it can. About fifty children have already developed AIDS as the result of transfusions of contaminated blood, and even the best current screening devices cannot ensure that blood supplies are safe. The first lawsuits against hospitals and the American Red Cross have already been filed.[17]

Within only the past fifteen years or so, the liability system has thus reached out to encompass the health and safety effects of virtually every enterprise and industrial undertaking. Courts are now positioned to redefine the broad social compact that defines rights and duties of employers

---

1984, p. 1. Claims were also filed on behalf of many children who claimed only that they stood at risk of developing disease in the future. The suits have been consolidated in the federal district court in Birmingham, Alabama, and are still in the discovery phase of litigation.

15. See Robert J. Cole, "Asbestos Suit Gain by Schools," *New York Times,* May 3, 1986.

16. Michael de Courcy Hinds, "Owning Unhealthy Homes Can Be a Lonely Business," *New York Times,* March 21, 1982. While most suits are for property damage, some allege that exposure to formaldehyde has caused health problems. See, for example, *Eckert* v. *Geurdon Industries,* No. 79-1627-8 (D.S.C. 1982), which alleged a 50 percent loss of lung capacity from exposure to formaldehyde.

17. See Margaret Engel, "Short, Joy-Giving Life Comes to an End for AIDS Victim," *Washington Post,* July 15, 1986.

and employees, industries and their locales, servicemen, military contractors, and the federal government. The multimillion-party personal injury suit has arrived; indeed the first such suit, over Agent Orange, has already been settled.

Legislative Initiatives

Federal and state legislation has encouraged many of the recent developments in environmental litigation. The Love Canal incident spurred Congress to enact the 1980 Superfund law, originally a $1.6 billion—and today a $9 billion—program to clean up abandoned dump sites.[18] The law was strengthened in 1984, and federal regulation of hazardous wastes became the Environmental Protection Agency's top priority. EPA identifies sites for cleanup and draws initial funding for the effort from a broad-based tax on the chemical industry.[19] Liability for the cost of cleanup can then be funneled back to waste generators and dump operators through liability suits. Liability standards, sketched out in the Superfund legislation as well as in the Resource Conservation and Recovery Act, impose strict liability with no effective time limitations on when suits for recovering cleanup costs may be brought.[20] The Superfund legislation was amended in 1986 to include community right-to-know, a provision under which manufacturers must notify local, state, and federal officials of both routine and accidental releases of any one of several hundred chemicals that may

18. The Comprehensive Environmental Response, Compensation, and Liability Act (CERCLA), 42 U.S.C. 9601 et seq.

19. *BNA Environment Reporter,* October 17, 1986, pp. 907–09. The Superfund will raise about $9 billion over five years from a new general tax on business, the oil excise tax, a tax on forty-two chemical feedstocks, and a tax on motor fuels.

20. Section 7003 of RCRA has been held to impose strict liability on owners and operators of waste sites and on postenactment off-site generators and transporters; see *United States* v. *Hardage,* 18 BNA *Environment Reporter Cases* 1685 (W.D. Okla. 1982); and *United States* v. *Ottati and Goss, Inc.,* 23 BNA *Environment Reporter Cases* 1705 (D.N.H. 1985). Liability under the Superfund is linked to the standard of liability under section 311 of the Federal Water Pollution Control Act, which like RCRA, is also silent as to the standard of liability. See, for example, *United States* v. *Chem-Dyne Corp.,* 572 F. Supp. 802, 804–07 (S.D. Ohio 1983); and *United States* v. *Northeastern Pharmaceutical and Chemical Company, Inc.,* 579 F. Supp. 823, 843–44 (W.D. Mo. 1984).

The government's preferred position is that no statute of limitations applies. See *United States* v. *Mottolo,* 605 F. Supp. 898 (D.N.H. 1985), which finds no CERCLA statute of limitations applicable to cost reimbursements. See also *Mola Development Corp.* v. *United States,* No. CV82-0819-RMT (JRX) (C.D. Cal. 1985), which grants a three-year statute of limitations by analogy to CERCLA section 112(d) and California state law.

cause acute or chronic health effects. These provisions will likely trigger still more litigation.

Personal injury claims have already routinely followed on the heels of EPA-initiated lawsuits for repayment of cleanup expenditures. The Superfund itself does not cover claims for personal injuries, but it does supersede state tort laws covering personal injury so that the statute of limitations for every state may start to run only when the victim discovers that the injury was caused by the hazardous substance in question. Many states have since enacted their own hazardous waste and toxic chemical laws, relying in large part on liability suits to provide funding. In 1986, for example, California voters passed the Safe Drinking and Toxic Enforcement Act, which, among other provisions, allows state and local governments and private citizens "acting in the public interest" to sue a business guilty of a violation.[21] New Jersey's Spill Compensation and Control Act imposes liability for both cleanup costs and third-party economic damages on anyone who owns or operates a hazardous waste facility, arranges or contracts for the treatment, storage, or disposal of a hazardous substance, or accepts the waste for transport while knowing that the disposal site is operating in violation of the law.[22] Minnesota's Environmental Response and Liability Act contains similar provisions but allows damages for cleanup costs, loss of real or personal property, economic and noneconomic losses, and all medical expenses.[23] Few other state statutes reach so broadly, but many contain similar provisions.

A common characteristic of federal and most state statutes has been the provision for joint and several liability of virtually all waste generators, transporters, and disposers connected in any way with a particular dump. Several courts have concluded that in pursuing a Superfund claim for an injunction and reimbursement of cleanup costs, the government need only prove that the defendant's waste was disposed at the site and need not link its costs to wastes created by the defendants.[24] This has far-reaching implications. Massachusetts, for example, has more than 5,000 disposers of hazardous wastes but only 50 dumps. The strict joint and several

21. *BNA Environment Reporter,* November 14, 1986, pp. 1175–76.
22. See *New Jersey Statutes Annotated,* title 58, section 10-23.11 (St. Paul: West Publishing, 1987 supp.).
23. See *Minnesota Statutes Annotated,* sections 115B.01-115B.37 (St. Paul: West Publishing, 1987).
24. See, for example, *United States* v. *Wade,* 577 F. Supp. 1326 (E.D. Penn. 1983). Compare *Superfund Improvement Act of 1985,* Hearings before the Senate Committee on the Judiciary, 99 Cong. 1 sess. (Washington, D.C., 1986), p. 36.

liability rules can reach firms that are cleaning up the pollution as easily as those that created it.

Linking Cause and Effect

Liability rules, which once lagged well behind the evolving toxicology and epidemiology of environmental contaminants, now far outpace them. The first toxic tort suits, implicating drugs and X-rays, involved individual plaintiffs exposed to comparatively high dosages of the toxic agent and diseases that could be traced with some confidence to the earlier exposure. The second generation workplace cases were already less well defined but still reasonably exact, at least when compared with what was yet to come. Occupational exposures to some toxic materials were high, and the affected populations fairly well defined. In the most recent phase of environmental litigation, however, exposure levels have dropped again by factors of a thousand or a million, while the numbers of individuals exposed have increased by similar multipliers.

The most vexing question in the latest generation of environmental litigation is also absolutely fundamental: Did the defendant's activity really cause the injury in question? Rarely can this question be answered with any precision in cases involving diffuse, mass-exposure, long-latency risks.

A first problem often lies in tracing a particular contaminant to its origins. With broadly dispersed pollutants the physical pathways linking suspected cause and realized effect can be very difficult to track. As the links grow longer and more attenuated, the cause-and-effect analysis is further complicated by a proliferation of competing possible sources and causes. Beyond this, causal agents can often also interact synergistically or counteractively to amplify or mute the effects that each would cause in isolation. As much as 90 percent of "asbestos-caused" lung disease, for example, could be eliminated without changing asbestos exposure levels at all—the poisonous synergy is between asbestos and cigarette smoke.[25] Synergistic interactions of this type enormously complicate environmental litigation, and the problems grow larger as the toxic agents grow more diffuse.

25. See U.S. Public Health Service, Office on Smoking and Health, *The Health Consequences of Smoking: Cancer and Chronic Lung Disease in the Workplace* (Rockville, Md.: Department of Health and Human Services, 1985), pp. ix–x.

Most frustrating of all, for all but a handful of chemicals the effects of low exposures on humans are unknown. Experiments exposing animals to high doses provide some information; large-population epidemiological statistics with humans provide somewhat more. But neither source of information resolves individual claims or provides useful measures of the incidence of disease for any class actions that do not embrace extremely large populations. Laboratory mice exposed to tce, the principal suspect chemical in the W. R. Grace litigation, have developed cancer of the lymph nodes, but they have not developed leukemia. A review of research published by the National Academy of Sciences showed no increased incidence of any kind of cancer among humans exposed to much higher concentrations of tce on their jobs.[26] Twelve scientists appointed to a Massachusetts advisory panel to investigate W. R. Grace's pollution of wells in Woburn, Massachusetts, concluded, "The hypothesis that the increase in leukemia incidence was associated with environmental hazards, and specifically with the contamination of drinking water supplies, is neither supported nor refuted by the study findings."[27] At the conclusion of the Agent Orange litigation, which turned on dioxin contamination of the herbicide, Judge Jack B. Weinstein flatly declared to the plaintiffs' lawyers, "In no case have you shown causality for the health effects alleged."[28]

Uncertainty of this order pervades almost every claim of injuries arising from dispersed environmental pollutants. Scientific developments in the past thirty years have shown convincingly that man-made environmental pollutants can cause serious disease. Epidemiological evidence with certain drugs and with extended high-level exposures to occupational hazards has vividly confirmed that possibility in a few tragic episodes. But the science and epidemiology of diffuse environmental pollutants are quite another matter. The best epidemiological estimates suggest that, tobacco aside, less than 5 percent of all cancers in the general public can be attributed to diffuse pollutants in air, water, food, building materials, consumer products, and the like.[29] This is still

26. Paula DiPerna, "Leukemia Strikes a Small Town," *New York Times,* December 2, 1984.

27. Quoted in Gene I. Maeroff, "Trial Set in Suit Over 7 Cancer Cases," *New York Times,* March 9, 1986.

28. Fred H. Tschirley, "Dioxin," *Scientific American,* February 1986, p. 35.

29. Richard Doll and Richard Peto, *The Causes of Cancer: Quantitative Estimates of Avoidable Risks of Cancer in the United States Today* (Oxford University Press, 1981).

a considerable amount of disease, however—perhaps as many as 15,000 to 20,000 new cancers a year. And some scientists arrive at considerably higher estimates—and are willing to testify positively on questions of cause and effect, notwithstanding the reservations of others in the mainstream of their profession. The statistical evidence weighs heavily against any individual claimant here. But unambiguously negative conclusions are equally elusive, and virtually any case contains enough doubt to be brought to a jury.

Every one of the major settlements of environmental cases reflects these difficulties. None of the plaintiffs in Love Canal, Jackson Township, Woburn, Triana, or Times Beach had a strong positive case linking cause and effect, nor could the defendants irrefutably prove the negative. Indeed, the only convincing defense in lawsuits of this kind involves a demonstration that some other factor or set of factors accounts for the plaintiffs' illnesses and complaints, a contention that always presents equally difficult questions of proof.

We cannot expect that scientific advances will ever answer the most fundamental questions that so trouble environmental liability litigation, and we cannot hope that advances in science will soon cure the problems. Whatever science can say about the hazards of particular pollutants at particular levels of exposure, there will always be a larger class of individuals exposed at a lower level whose complaints fall below the threshold that science can confidently address.[30] Near zero risk and infinite exposure can multiply out to large finite injury. Science inevitably breaks down when it deals with singularities of this order. The most far-reaching environmental cases will therefore always extend into what Alvin M. Weinberg has labeled trans-science, that ocean of speculation, hope, fear, myth, and monsters surrounding the small island of firm scientific knowledge.[31] Few of these problems were weighed or anticipated as the courts drifted into the new regime of environmental liability in the past decade.

---

30. Rosenberg, "Causal Connection in Mass Exposure Cases," suggests that problems of proof in environmental liability cases can be resolved by broader use of large class actions because low-risk, mass-exposure environmental litigation can then successfully draw on modern epidemiological tools to identify the excess risks created by particular activities or technologies. For a different view, see Peter Huber, "Safety and the Second Best: The Hazards of Public Risk Management in the Courts," *Columbia Law Review,* vol. 85 (March 1985), pp. 277–337.

31. Alvin M. Weinberg, "Science and Its Limits: The Regulator's Dilemma," *Issues in Science and Technology,* vol. 2 (Fall 1985), pp. 59–72.

Judgment without Verdict

The established legal rule in the new-generation environmental cases is clear: there is absolute liability for all harm caused by toxic releases of any sort. No one, however, is at all sure just what harm, if any, these releases actually cause. The judgment in these cases is thus very much clearer than the verdict.

Some courts have attempted to sidestep the intractable questions of cause and effect. If the hazards of a toxic pollutant are uncertain, the lawsuit comes to center upon warnings that were or were not provided by its seller. Warning can also become the crux of the debate in cases involving waste dumps if the site in question was sold after the dump was established. A diffuse environmental problem is thus converted into a concrete claim against a "defective" product, building, or piece of land. The defect in turn is identified not with the good itself but with its packaging—the absence of a warning about possible, though highly speculative, risk. Other courts have attempted to finesse questions of cause and effect by readjusting burdens of proof.[32] Plaintiffs' lawyers in the Agent Orange case argued that chemical companies' failures to warn of a possible hazard meant that the companies rather than the plaintiffs should bear the burden of proving that the hazard did not in fact exist. A district court allowed a similar argument in the cases arising from the federal government's atomic bomb tests in Nevada and Utah.[33]

But these are lawyers' games, not serious solutions. No legal refinement can resolve the most fundamental question in any liability case, which is whether the defendant in fact caused the injury. With information about cause and effect both essential and unobtainable in almost equal measure, many courts have attempted to make a virtue of necessity: the brooding uncertainty about the risk becomes a lawsuit in itself. Plaintiffs have been injured, some courts have elliptically concluded,

32. "[Another] means that has been used to undermine causation—increasingly common in toxic torts cases—is the use of presumptions or burden-shifting techniques to force the defendant to prove the lack of causation in order to avoid liability. Frequently, this amounts to asking the defendant to meet an impossible burden of proving the negative." U.S. Department of Justice, *Report of the Tort Policy Working Group on the Causes, Extent and Policy Implications of the Current Crisis in Insurance Availability and Affordability* (Washington, D.C., February 1986), pp. 34–35. See also "Comment on the Burden of Proof in Environmental and Public Health Litigation," *UMKC Law Review,* vol. 49 (Winter 1981), pp. 208–09.

33. *Allen* v. *United States,* 588 F. Supp. 247 (D. Utah 1984), *rev'd,* 816 F.2d 1417 (10th Cir. 1987).

precisely because they fear but cannot determine that they have in fact been injured. Compensation is then awarded to pay for the costs they may incur in the future to find out whether they have really been hurt.

Courts accepting this logic have awarded damages or approved settlements tied to three major elements of loss. Medical monitoring has been the most important. The award covers the cost of medical surveillance and diagnostic testing. Medical monitoring and primary health care provisions figure, for example, in the settlements covering Three Mile Island, Agent Orange, Jackson Township, and Triana.[34] And because settlements and verdicts have also commonly included damages for emotional distress, claims for "disease phobia" in toxic chemical cases have grown increasingly common.[35] Finally, some courts have begun seriously to consider adjusting an award to reflect the increased risk that disease may develop in the future as a result of past toxic exposures.[36]

The new generation of environmental suits and settlements is thus an edifice of compromise, the product of ignorance and emotion, not knowledge or understanding. Cause may be uncertain, but plaintiffs nevertheless come to court with real, sometimes grievous injuries. Defendants almost always have the weight of the evidence (usually negative) on their side. Plaintiffs have sympathy on theirs. For very different reasons both sides are horrified at the prospect of taking matters to a jury. Plaintiffs fear that a jury might look at the facts carefully; defendants fear that it will not. The result has been a series of settlements detached from any objective measure of harm. Hundreds of millions of dollars have now changed hands in such settlements, but not one has involved evidence linking alleged cause and observed effect in a way that epidemiologists and public health experts in the mainstream scientific community consider close to convincing.

34. For the settlement on Three Mile Island, see Ruth Simon, "The New Age of Nuclear Law," *National Law Journal*, January 3, 1983, p. 1. For Jackson Township, see *Ayers* v. *Township of Jackson*, 461 A.2d 184, 190 (N.J. Super. Ct. Law Div. 1983). For Triana, see "Olin Corp. to Pay for DDT-Cleanup Costs in Triana, Ala.; Health Care Is Included," *Wall Street Journal*, April 22, 1983. The $24 million settlement included $5 million for primary health care and monitoring, $19 million to settle personal injury claims, and an additional amount, as yet undetermined, for cleanup costs.

35. See "Comment on Emotional Distress Damages for Cancerphobia: A Case for the DES Daughter," *Pacific Law Journal*, vol. 14 (July 1983), p. 1215, note 1; and Terry Morehead Dworkin, "Fear of Disease and Delayed Manifestation Injuries: A Solution or a Pandora's Box?" *Fordham Law Review*, vol. 53 (December 1984), pp. 527–77. See also *Martinez* v. *University of California*, 601 P.2d 425 (N.M. 1979), in which recovery was allowed for phobias that continued exposure to radioactive material would result in death.

36. *BNA Environment Reporter*, August 10, 1984, p. 576.

Insurers Depart

Insurers, unsurprisingly, have all but abandoned this unruly field. In the early 1970s most general liability commercial policies expressly excluded coverage for pollution except for that arising from "sudden and accidental" releases. From the beginning, insurers were thus unwilling to grapple with ubiquitous, routine, and low-level emissions, the classic nuisances addressed by the old liability rules. They were, however, prepared to cover sudden, discrete accidents—spills and releases during transportation or storage, for example—that could comfortably be slotted into the *Rylands* pigeonhole of litigation. Problems of gradual, long-term leakage or migration were occasionally covered under separate environmental impairment liability (EIL) policies but often only at a high price. Many of those insured did not buy this second class of coverage.

Courts, however, often had a different agenda, one that called for generous compensation for toxic environmental exposures, and a few boldly attempted to rewrite insurance policies accordingly. Jackson Township's liability policy, for example, excluded pollution coverage for all but sudden and accidental occurrences. But when the town dump was blamed for polluting groundwater over a twelve-year period, a court nevertheless held the town's insurer liable.[37] Through no more than creative reading, twelve-year seepages were smoothly transformed into sudden and accidental events. Courts in several other states have adopted similar reasoning, though some federal courts have continued to apply policy language as written.[38]

The most common reaction of insurers to such uncertainty has simply been to exclude all pollution liability coverage—sudden, accidental, gradual, or otherwise. Most have now concluded that links between pollution and damage are so highly speculative, at least in the courts, that policies cannot be rationally priced. "Two major companies dropped out of the [EIL] market in 1985, and by the end of the year only two companies were offering EIL coverage."[39] Most businesses handling

37. *Jackson Township Municipal Utilities Authority* v. *Hartford Accident and Indemnity Company,* 451 A.2d 990 (N.J. Super. Ct. Law Div. 1982).

38. For the interpretations of state courts, see Dennis R. Connolly, "Insurer Perspectives on Causation and Financial Compensation," *Regulatory Toxicology and Pharmacology,* vol. 6 (June 1986), pp. 80–88. For federal courts, see *Great Lakes Container Corporation* v. *National Union Fire Insurance Company of Pittsburgh, Pennsylvania,* 727 F.2d 30 (1st. Cir. 1984).

39. Department of Justice, *Report of the Tort Policy Working Group,* p. 6.

hazardous waste are now turning toward captive insurers or self-insurance. Prices have increased drastically in the few instances that insurance is still being offered at all.

Expanding liability and shrinking insurance for that liability have produced predictable consequences, ones most immediately evident in situations for which federal or state statutes make liability insurance mandatory. Federal law now requires operators of hazardous waste facilities to carry several million dollars of liability insurance, the exact amounts varying with the type of facility. Many laws and contractual arrangements for the operation or cleanup of these facilities impose similar insurance requirements. The insurance itself, however, is often not available, which means that the activities must be curtailed.

Forty-seven companies were forced to close hazardous waste management facilities for lack of EIL coverage in 1985.[40] A 1986 news report noted that most of the country's 400 largest consulting engineering firms that do pollution control work are "refusing to handle toxic-waste sites unless their clients protect them from lawsuits."[41] These firms "have been unable to purchase pollution liability insurance in any amount, or at any price."

Options

Environmental cases represent the liability system's most severe challenge. In every other area of liability law the debate concerns comparatively fine legal questions—fault, noneconomic injury, joint liability, punitive damages. These same issues surface in environmental cases too, but they pale beside the unresolved and—at the boundaries—unresolvable questions of cause and effect.

The resulting uncertainty eviscerates the liability system of all purpose and justification. The principal objectives of the modern liability system are said to be deterrence and compensation, though one must at least note that until very recently the system was rationalized in much more modest terms of individual, corrective justice. But even if one frames the inquiry in the contemporary terms, the linkage of cause and effect is absolutely fundamental.

A conclusion about cause and effect links the claimant who "de-

40. Ibid.
41. "New Snag in Toxic Cleanups," *New York Times,* September 8, 1986.

serves" to be compensated to the defendant who "should" do the compensating within the liability system. It is easy enough to call for generous financial assistance for those who are grievously sick and in need of help, whatever the cause of their illness. But neither businesses nor their insurers can or will provide such assistance for very long if payments are not systematically and predictably linked to specific patterns of conduct. Insurers were the first to distance themselves from the possibility of litigation involving environmental hazards. Companies involved in cleanup or disposal are now walking the same path, either by demanding indemnity coverage from government or by abandoning the business altogether. Chemical manufacturers, transporters, and handlers could soon follow. In the long run the liability system's compensation objectives cannot be achieved without appropriate scrutiny of cause and effect. No industry or insurance company is large enough or wealthy enough to serve as a general first-party insurer against any and all diseases or injuries of unknown origin.

An accurate understanding of cause is equally essential in fulfilling the liability system's deterrence objectives. Liability will effectively deter unsafe behavior only if it is brought to bear more against activities that do in fact cause disease than against those that do not. A system that is largely random in its choice of targets is as likely to make life more dangerous as it is to make life safer. Indeed, regression may be the more probable outcome because the most popular liability targets are large, stable, and for the most part cautious enterprises.

We now confront two sharply diverging trends. Demand for personal injury compensation based on environmental claims is growing steadily. The common assumption in the legal literature, the public mind, and in an increasing number of courtrooms is that disease, especially cancer, of unknown origin is likely to have been caused by exposure to diffuse, man-made, environmental pollutants. Increasingly common, as well, are financial responsibility laws, which decree that particular activities may not be conducted without solid insurance against the injuries that pollution is likely to cause. More personal injury cases are being filed and are sweeping more plaintiffs into court. Awards and settlements are growing steadily larger. At least when confronted by persistent plaintiffs with well-publicized fears, most courts are now committed to engineering settlements and upholding compromise awards. In practical terms, the absence of serious, positive evidence of actual physical harm now counts for little. The contest turns on hot publicity and emotion, not on cool scientific inquiry.

The response of those who supply compensation, by contrast, has been altogether cold-blooded and rational. Many reinsurers, especially from outside the United States, will no longer underwrite U.S. environmental liability coverage of any description. Most primary insurers in the country are also backing out of the market. The total pool of private funds earmarked for environmental liability claims is therefore contracting.

With demand for payments growing and supply of insurance decreasing, environmental liability law is on an unstable course that cannot long be sustained. What are the options for successful outside intervention? One, at least in theory, is to return environmental liability law to its common-law roots and insist on truly rigorous courtroom proof of cause and effect.[42] The practical consequence would be to cut off virtually all environmental lawsuits. As Jerry L. Mashaw has pointed out, "Good science in the courts, of course, favors defendants in toxic torts litigation. If taken seriously in litigation, all the imponderable causation issues are going to prevent many wealth transfers from defendants to plaintiffs."[43] With a return to serious standards of proof, the awards and settlements from Agent Orange, Three Mile Island, Love Canal, and other such cases would soon be forgotten as temporary aberrations in liability jurisprudence. In time, insurers would return to the environmental liability market to cover both cleanup expenses after accidental releases and the very rare claims of personal injury that could meet honest burdens of proof. The resurrection of environmental liability insurance would of course also depend on restoring judicial respect for the language of the insurance contract. Insurers wishing to cover only sudden and accidental environmental incidents must be allowed to do so or they will end up where they are now, not covering any environmental incidents of any description.

Rigorous standards of proof could restore coherence and stability to a system that currently has neither characteristic. Yet such standards are not unconditionally favored by higher principles of optimal deterrence, economic efficiency, equity, or moral justice. Most disease of untraceable origin is not caused by man-made environmental pollutants, but some undoubtedly is. As mentioned before, Doll and Peto's estimates

---

42. An excellent outline of the elements of scientifically rigorous proof in toxic tort litigation appears in Bert Black and David E. Lilienfeld, "Epidemiologic Proof in Toxic Tort Litigation," *Fordham Law Review,* vol. 52 (April 1984), pp. 732–85.

43. Jerry L. Mashaw, "A Comment on Causation, Law Reform, and Guerilla Warfare," *Georgetown Law Journal,* vol. 73 (August 1985), p. 1396.

suggest that perhaps 15,000 to 20,000 U.S. cancers (a few percent of the annual total) are caused by artificial chemical pollutants in the environment.[44] Conventional pollutants like noise, dust, smoke, particulates, sewage, and solid waste undoubtedly also contribute to physical and psychic stress and disease. A strict standard of proof in the liability system would eliminate the false positives—the cases in which plaintiffs recover damages when they should not—but it would also increase the false negatives. Those who favor broader liability are probably correct in their general claim that the total environmental liability payments currently made by all industrial defendants are lower than the total external environmental costs their activities generate, since most low-level releases still go unnoticed. At some level of simplistic group justice, in which undifferentiated industries and their insurers are viewed in a polar alignment against the public at large, one may plausibly argue that we have too little environmental liability rather than too much.

And that hazy perspective appears to be the preferred one in most political and judicial circles. Man-made environmental pollutants are the prime suspects when other explanations for disease cannot be found. The consensus in both state and federal legislatures is in step with popular sentiment. And the steady trend in the courts is toward expanding liability, if only through the vehicle of a brokered judgment rationalized by the absence of any real verdict.

Demands both for the regulation of polluting activities and for the compensation of injuries that may be related are thus likely to continue growing. Yet private industry and insurance companies will not willingly fund an insurance program administered through a liability system unhinged from any accurate assessment of cause and effect. How is this impasse to be resolved?

One possibility is a steady retreat by those industries most directly in the path of the advancing liability system. Chemical companies, handlers and disposers of hazardous wastes, and countless smokestack industries will be among the ones most immediately affected. But today's environmental liability law is not carefully selective in its choice of targets. Companies that generate wastes will certainly curtail their activities, but so will companies that develop innovative incineration, cleanup, and disposal alternatives. The villains of *Silent Spring* will move on to other enterprises, but so will the new-generation biotechnologists who could offer more benign alternatives. Almost every man-

44. Doll and Peto, *Causes of Cancer.*

ufacturing or industrial processing activity is in fact a potential target of the new environmental litigation, whether its net contribution to environmental quality is positive or negative.

Industrial activity within stable and rationally defined social rules is essential, however, not only to economic welfare but also, ironically, to environmental protection and restoration. This suggests that in coming years the growing demand for what the environmental liability system is unsuccessfully struggling to provide—regulation of possibly hazardous activities and compensation of possibly injured claimants—must finally be provided by government institutions other than the courts. Administrative oversight by the EPA, OSHA, and their state counterparts must surely assume the dominant role in regulating, promoting, and deterring activities according to their environmental risks and benefits. Of course, uncertainty about cause complicates the regulation of environmental hazards in the administrative agencies just as it does in the courts. But the financial stakes grow exponentially larger as one moves down the chain from containment and proper disposal of toxic products in the first place, to cleanup after improper disposal, to broad compensation for victims that may or may not have been injured by the pollutants in question. Administrative agencies, operating earlier in this chain, can perhaps afford to err consistently on the side of caution without imposing intolerable social costs as a result. The courts, arriving on the scene much later, cannot.

All the major state and federal legislative initiatives so far have sensibly focused on containment and cleanup led through the administrative agencies rather than the courts. In addressing both Agent Orange and atom bomb fallout, for example, Congress expressly stopped short of providing any compensation for personal injury until causal links had been solidified. Attempts to expand the Superfund to cover personal injury claims have also consistently been rejected. So far, at least, Congress has recognized better than have some courts that environmental liability cases are not yet real cases at all and may never become so if science and epidemiology either cannot determine cause and effect or remain ambivalent.

Compensation for disease said to have been caused by environmental assault is a vastly more complex and difficult matter. The modern liability system both accommodates and promotes growing demands for such compensation. Channeling an ever-growing river of no-fault compensation insurance through the liability system will not only overwhelm the courts but also guarantee the financial collapse of the defendants selected as the source of funds. The latter result may be desirable if the hazards in question are as large as the most pessimistic advocates maintain. But the result will be very wasteful economically and will also extend far beyond the particular companies directly targeted if the risks are indeed much smaller, as the weight of the epidemiological evidence in fact suggests.

This means that in coming years the demand for compensation will end up being funded outside the traditional markets for private insurance. Indeed, it seems likely that the United States is now committed to march steadily toward the complete socialization of liability insurance.

The Superfund program already operates as a sweeping system of mandatory government-prescribed insurance. Premiums are now styled as a tax; broad industry participation in a single, loosely defined insurance pool is mandatory, the taxes collected are not linked to the possible misconduct of any particular tax-paying company, and cost controls within the new insurance pool have all but disappeared.[45] Although the Superfund does not yet cover claims for personal injury, there have been repeated proposals to broaden its scope. A 1982 report prepared pursuant to the original law concluded that "the present system for compensating victims for damages from toxic pollutant exposure is 'inadequate' " and that Congress should enact a federal program financed by industry taxes to deal with the problem.[46] Three major studies, one in Minnesota, one in Massachusetts, and one prepared at the Keystone Center, have made similar compensation proposals, though each begins by acknowledging that we are as yet unable to quantify the personal injuries from hazardous wastes in any way.[47] Congress and most state legislatures have so far resisted proposals of this character, but pressure for the adoption of such a program can only grow.

45. A similar socialization of insurance is inching forward in other areas, and for similar reasons. See Peter Huber and Donnamarie McCarthy, "Singular Remedies for Plural Catastrophes," *Issues in Science and Technology,* vol. 3 (Fall 1986), pp. 41–48. For example, the national swine flu vaccination program in 1976, followed by the National Childhood Vaccine Injury Act of 1986, set up government-supervised and funded insurance programs to fill a need that private insurers were flatly unwilling to meet.

46. *BNA Environment Reporter,* October 1, 1982, p. 742. The new fund, similar to the existing Superfund, would be financed by contributions from or taxes on production of hazardous or toxic chemicals and crude oil, and a tax on the deposit of hazardous wastes. The fund would cover medical expenses in full and lost earnings in substantial part.

47. *Potential Approaches for Toxic Exposure Compensation: A Report on the Conclusions of a Keystone Center Policy Dialogue* (Keystone, Colo.: Keystone Center, January 1985). See generally Connolly, "Insurer Perspectives on Causation."

We thus appear to be headed toward the complete preemption of environmental compensation by governmental programs, styled after the Superfund or the recent vaccine compensation legislation.[48] Common-law liability is supplanted by legislatively prescribed entitlement. Voluntary private insurance gradually gives way to a mandatory tax.

Government compensation programs enjoy one obvious advantage. Given sufficient funding, they can simply ignore most questions of cause and effect and tie payments to the occurrence of the disease itself rather than its origin. A system of this sort works, in a manner of speaking, but it is also notoriously incapable of containing costs. Although a few programs such as workers' compensation, created with strict attention to costs and benefits, have indeed achieved financial stability, many others, exemplified by the federal black lung program and the Superfund, have experienced runaway costs, increasingly voracious demands for new revenues, and no commensurate public benefits. Disease remains very common; indeed it is in the end a certainty of the human condition. Any government-administered program for injury of allegedly environmental origin will, in actual practice, end up covering very much more.

Conclusion

One must conclude on a note of pessimism. The United States is currently on a course of steady expansion of environmental liability undisciplined by rigorous attention to questions of cause and effect. The public is widely convinced that environmental pollutants are significant causes of cancer and other disease, and those convictions are mirrored in the jury box. The weight of the statistical scientific evidence does not support this view, but cause and effect in any particular case involving claimed environmental injury is usually uncertain. The uncertainty has created a sufficient opening for the courts, and liability judgments have followed in increasing numbers and size. New financial responsibility legislation is further increasing demand for environmental liability coverage.

Few private insurers, however, believe that they can profitably cover

48. Compare Peter Huber, "Catastrophe and Compensation: Reassembling the Pieces," in Huber and others, *The Legal System Assault on the Economy*, vol. 3 (Washington, D.C.: National Legal Center for the Public Interest, 1986), pp. 19–32; and Huber and McCarthy, "Singular Remedies for Plural Catastrophes."

environmental hazards. An insurer must know what risk is being insured. The liability system as it currently resolves environmental claims provides no coherent answer. It is doubtful that private insurance can provide stable coverage against a legal process that accepts deep-rooted ignorance as a sufficient basis for multimillion dollar awards.

By all appearances, the demands of the environmental liability system are fast outpacing the supply of funds from private insurance. If demand for coverage continues to grow while supply continues to shrink, federal and state governments are likely to intervene. The federal government has in fact already taken the first step with the $9 billion Superfund, which operates as broad, mandatory, retroactive insurance for cleanup costs. The next step, urged since 1980 though so far resisted by Congress, may be to extend the program to cover personal injury claims as well.

Government programs of this type are notoriously costly. The swine flu vaccination insurance program, undertaken by the government in 1976 when private insurers declined the invitation, cost vastly more than originally projected. A similar mushrooming of costs appears likely under the National Childhood Vaccine Injury Act, if that program is ever funded.[49] Experience with the black lung program points to a similar conclusion. The exact origin of most cancers and many other chronic or degenerative diseases is still unknown. Without rigorous attention to cause and effect, a broad government plan for compensating all claims of environmentally induced disease is thus likely to be transformed quickly into an unselective program of general health insurance for all disease of uncertain cause.

Whether compensation of suspected environmental injuries is left in the liability courts or the process is moved into an administrative compensation program, the United States will be forced sooner or later to stop prevaricating on the question of environmental cause and effect. Evasion of this core issue has already eviscerated the insurance backing that makes third-party liability possible. A government compensation program that repeats the same error will quickly find itself deluged with claims not clearly linked to man-made environmental pollutants.

The simplest and most readily available solution that is affordable, stable, and predictable is a return to rigorous standards of proof within the liability system. Regrettably, that also appears to be socially unacceptable to both the public and the courts.

49. There is, for example, already a wide divergence between committee estimates of the likely costs and much more pessimistic estimates provided by the Congressional Budget Office.

CHAPTER SIX

Liability for
Occupational Accidents and Illnesses

W. Kip Viscusi

INTEREST in maintaining health and safety in the workplace has surged dramatically since the early 1970s. In 1971 the Occupational Safety and Health Administration was created within the U.S. Department of Labor to control job-related risks. Throughout the 1970s, states boosted the level of workers' compensation benefits. And the courts have dealt with an increasing number of products liability suits for victims of occupational disease.

In terms of current policy considerations the role of the judicial system is most important, and debate focuses on three classes of concerns. First, how should the liability system be restructured, if at all, to address the new issues that have arisen in mass toxic tort cases? Second, to what extent should laws pertaining to job injuries be overhauled? Finally, given the advent of stiffer job safety regulations and more generous compensation levels for accident victims, should the United States reconsider the role of the liability system? Thus, how have recent policy changes altered the appropriate division of labor among these major institutions?

Policy Objectives and Instruments

Although the specific context may differ from that of other accidents, such as those that are product-related, society's broad objectives in dealing with job-related injuries and illnesses are the same. First, it is desirable to promote an efficient level of accident prevention. The employer takes actions to make the technology of production, the materials used, and workplace operations safer. Workers affect safety through their behavior on the job and sometimes off (smoking, for example). Ideally, a policy should encourage awareness of safety practices among all participants in the workplace. At the same time, the optimal level of job safety will not provide a risk-free environment. Actions to improve safety are costly to the firms that must spend money for them and to the workers who must expend effort or forgo activities such as smoking cigarettes. Some trade-offs are required.

A second objective is to provide an efficient level of insurance for workers exposed to the risk of injury or illness. In instances when workers experience financial losses for which they are not responsible, the optimal level of insurance that will provide for full replacement of income is the level that gives them the same marginal utility when they are injured as when they were not. Such a policy of "making one whole" is not generally ideal, however.[1] Less than full compensation is desirable if the accident decreases the marginal utility of income and more if the accident increases its marginal utility.

To see why this is the case, consider the extreme situation of death. In an economic manner of speaking, dying alters a worker's utility function by dropping both the level of utility and the marginal utility of income to zero; in effect, death replaces the utility function with a bequest function. It would not be rational to provide for the same level of income after death that a worker would have chosen when alive, since he or she would not be alive to enjoy or need it.

Similarly, if there are other types of health impairments that affect the ability to derive utility from income, the replacement of less than full welfare loss will be desirable. If one becomes a paraplegic, one would wish to have insured enough income replacement so that a dollar of income provides the same marginal utility as it would have if one had remained healthy. But no reasonable amount of compensation may eliminate the irreplaceable loss in welfare that a deterioration in health entails. The

---

1. For a discussion of the effects of changes in utility function see Richard J. Zeckhauser, "Coverage for Catastrophic Illness," *Public Policy*, vol. 21 (Spring 1973), pp. 149–73; Michael Spence, "Consumer Misperceptions, Product Failure and Producer Liability," *Review of Economic Studies*, vol. 44 (October 1977), pp. 561–72; Philip J. Cook and Daniel A. Graham, "The Demand for Insurance and Protection: The Case of Irreplaceable Commodities," *Quarterly Journal of Economics*, vol. 91 (February 1977), pp. 143–56; W. Kip Viscusi, *Employment Hazards: An Investigation of Market Performance* (Harvard University Press, 1979); and Viscusi, "Imperfect Job Risk Information and Optimal Workmen's Compensation Benefits," *Journal of Public Economics*, vol. 14 (December 1980), pp. 319–37. An extensive discussion of appropriate compensation and incentives in accident situations is provided in Guido Calabresi, *The Cost of Accidents: A Legal and Economic Analysis* (Yale University Press, 1970).

underlying reference point is the level of insurance that accident victims would have selected if they had purchased full coverage at actuarially fair rates before the accident.

It has been generally assumed that an accident leading to disability or otherwise undermining health lowers a person's marginal utility of income, which implies that less than full compensation is desirable. Recent empirical evidence supports this assumption.[2] As a result, the optimal level of compensation that a worker would choose in a fully efficient market would not restore his or her welfare to its preaccident level.

In addition to accident prevention and efficient compensation, society also wishes to ensure equitable treatment for its members. This takes several forms. First, there may be an altruistic concern with the risks workers face, particularly inordinately large risks. Society may view the situation of one worker facing an annual death risk of 1 in 10 much differently than it views 10,000 workers, each of whom faces a death risk of 1 in 100,000, even though the expected percentage of lives lost is the same in each case.

Second, the manner in which the risk is generated may be of consequence. Society tends to place greater value on assisting individuals who are victims of involuntary risks than on assisting those who incur risks voluntarily.

Third, society is concerned with all classes of accident victims. Victims of job accidents and illnesses presumably are no more deserving of compensation than are victims of product-related accidents or risks whose source cannot be identified.

Finally, society may wish that accident prevention and compensation policies be used to redistribute resources toward those in low-income groups. This objective is controversial because income transfer programs that are more broadly based are better suited to this purpose. Requiring wrongdoers to be responsible for society's broader desire to ensure equitable income distribution may be inefficient, since it will weaken the effectiveness of litigation to help achieve the other objectives, such as providing efficient incentives for preventing accidents. As a result, the broad-based concern for equitable income distribution is best excluded from a discussion of improving ways to meet society's objectives except as it may specifically relate to income inequities caused by health and safety risks.

2. W. Kip Viscusi and William Evans, "Utility Functions That Are Dependent on One's Health State: Estimates and Economic Implications," working paper (1988).

Society's objectives with respect to job-related health and safety are promoted by various institutional mechanisms—market forces, notably implicit or explicit bargains between workers and employers, occupational safety and health regulations, social insurance programs for job-related illnesses and injuries (workers' compensation, for example), and the civil liability system. Since no single mechanism need serve all functions, a division of responsibility is possible. The workers' compensation system, for instance, may be effective in compensating victims of accidents in the workplace but may provide little incentive to improve safety; the civil liability system, however, may very well help to improve safety by holding out the possibility of damages assessed against employers if they do not cooperate. The relative strengths of the different tools should be recognized and exploited.

Thus the civil liability system cannot be viewed in isolation. One must take into account what is accomplished by other mechanisms before suggesting any changes in its function. Indeed, these mechanisms do more than provide the pertinent backdrop against which the system operates. For accidents in the workplace, they are the driving force behind the compensation that injured workers receive and the determination of the level of risk on the job.

The Role of the Market

The most useful starting point for discussing safety risks on the job is to review the effects of the market.[3] Unlike broad environmental hazards that may be borne by an individual who has a remote relationship to the party generating the risk, job hazards arise in an employment relationship. The employer that controls both the work environment and overall work operations hires the worker at some wage rate to perform certain tasks. Implicitly if not explicitly, the worker accepts the job and its associated characteristics, including the risk level and the remuneration associated with it. Thus if risks are known, workers will demand additional compensation for the hazards. This compensation could be provided through a higher base wage rate or, after an injury, through insurance benefits.

With perfect markets, the mix of the various forms of compensation

3. For a broader perspective, see W. Kip Viscusi, *Risk by Choice: Regulating Health and Safety in the Workplace* (Harvard University Press, 1983); and Viscusi, *Employment Hazards.*

will be optimal and the risk level will be efficient. Employers will continue investing in safety until the cost incurred just equals the savings achieved in compensation and injuries avoided. Workers will be fully compensated before any accidents for the expected welfare loss to which they are exposed. The additional wage and insurance benefits will equal or exceed the value of their expected loss from injury. Although compensated ex ante, workers will not generally be fully compensated after an injury except when losses are purely financial, in which case risk-averse workers will obtain full insurance for their potential loss in earnings. Because of the wage premium they receive, workers will, however, be better off if no injury occurs, and overall they will not be worse off because of the presence of job risks.

By almost any standard the wage adjustment that workers receive for risk is substantial—an estimated $90 billion in 1985 dollars for the private sector as a whole.[4] Ex ante compensation is substantial on a unit risk basis as well. Table 6-1 summarizes estimates of the implicit values of life and injury reported in various studies of worker earnings. Consider, for example, results from the 1970–71 Survey of Working Conditions. A $3.2 million value of life means that workers receive compensation at the rate of $3.2 million for each expected life lost. Thus a worker facing the average blue-collar death risk of 1 in 10,000 receives extra annual compensation of $3.2 million × 1/10,000, or $320. Similarly, every death at a workplace alters workers' perceptions of the risk and boosts wage levels employers must pay, thus providing a powerful incentive for firms to operate safely. Estimates of the implicit compensation value of nonfatal job injuries are roughly two orders of magnitude lower than the values of fatalities.

A major criticism of looking to additional compensation for a measure of the implicit values of job risks is that workers may not be fully aware of the risks of a given job when they decide to accept it. Such lack of information is no doubt important, particularly with respect to dimly understood health risks. Nevertheless, employers do provide substantial wage compensation for jobs with increased risks. And survey evidence indicates widespread awareness among workers of many risks they do face.[5]

4. This estimate updates to 1985 prices my estimate of $69 billion in 1980 prices; see chapter 3 of Viscusi, *Risk by Choice*.

5. Ibid.; and W. Kip Viscusi and Charles J. O'Connor, "Adaptive Responses to Chemical Labeling: Are Workers Bayesian Decision Makers?" *American Economic Review*, vol. 74 (December 1984), pp. 942–56.

Table 6-1. *Summary of Labor Market Studies of Wage Premiums for Job Risks*
Thousands of constant 1985 dollars

Investigator	Sample	Implicit value of life	Implicit value of nonfatal injuries
Brown	National Longitudinal Survey, 1967–73	1,100–1,700	n.a.
Olson	Current Population Survey, 1973	8,100	n.a.
Smith	Current Population Survey, 1967	8,300	n.a.
	Current Population Survey, 1973	3,600	n.a.
Thaler and Rosen	Survey of Economic Opportunity, 1967	638	n.a.
Viscusi	Survey of Working Conditions, 1970–71	3,200–4,300	25–37
Viscusi	Panel Study of Income Dynamics, 1976	8,000–12,000[a]	35–39
Viscusi and Moore	Quality of Employment Survey, 1977	n.a.	37–45
Viscusi and O'Connor	Survey of Chemical Industry Workers, 1982	n.a.	11–14

Sources: Charles Brown, "Equalizing Differences in the Labor Market," *Quarterly Journal of Economics*, vol. 94 (February 1980), pp. 113–34; Craig A. Olson, "An Analysis of Wage Differentials Received by Workers on Dangerous Jobs," *Journal of Human Resources*, vol. 16 (Spring 1981), pp. 167–85; Robert S. Smith, *The Occupational Safety and Health Act: Its Goals and Its Achievements* (American Enterprise Institute, 1976); Richard Thaler and Sherwin Rosen, "The Value of Saving a Life: Evidence from the Labor Market," in Nestor E. Terleckyj, ed., *Household Production and Consumption* (Columbia University Press for the National Bureau of Economic Research, 1976), pp. 265–301; W. Kip Viscusi, *Employment Hazards: An Investigation of Market Performance* (Harvard University Press, 1979); Viscusi, *Risk by Choice: Regulating Health and Safety in the Workplace* (Harvard University Press, 1983); Viscusi and Charles J. O'Connor, "Adaptive Responses to Chemical Labeling: Are Workers Bayesian Decision Makers?" *American Economic Review*, vol. 74 (December 1984), pp. 942–56; and Viscusi and Michael J. Moore, "Workers' Compensation: Wage Effects, Benefits Inadequacies, and the Value of Health Losses," *Review of Economics and Statistics*, vol. 69 (May 1987), pp. 249–61.
n.a. Not available.
a. Evaluated at the mean risk level for the sample for a model in which the heterogeneity in wage-risk trade-offs was assessed.

When workers accept jobs whose risks are not fully understood, additional market forces come into play. They may often learn about the risk through on-the-job experience, and if the information is sufficiently unfavorable, they can quit. Indeed, as many as one-third of all resignations among manufacturing workers may be due to job risks.[6] Of course, such learning may involve experiencing a disabling on-the-job injury. And there is no assurance that workers will ever be fully informed.

Still, the market plays a central role in determining job safety outcomes.

6. See Viscusi, *Employment Hazards;* and Viscusi, *Risk by Choice.*

Decisions by workers and employers dictate the jobs workers take and the risks to which they are exposed. Wage premiums for additional risk and such fringe benefits as sick leave, life insurance, and medical insurance provide the primary compensation they receive. Although their welfare typically will be reduced after experiencing an injury, in many cases workers receive compensation ex ante. Those who are exposed to risk but who are not injured will be paid more than they would have received in a risk-free job. And before an injury takes place, they will find the position attractive, given their perceptions of the risk.

Direct Regulation of Risk

Since workers typically will not be fully informed of all the risks they face, market incentives for improving safety may be inadequate. Even if full information were available and risk levels were efficient, society might wish to promote additional reductions in risk to reflect its altruistic concern with individual health.

Control of risks on the job is the primary function of the Occupational Safety and Health Administration, whose mandate is "to assure so far as possible every working man and woman in the Nation safe and healthful working conditions."[7] Compensating accident victims is excluded from the agency's functions and must be met by market forces, workers' compensation, and the civil liability system.

OSHA's primary regulatory strategy has therefore been to issue health and safety standards, which are then enforced by its inspectors, who have the authority to levy fines on firms that do not comply. The agency began operating by adopting industry consensus standards, such as those of the American National Standards Institute, which pertained largely to safety concerns rather than health risks. OSHA's more recent activities have emphasized setting standards for health risks not covered by the initial standards. Table 6-2 summarizes major OSHA regulations that have been issued or proposed since 1972. The standards have been ranked according to diminishing cost-effectiveness as measured by the cost per life saved.

While most of the standards listed in table 6-2 concern health hazards, the most cost-effective standards concern safety. It is also striking that the cost per life saved for roughly half of these regulations greatly exceeds estimates of the value of life revealed by workers' labor market decisions.

7. Section 26 of the Occupational Safety and Health Act of 1970, 29 U.S.C. 651 (1982).

Table 6-2. Cost per Life Saved for OSHA Standards

Regulation	Year	Status[a]	Nature of risk	Initial risk (annual)	Lives saved (annual)	Cost per life saved[b]
Oil and gas well servicing	1983	P	Safety	1.1×10^{-3}	50.000	0.1
Underground construction	1983	P	Safety	1.6×10^{-3}	8.100	0.3
Servicing wheel rims	1984	F	Safety	1.4×10^{-5}	2.300	0.5
Crane suspended personnel platforms	1984	P	Safety	1.8×10^{-3}	5.000	0.9
Concrete and masonry construction	1985	P	Safety	1.4×10^{-5}	6.500	1.4
Hazard communication	1983	F	Safety	4.0×10^{-5}	200.000	1.8
Grain dust	1984	P	Safety	2.1×10^{-4}	4.000	2.8
Asbestos	1972	F	Health	3.9×10^{-4}	396.000	7.4
Benzene	1985	P	Health	8.8×10^{-4}	3.800	17.1
Ethylene oxide	1984	F	Health	4.4×10^{-5}	2.800	25.6
Acrylonitrile	1978	F	Health	9.4×10^{-4}	6.900	37.6
Coke ovens	1976	F	Health	1.6×10^{-4}	31.000	61.8
Asbestos	1986	F	Health	6.7×10^{-5}	74.700	89.3
Arsenic	1978	F	Health	1.8×10^{-3}	11.000	92.5
Acrylonitrile	1978	R	Health	9.4×10^{-4}	0.600	308.0
EDB	1983	P	Health	2.5×10^{-4}	0.002	15,600.0
Formaldehyde	1985	P	Health	6.8×10^{-7}	0.010	72,000.0

Source: John F. Morrall, "A Review of the Record," *Regulation*, vol. 10 (November–December 1986), p. 30
a. F = final rule; P = proposed rule; R = rejected rule.
b. Millions of 1984 dollars.

Although the exact cutoff for excessively stringent standards may not be clear, all standards following asbestos appear to impose costs that well exceed the benefits generated. The least cost-effective of OSHA's regulations in force is the arsenic standard, which imposes estimated costs of $92.5 million per life saved. More lives could be saved at less cost by redirecting the emphases of OSHA's policies.

The most ambitious of OSHA's regulatory initiatives in the 1980s has been its requirement that manufacturers label their hazardous chemicals and meet other informational requirements. The agency adopted the requirement because it believed that substance-by-substance regulation of the thousands of hazardous chemicals in the workplace was not feasible. From an economic standpoint the labeling strategy is attractive because it addresses directly the market's failure to provide adequate information. Although employers began to comply with this regulation only in 1986, and so it is too early to assess its effectiveness, a field study of the responses

Table 6-3. *Worker Responses to Hazard Warnings*

Item	Asbestos	Chloroacetophenone
Annual probability of injury before warning	.09	.10
Annual probability of injury after warning	.26	.18
Fraction of workers requiring a wage increase	.71	.48
Risk premium (dollars)	2,995.59	1,919.01
Probability of quitting before warning	.13	.10
Probability of quitting after warning	.65	.23

Source: W. Kip Viscusi and Charles S. O'Connor, "Adaptive Responses to Chemical Labeling: Are Workers Bayesian Decision Makers?" *American Economic Review,* vol. 74 (December 1984), pp. 942–56.

of workers from different plants suggests that the information may be having a dramatic effect. The general nature of the results is reflected in representative statistics in table 6-3 for two health hazards: asbestos, a well-known carcinogen, and chloroacetophenone, an industrial chemical that causes eye irritation. In each case, workers were shown a label of the type now used by chemical firms with labeling systems. For both hazards the perceived annual risk level, which is scaled in frequency terms comparable to the Bureau of Labor Statistics injury and illness rates, was about one chance in ten before seeing the label. The hazard warning almost tripled the perceived risk in the case of asbestos and doubled it for chloroacetophenone. The fraction of workers who viewed their jobs as high risk (above the national injury risk) also escalated. These increases in risk perceptions were accompanied by a desire for additional wage compensation in many instances (over 70 percent for asbestos), the average premium being $3,000 for working with asbestos and $1,900 for chloroacetophenone. Finally, if the workers did not receive additional pay, they would be more likely to quit their jobs, particularly if they worked with asbestos.

Although the hazard communication standard has substantial promise, OSHA standards generally have not yet had the dramatic effects that policymakers envisioned. The most favorable empirical evidence of the agency's efficacy suggests that from 1973 to 1983 its regulations reduced all work injuries and illnesses by 2.6 percent, injuries and illnesses causing lost days of work by 3.6 percent, and the rate of total lost workdays by 6.1 percent.[8] The percentage reduction in injuries is largest for the more severe types, which suggests that OSHA targets more severe hazards disproportionately. Nevertheless, because the agency's rate of inspections and

8. These are the strongest of the set of results reported in W. Kip Viscusi, "The Impact of Occupational Safety and Health Regulation, 1973–1983," *Rand Journal of Economics,* vol. 17 (Winter 1986), pp. 567–80.

the number of penalties assessed have remained low, its regulations have had at best only a moderate effect on workplace health and safety.

OSHA's role can thus be viewed as augmenting that of the market in providing incentives to control risks in the workplace. Unfortunately, its regulations have not fulfilled their initial promise because the standards have often focused on small risks that are expensive to reduce and the enforcement effort has been relatively weak. Many of these shortcomings could be remedied by more effective agency leadership that would recognize there are simply too many hazards to control comprehensively. The issuance of the hazard communication standard was in part an admission of this inadequacy.

Workers' Compensation

Before the twentieth century, workers who suffered accidents on the job and sought compensation could do so only by filing a lawsuit against their employers and could win only by showing that those employers were careless or negligent. Reliance on the traditional remedies of liability litigation posed a variety of difficulties, however, which no doubt led to the creation of the no-fault system of workers' compensation. An average of one in twenty-five workers suffers an accident each year that leads to lost work time. The lawsuits resulting from such injuries could cause a considerable judicial burden, impose sizable legal costs on employers, and create impediments through legal fees and time delays in workers' obtaining compensation. Tort remedies also do not ensure compensation, since employers can invoke several defenses: contributory negligence, assumption of risk, and the fellow servant rule.[9] Finally, judicial remedies put employer and worker in an adversarial relationship. Since most workplace injuries are temporary, after which the worker returns to his job, filing a lawsuit may damage a relationship that both parties would have liked to preserve.

In large part because of such factors, states have established workers' compensation programs. These statutes typically cover all injuries aris-

---

9. For a discussion of these principles, see W. Page Keeton, ed., *Prosser and Keeton on the Law of Torts* (St. Paul: West Publishing, 1984), p. 573. Thus the employer could argue that the worker's carelessness contributed to the accident (contributory negligence), that the worker was aware of the risk and incurred it voluntarily (assumption of risk), or that the worker assumed the risk posed by his "fellow servants" upon accepting employment from the "master" (fellow servant rule).

ing out of and in the course of employment, regardless of fault. For the injuries it covers, workers' compensation represents the sole remedy; the worker is generally barred from seeking a recovery from the employer through common law.[10]

These restrictions do not imply that litigation has no function but only that it has a subsidiary one. In some cases of extreme negligence or intentional misconduct, workers can sue employers. They can also sue third parties who manufactured the products contributing to the injury. Thus a forklift driver injured on the job can sue the manufacturer if, for example, a defect in the forklift led to the accident. On balance, however, workers' compensation programs require employees to sacrifice their right to sue employers for the costs imposed by on-the-job injuries in return for receiving some amount of compensation. To receive compensation, workers must show they suffered an injury arising out of and in the course of employment—and that requirement is not innocuous. For example, causality is much simpler to show for accidents than for illnesses, and as a result, workers' compensation benefits serve primarily as accident compensation. The adverse effects of health hazards, particularly those with long gestations, are often not compensated.

For injuries that are covered, the level of compensation is reasonably generous. The typical state formula provides for replacement of two-thirds of wages, subject to various constraints on minimum benefit levels, maximum benefit levels, and benefit duration.[11] Since these benefits are not taxable, their value is often comparable with the value of the worker's net earnings before the injury.[12] The levels of benefits under workers' compensation, however, are somewhat lower than those in products liability awards because workers are paid regardless of fault.[13]

Employers bear the cost of workers' compensation by paying insurance premiums, whose costs provide a financial incentive to maintain a

10. Ibid., pp. 574–75.

11. See U.S. Chamber of Commerce, *Analysis of Worker Compensation Laws* (Washington, D.C., 1986).

12. For a comparison of workers' compensation benefits and products liability settlements, see W. Kip Viscusi, "Alternative Approaches to Valuing the Health Impacts of Accidents: Liability Law and Prospective Evaluations," *Law and Contemporary Problems*, vol. 46 (Autumn 1983), pp. 49–68.

13. A substantial level of replacement was provided for workers included in the University of Michigan Quality of Employment Survey analyzed in W. Kip Viscusi and Michael J. Moore, "Workers' Compensation: Wage Effects, Benefit Inadequacies, and the Value of Health Losses," *Review of Economics and Statistics,* vol. 69 (May 1987), pp. 249–61. Taking into account the tax status of benefits, the rate of wage replacement for this 1976 sample was 0.835.

Table 6-4. *Workers' Compensation Benefits and Related Financial Effects, 1976–83*
Billions of dollars

Year	Total premiums	Total payments[a]	Wage reduction	Net employer savings
1976	10.9	7.6	29.9	22.3
1977	14.0	9.8	36.1	26.3
1978	16.6	11.6	39.4	26.8
1979	20.0	14.0	43.9	29.9
1980	22.0	15.4	44.3	28.9
1981	22.9	16.0	41.8	30.0
1982	22.5	15.8	37.0	21.2
1983	22.9	16.0	33.5	17.5

Source: Michael J. Moore and W. Kip Viscusi, "Have Increases in Workers' Compensation Benefits Paid for Themselves?" in National Council for Compensation Insurance workers' compensation conference volume, forthcoming, table 5.

a. Amounts have been adjusted to reflect after-tax costs to the firm.

safe workplace. Employers that self-insure or those large firms that are strongly merit-rated will be most influenced by these incentives. The provision of such benefits, however, also reduces workers' incentives to avoid accidents, since, after all, they are not footing any part of the premium. Several recent studies suggest that the effect on these incentives may be significant.[14]

The costs of workers' compensation have increased greatly since the 1970s because benefit levels have become more generous. In 1983, the latest year for which data are available, workers received $22.9 billion in benefits. Table 6-4 shows yearly workers' compensation payments and after-tax premium costs paid by employers. Both payments and premiums have escalated dramatically since the mid-1970s and have led some observers to voice alarm.

The increasing premiums paint an overly simplistic portrait of the program's actual burden, however. Since workers value benefits both for their insurance aspects and their tax-exempt status, they would be

14. See in particular John W. Ruser, "Workers' Compensation Insurance, Experience-Rating and Occupational Injuries," *Rand Journal of Economics,* vol. 16 (Winter 1985), pp. 487–503, for high estimates; Thomas J. Kniesner and John D. Leeth, "Workers' Compensation with Imperfect State Verification: The Long-Run Impact on Injuries and Claims," paper presented at 1986 summer meeting of the Econometric Society, for estimates of a weaker effect; and James R. Chelius, "The Influence of Workers' Compensation on Safety Incentives," *Industrial and Labor Relations Review,* vol. 35 (January 1982), pp. 235–42, for estimates of no such relationship.

willing to accept lower wages in return for additional benefits. Indeed, unless benefit levels are excessive, the wage reduction will exceed the actuarial value of benefits because risk-averse workers will value the insurance provided by workers' compensation by more than the expected payout. The estimates for two large samples of workers used to generate the wage reduction statistics in table 6-4 indicate that higher benefits lead to a wage offset more than double the current level of premiums. Thus, far from being a financial burden, workers' compensation actually produces net compensation cost savings for employers.[15]

These empirical results can also be used to ascertain the optimal level of benefits.[16] In 1976 benefits were substantially underprovided because the wage reduction workers accepted greatly exceeded the cost of the benefits. But by 1983 levels of compensation had led to benefits close to their optimal level. In terms of efficient insurance, workers' compensation now fulfills its role for those adverse health outcomes covered by the program.

The key remaining inadequacy of workers' compensation is that victims of health hazards often have difficulty obtaining appropriate compensation. Because this problem plagues any compensation program, including civil liability litigation, it is instructive to explore it in detail. The central difficulty is that workers must prove their conditions are job-related. Meeting this test is straightforward when injuries are the result of accidents, but when occupational disease is involved, making an acceptable case for compensation is more difficult. Workers must not only prove they have the disease and that it has adverse health effects but must also prove the link between the disease and the job. Ascertaining such links is often difficult because diseases may have multiple causes, notably those stemming from the workers' own behavior (smoking, say, or alcohol consumption), and because the relative seriousness of different exposure levels may not be well understood. Except for a few "signature" diseases such as asbestosis or mesothelioma, which are caused by exposure to asbestos, the link to the job will be difficult to prove.

15. One possible offset to these savings is the moral hazard problem that may result if higher benefit levels lead to more accidents.
16. See Viscusi and Moore, "Workers' Compensation"; and Michael J. Moore and W. Kip Viscusi, "Have Increases in Workers' Compensation Benefits Paid for Themselves?" in National Council for Compensation Insurance workers' compensation conference volume, forthcoming.

Even if the underlying medical relationship between substance and injury is clear, the worker's history of exposures may not be known. With diseases that occur after gestation of a decade or more, a variety of factors both on and off the job may have contributed. Since record-keeping over long time periods is often nonexistent, it may not be possible to ascertain, for example, what the worker's history of exposure to toxic chemicals has been. Indeed, until the advent of the OSHA hazard communication regulation, it might not have been possible to discover the nature of workers' present exposures. More fundamentally, it may not be possible to verify workers' plant locations and the nature of their jobs.

Workers' compensation statutes impose strict requirements for establishing the relationship between injury and entitlement to benefits. They typically stipulate that a worker must prove the disease is not one of the "ordinary diseases of life" but is "peculiar to the worker's occupation." Some statutes require a worker to have been exposed to the hazard for a specific length of time before granting eligibility for compensation, even though the disease may be caused by a briefer exposure.[17]

If these requirements are met, a worker still may not be able to collect because the statute of limitations may have expired. Some statutes require the worker to file for compensation within a particular period after disablement. Such tests do not appear to be overly restrictive except when the worker does not realize the disease is job-related. Although the usual period is one or two years, if only a short time is allowed, the worker may not have sufficient time to identify the cause of the ailment.[18] The first incidents of liver cancer caused by exposure to polyvinyl chloride, for example, did not lead to widespread awareness of the job risk because they were very rare and were dismissed as random occurrences. Only after diseases become more widespread and better publicized do people become sufficiently aware of their jobs' role in causing the injury.

Much more restrictive in their effects are requirements that workers be employed at the firm where the disease occurred for a minimum period of time—the average is eight years.[19] This is much shorter than

17. See "Note: Compensating Victims of Occupational Disease," *Harvard Law Review,* vol. 93 (March 1980), pp. 921, 923.

18. The period is only ninety days in New York. See National Council on Compensation Insurance, *The Asbestos Crisis—Yesterday, Today and Tomorrow* (New York: NCCI, 1983), p. 16.

19. Government Research Corporation, *Victim Compensation: The Policy Debate* (Washington, D.C., 1983), p. 6.

the usual gestation period for cancer. If workers have changed jobs or retired, they may be unable to qualify for benefits.

These difficulties in the structure of workers' compensation are reflected in compensation payments. Employers are six times as likely to contest a disease-related claim as they are an accident-related one, and they win in two-thirds of these cases, usually on the issue of compensability.[20] Even cases that do result in a compensation payment often involve a prolonged administrative battle; indeed, 60 percent of all such awards are initially denied.[21]

The net effect is that few victims of diseases that workers believe to be occupationally related receive compensation. For disabling illness, estimates of workers compensated range from one in thirty to one in twenty.[22] Five percent or less of these cases are covered. The successful claim rate is higher when the worker has died; about one-third of these cases receive compensation.

When a clear link between the job and the disease is apparent, the success rates for claims may be much higher. For example, one survey of fatality claims based on exposure to asbestos stated that 61 percent of the claims had been awarded, 25 percent had resulted in an agreement to a modified compensation level, 3 percent had been denied, 6 percent were pending, and 1 percent had been dropped.[23] But cases of diseases related to asbestos have received widespread publicity; the success rate of these claims is much higher than for occupational diseases overall. In this sense, asbestos might be viewed as a "best case" for the functioning of workers' compensation.

The low level of benefits received for occupational disease claims often results from the tendency of claimants to negotiate settlements in contested cases. To the extent that there are causes of the disease that are not job-related, this practice may simply reflect the degree of exposure on the job. Public and private compensation combined replace 40 percent of all wages for severely disabled victims of occupational diseases; they replace 60 percent of the wages for all injury classes combined.[24]

20. "Note: Compensating Victims," p. 923.
21. U.S. Department of Labor, *An Interim Report to the Congress on Occupational Diseases* (Washington, D.C., 1980), p. 3.
22. "Note: Compensating Victims," p. 923; and U.S. Department of Labor, *Interim Report,* p. 3.
23. U.S. Department of Labor, *Interim Report,* p. 2.
24. Ibid.

These statistics, however, suggest a much higher level of income support for those with occupational diseases than did the workers' compensation statistics cited earlier. The reason for the discrepancy is that workers' compensation is only a minor source of support for the disabled. The main source is social security (53 percent); others include pensions (21 percent), veterans' benefits (17 percent), and private insurance (1 percent).[25] Workers' compensation accounts for the remainder, or only 5 percent of compensation for occupational diseases.

The relatively small contribution of workers' compensation no doubt results from the difficult practical and legal task of establishing a causal link between a job-related exposure and a particular disease. Although existing statistics on self-assessed occupational disease are inherently arbitrary, they do suggest that few such cases are compensated while the worker is ill. More are compensated after death.

Since the major factor limiting compensation is the issue of causality, occupational diseases often get treated much like nonoccupational ailments. Private pension and insurance provide income support, as do social insurance efforts such as social security. From the standpoint of the individual's welfare, the source of the compensation is not of great consequence; it is the level that matters. Social security disability insurance provides income support for workers with long-term disabilities, irrespective of cause. The extent of earnings replacement hinges on a formula linked to the worker's past earnings. These benefits take the form of an annuity payable for life.

In terms of equity, victims of occupational diseases do better than victims of other illnesses but worse than victims of accidents on the job. To the extent that victims of occupational disease can receive workers' compensation benefits whereas victims of nonoccupational injuries and illnesses cannot, they can fare better overall. In accident cases, however, workers' compensation serves an additional function: it encourages employers to provide a safe workplace because premium levels are tied to accident rates. Occupational disease payments provide less incentive since causality is more difficult to ascertain.

Nevertheless, workers' compensation may result in overpayment for victims of occupational disease who collect from more than one source. Since workers' compensation benefits are not automatically deducted from product liability awards, a victim could potentially collect workers' compensation and reap the benefits for a successful product liability

25. Ibid.

lawsuit. To avoid such duplication, proposals have been made to reduce the level of the settlements in civil suits by the amount of workers' compensation benefits received.[26] Variations of this proposal are discussed in chapter 8.

Civil Liability Litigation

Institutional Interactions

Workers' compensation is so dominant a force in compensating for accidents on the job that some observers have questioned whether compensation provided through civil litigation will be of any consequence whatsoever in the long run. Indeed, Keeton and his colleagues have predicted the eventual demise of such litigation:

> There is thus a substantial and still important area of labor litigation in which the older law still has significance and vitality. The whole trend is toward cutting it down, making further inroads upon it by bringing as much as possible within the compensation acts; and its ultimate extinction appears only to be a question of time—which, however, may not mean anything immediate.[27]

Although the workers' compensation system is well suited to addressing workplace injuries, illnesses plausibly connected to occupational exposure pose continued problems. Workers not only have difficulty in proving that their diseases were caused on the job, but the benefits they receive if they can establish eligibility may not compensate for the economic and noneconomic (pain and suffering) costs they experience. Accordingly, workers have strong incentives to explore other options for obtaining compensation for severe job-related illnesses and injuries. Chief among these options is a third-party lawsuit against the maker of a product involved in a job accident. Because this option is being increasingly pursued, remedies provided through liability litigation will continue to be important to workers.

Is this desirable? From the standpoint of optimal compensation, accident victims should obtain efficient insurance reimbursement from whatever source might provide it. Thus if they cannot obtain adequate income support and medical reimbursement from workers' compensa-

26. One such initiative was the proposal of Senator Robert Kasten of Wisconsin, the Product Liability Act, S2631, introduced in June 1982.
27. Keeton, *Prosser and Keeton on the Law of Torts*, p. 575.

tion, additional reimbursement through a product liability award is desirable.

Workers may, however, do more than use product liability suits to fill the gaps left by workers' compensation. Although workers' compensation is the employee's exclusive remedy against an employer for injuries covered by the program, such coverage in no way precludes an additional claim against a third party involved in an accident. Recent evidence suggests that efforts to boost levels of workers' compensation have raised benefits for injuries from an inadequate level to roughly their optimal amount.[28] Thus from the standpoint of efficient insurance against income losses, a multiple recovery for injury may lead to over-compensation. For diseases, however, compensation may remain insufficient because benefits are subject to caps and duration limits. Such caps may be particularly important in cases of job-related fatalities, since the death benefits under workers' compensation are very limited. In addition, the quality and level of medical care provided through workers' compensation tends to be minimal. Injuries requiring extensive medical expenditures, such as repeated plastic surgery or specialized vocational rehabilitation, are not well handled. Nor is the best possible care generally provided. In situations in which highly specialized and expensive treatment would have a clear benefit, the court can provide for such care, but these determinations can add costs and delays to treatment.

A second objective of litigation is to provide proper incentives for risk reduction. Workers' compensation awards consist exclusively of compensation for loss of income and medical expenses. Product liability awards cover these losses as well as compensation for pain and suffering. Making the employer or producer of workplace equipment responsible for these expenses provides some financial incentive to encourage safety on their part. Nevertheless, in practice, these incentives appear muted.

Table 6-5 summarizes the average levels of compensation provided in court awards and out-of-court settlements in product liability cases concluded in 1977 (updated in 1985 prices). Although the levels of compensation are not negligible, they are below the values workers have assigned for prevention of these health outcomes, particularly fatalities. Product liability awards for fatalities average roughly one-tenth of the

---

28. See Moore and Viscusi, "Have Increases in Workers' Compensation Benefits Paid for Themselves?"

Table 6-5. *Distribution of Liability Awards by Severity of Bodily Injury, 1977*

Severity of injury	Percentage of parties with payment	Average payment (1985 dollars)[a]	Percentage of total payments
Death	3.6	219,237	18.8
Permanent total disability	3.0	421,374	29.9
Permanent partial disability	2.3	259,443	14.2
Temporary total disability	23.0	27,316	15.0
No disability	68.2	13,626	22.2
Full sample	100.0	41,894	100.0
Unknown	...	69,836	...

Source: Insurance Services Office, *Product Liability Closed Claim Survey: A Technical Analysis of Survey Results* (New York, 1977), p. 113.

a. The 1977 average payment figures were updated to 1985 values using the CPI.

value of life reflected in the wage-risk trade-offs summarized in table 6-1 and as a result provide too little incentive for safety. Moreover, the safety incentives that are created are dampened by employers' insurance arrangements. Workers' compensation rates for employers who do not self-insure are often governed by industry average risks, so that a firm's specific performance is, at best, only partly reflected in the rates. Similarly, many employers insure against adverse product liability judgments, thus reducing the incentive. The possibility of multiple benefit recoveries encourages safety precautions, but it does so less efficiently than could be achieved through direct OSHA regulation.

A related aspect of workers' compensation and product liability awards is that subrogation and indemnification rules permit the party reimbursing a victim for accident losses to sue a third party to recover his losses. Consider, for example, a worker who is injured while driving a defective forklift and obtains a workers' compensation award. A subrogated fund acquires the employee's right to sue the manufacturer for losses imposed by the defective product. While this legal remedy is feasible, the cost of litigating such a claim reduces its usefulness except when the potential award is very large.

Civil litigation also interacts with government safety regulations. Under current products liability law, the plaintiff can cite a violation of an OSHA safety standard as evidence of failure to adhere to the proper strict liability or negligence standards, thus greatly enhancing the chance of a successful suit.[29] Some observers have suggested that compliance with OSHA and Consumer Product Safety Commission regulations

29. Keeton, *Prosser and Keeton on the Law of Torts,* pp. 220–33.

might be used as a defense in such cases. But compliance may not be sufficient because these regulations are not comprehensive. In some instances there may be no regulation at all addressing a particular hazard; in others the regulation may not be sufficiently specific. For example, OSHA's hazard communication regulation requires that hazardous chemicals used by manufacturing workers be labeled, but it does not specify the label content or format. A products warnings case would explore intensively the adequacy of the label of a specific product.

Nevertheless, it may be sensible to rely on compliance with government regulations as a defense when the relevant regulation constitutes a highly specific design standard. The OSHA standard for ladders, for example, imposes meticulous design constraints.[30] If these standards limit the manufacturer's discretion to such an extent that it cannot greatly alter the product's safety-related attributes, then regulatory compliance takes on added significance.

The chief mechanisms that must establish effective incentives for safety are market forces and government regulation. If these institutions do not establish such incentives, then one cannot rely upon the compensation-oriented institutional approaches to do so.

The joint influence of workers' compensation and tort liability may be nil if a successful claim cannot be filed. If claimants succeed with respect to other remedies, there will be potential overcompensation of victims, leading to dual recovery and inadequate incentives to work safely. This seemingly paradoxical combination of possible overinsurance and inadequate prevention stems from the fact that health risks involve nontransferable, nonmonetary outcomes. The optimal level of insurance compensation for a fatality may be an amount such as $300,000, depending on the victim's age and family composition, but the appropriate value of life from the standpoint of prevention may be an order of magnitude larger. This divergence between the values for prevention and compensation highlights the need for relying on more than a single institution to meet multiple objectives.

Liability Criteria

Over the past decade third-party lawsuits to obtain compensation for job-related diseases have become increasingly prominent. The asbestos lawsuits and the Agent Orange lawsuits filed by Vietnam veterans are

30. 29 CFR 1910.25.

key examples. Yet many of the limitations of the workers' compensation system also plague products liability litigation, even under the strict liability doctrine increasingly used to resolve such disputes.

To make a successful case under strict liability, one must show that the product was defective, that the defect caused the injury, and that the defendant was responsible.[31] Defendants can defeat such claims by showing that at least one of these conditions has not been met. It is instructive to explore each of these criteria in turn, particularly with respect to the difficulties posed in disease cases.

PROVING A DEFECT. The principal test for whether a product is defective is whether the activity involving its use is "abnormally dangerous."[32] The American Law Institute suggests that this standard will be met where the risk is large, severe, and arises from some inappropriate aspect of the activity. Although disease victims are required to exercise "reasonable care," and therefore defendants' liability is not absolute, contributory negligence is not generally a successful defense in cases involving on-the-job exposures.[33]

PROVING CAUSATION. The plaintiff must also demonstrate that the product defect caused the injury. In situations involving diseases such as cancer there are typically multiple causes that cannot be readily distinguished. Indeed, the prominence of asbestos-related lawsuits was certainly due in large part to the clear scientific evidence linking exposure to asbestos with mesothelioma and asbestosis. In many other situations, however, the evidence is far less clear; the long gestation for many diseases makes the process of inferring causal linkages especially difficult.

These lags have additional implications for applying statutes of limitations. The time limits vary, but they typically run from one to six years after the date of injury or exposure in negligence and strict liability lawsuits and from three to twenty years from the date of sale in warranty cases.[34] In states where the time period begins at the date of exposure to the hazard, these limits undermine many attempts to secure compensation.

Courts and legislatures in more than forty states have responded to this problem by ruling that the statute of limitations does not begin to run until the injury has been discovered. In thirteen of these states, the

31. *Injuries and Damages from Hazardous Wastes—Analysis and Improvement of Legal Remedies,* Committee Print, 97 Cong. 2 sess. (GPO, 1982), p. 44.
32. American Law Institute, *Restatement (Second) of Torts,* 520.
33. Government Research Corp., *Victim Compensation,* p. 45.
34. "Note: Compensating Victims," p. 920.

time begins after the individual has ascertained or could reasonably have ascertained the causal connection between the job and the illness.[35] Such provisions reduce the formal legal barriers that must be hurdled before a plaintiff can win a case, but they do not eliminate the more general problem of establishing the link between a particular exposure and the disease.

PROVING THE DEFENDANT'S RESPONSIBILITY. Plaintiffs must show that defendants are responsible for the risk. In practice plaintiffs must show that they were exposed in some way to the product of a specific manufacturer that carried the risk. Because of the long time lags involved in many occupational disease cases, plaintiffs may have great difficulty in meeting this test, especially in linking a particular producer with the risk. A worker who used asbestos in manufacturing fireplaces, for example, might not know the identity of the supplier.

Some courts have resolved the identification problem by finding that all producers of a particular substance should be held liable.[36] But this resolution raises still other problems: how should liability be allocated? One practical procedure is to assess liability on the basis of market share.[37]

In some cases the costs are borne by insurance companies as well as producers, but this not only increases the number of parties involved, it also complicates the informational requirements, since courts must ascertain which insurer should be held liable and in what amount. In many cases insurance has been sold off to excess carriers or reinsurance companies, introducing additional parties. And the courts' task may be further complicated if such coverage has been written decades ago.

Producers can still avoid liability, however, if they can establish that plaintiffs assumed the risk of injury, that they were aware of the risk and incurred it voluntarily. Much of the impetus for the voluntarily adopted chemical labeling efforts has come from a desire to inform users of the chemical of the risks they face, thus reducing the prospects that producers will be held liable for workers' injuries.

OTHER COMPLICATING FACTORS. Even if the victims must be able to make a case for compensation, they may not be able to collect. The party found responsible may not have sufficient funds to pay all the claims. Or the firm may have closed—indeed, over several decades firms

35. *Injuries and Damages from Hazardous Wastes,* pp. 43–44.

36. *Sindell* v. *Abbott Laboratories,* 26 Cal. 3d 588 (1980), 163 Cal. Rptr. 132, 607 P.2d 924, *cert. den.,* 449 U.S. 912, 101 S.Ct. 286, 66 L. Ed. 2d 140.

37. *Injuries and Damages from Hazardous Wastes,* pp. 61–62.

face a reasonably high probability of closure. But even if the firm remains in business, a surge in the number of lawsuits may threaten its financial viability. Many risks, such as those posed by asbestos or a nuclear power plant catastrophe, will affect a large number of people simultaneously. In the absence of legally mandated caps on awards or unusual insurance protection, resources will be insufficient to meet all valid compensation claims. Claims involving diseases may well be in the billions of dollars—possibly over $38 billion for asbestos alone.[38] Very large levels of payoffs might threaten the viability of the insurance industry and would even have a sizable fiscal impact if the government were the insurer. Opportunities for reorganization under bankruptcy laws enhance the possibility that there will be a limit on the potential liability lower than the total value of legitimate compensation claims.

Despite these shortcomings, products liability provides an important source of compensation for job-related diseases. Almost one-third of all products liability claims are for industrial accidents.[39] But only 11 percent of those who received payment in products liability claims for bodily injury received it for job-related causes.[40] These claims were, however, for much larger amounts than the typical bodily injury award. Roughly 42 percent of total payments were for accidents caused by industrial hazards, and the average payment was $98,000 (in 1976 dollars).

Much of the average award, however, goes toward legal fees, expert witnesses, and court costs. Overall, only 37.5 cents of every product liability insurance premium dollar goes to claimants.[41] In part, this reflects traditional insurance company administration and overhead, which reduces the amount of the total premium that is paid out to resolve claims. The victims' share of the actual award devoted to legal and other expenses is much greater. In one small sample of asbestos settlements, which differs from the aggregative sample for all injuries cited above, 41 percent of all compensation was used to pay legal fees and other litigation expenses.[42] The average performance of the products liability compensation system may be much better. Indeed, the

38. Paul MacAvoy, "The Economic Consequences of Asbestos-Related Disease," working paper 27 (Yale School of Organization and Management, 1982), p. 4.

39. "Note: Compensating Victims," p. 918.

40. Insurance Services Office, *Product Liability Closed Claims Survey: A Technical Analysis of Survey Results* (New York, 1977), p. 60.

41. "Note: Compensating Victims," p. 928.

42. James S. Kakalik and others, *Costs of Asbestos Litigation* (Rand Corporation, Institute for Civil Justice, 1983), p. v.

litigation cost per case should decrease as the legal precedents in these cases become clear-cut and the outcomes more predictable. As a result, legal costs should constitute a decreasing share of total products liability awards.

Asbestos Claims

As just noted, firms may not have the resources to pay all valid products liability claims, especially as liability doctrines result in greater awards. The asbestos claims provide the most dramatic and best documented illustration of this problem.

Exposure to asbestos poses several risks. It may lead to asbestosis, which involves scarring of the lungs and pulmonary insufficiency that may be fatal. This is a chronic, noncancerous disease. Asbestos may also lead to lung cancer, which is the cause of death for one-fifth of all asbestos workers. This risk may interact with cigarette smoking, which is believed to increase the incremental asbestos mortality rate (relative to nonsmoking workers not exposed to asbestos) by ten times. Asbestos is also the principal cause of mesothelioma, a cancer that affects the lining of the lung or abdominal wall. Finally, a number of other types of cancer (for example, gastrointestinal cancer) have also been linked to asbestos, but no dose-response relationship has been estimated. As in the case of lung cancer, there are other possible causes of these diseases so that it is often difficult to infer the contributory role of asbestos exposures.[43]

Even in situations of multiple causality, the extremely potent carcinogenicity of asbestos makes it a strong candidate for causing the disease. A nonsmoking asbestos worker, for example, faces five times the mortality rate from lung cancer as workers who do not smoke and who are not exposed to asbestos, and faces roughly half the risk of a cigarette smoker.[44] If, however, a worker smokes cigarettes and is exposed to asbestos, his mortality rate from lung cancer is fifty times that of a nonsmoker who does not work with asbestos. The net effect of such powerful risks is that asbestos may account for up to one-half of all cases of occupational cancer.

These potent hazards in turn have given rise to a rapid increase in

43. For medical information, see Irving J. Selikoff, *Disability Compensation for Asbestos-Associated Disease in the United States* (Springfield, Va.: National Technical Information Service, 1981), pp. 19–29.
44. Ibid., pp. 332–35.

asbestos-related lawsuits that began in 1973 with the application of strict liability principles in products liability lawsuits. One leading as-bestos producer, the Manville Corporation, had 16,500 suits pending against it in 1982, with an estimated potential cost of $660 million.[45] Over 100,000 additional suits against Manville are anticipated by 1992.

The settlements in asbestos-related cases averaged $72,000 from 1967 to 1976, of which an average of $28,500 was spent to cover legal fees.[46] The total price tag to the industry of the settlements and litigation expenses up to 1982 has been estimated to be $1 billion. One-third of this amount has been borne by asbestos producers and two-thirds has come from insurance firms.[47]

As significant as these amounts may seem, the primary costs imposed by asbestos-related diseases will appear in lawsuits that have yet to be resolved or settled. The best estimate of the financial liability of the asbestos industry, based on compensation payments made to claimants thus far, is $38.2 billion.[48] The range of estimates is $7.6 billion to $87.1 billion, a disparity caused by the possibly substantial variation in several key parameters—the incidence of the disease, the average settle-ment, and the rate of growth in claims.

To put the asbestos costs in perspective, it is instructive to compare them with the potential resources available for compensating victims. The combined net worth as of 1982 of the fifty-one insurance companies involved in asbestos claims was $11.5 billion. The net worth of the asbestos industry was $15.6 billion, but the pertinent amount will be less than this figure to the extent that firms create asbestos-related subsidiaries, as has Manville, giving it protection from some claims under Chapter 11 of the federal bankruptcy laws.[49]

In short, the financial resources available to pay asbestos claimants are not likely to be sufficient to cover the cost. Even the combined net worth of the asbestos industry and all insurance companies that have paid asbestos claims will not suffice.

For this and other reasons, alternative approaches involving govern-ment action have been suggested. These include shifting the burden of the claims to the federal government, establishing a more modest com-pensation system, and setting up a pool of funds to pay future claimants.

45. Government Research Corp., *Victim Compensation,* pp. 12–13.
46. Selikoff, *Disability Compensation,* p. 11.
47. Kakalik, *Costs of Asbestos Litigation,* p.v.
48. MacAvoy, "Economic Consequences of Asbestos-Related Disease," p. 66.
49. Ibid., pp. 77–78.

Toxic Tort Compensation Schemes

The genesis of the recent compensation proposals for victims of occupational disease can be traced to insurance arrangements mandated for hazardous wastes, as well as to the longer-term role of workers' compensation in supporting victims of job accidents. Under the Resource Conservation and Recovery Act, the owner of a landfill or hazardous waste site must maintain insurance coverage for liability up to $6 million, excluding legal fees.[50] The Comprehensive Environmental Response, Compensation and Liability Act imposes similar requirements on vessels that transport hazardous substances: they must have insurance coverage up to the maximum of either $300 per gross ton of hazardous waste carried or $5 million.[51] The Superfund Study Group has proposed changes in mechanisms of compensation that would alter the legal structure to make compensation for exposure to hazardous waste more like the workers' compensation system.[52]

Occupational Disease Compensation

The concept of targeting a compensation program on victims of occupational disease is not new. Since its establishment in 1969 the black lung program has provided income support to coal mine workers disabled by the disease.[53] This program differs from workers' compensation in that the eligibility criteria are generous. A worker was initially presumed to be totally disabled from black lung disease if he had worked in a coal mine for at least ten years and had medical evidence of complicated pneumoconiosis. The program was later expanded to include respiratory and pulmonary impairment (plus fifteen years of coal mining employment). Benefits took the form of an annuity that was not tied to worker wages. The associated costs mushroomed from $150 million in 1970 to more than $1 billion by the late 1970s, in large part because of the increased number of claims. This unexpectedly rapid growth should provide a cautionary signal for all those who project costs for any disease compensation program. The estimates should be sufficiently large to include unexpected growth in claims.

In 1977 the financing of the black lung effort from general revenues

50. 29 CFR 264.147(b), as revised in 47 *Federal Register* 16555 (April 16, 1982).
51. 42 U.S.C. 9608(a)(1) (1982).
52. *Injuries and Damages from Hazardous Wastes*, pp. 196–271.
53. U.S. Department of Labor, *Interim Report*, pp. 85–91.

was abandoned and a tax on coal production instituted (50 cents a ton for underground mines and 25 cents a ton for surface mines). Because this tax is not explicitly linked either to workplace conditions or to incidence of the disease, it creates no explicit incentives for particular mine operators to operate more safely. However, the tax will reduce coal output.

The basic outlines of the black lung program were found in the most prominent asbestos compensation policy proposed thus far—the Occupational Disease Compensation Act of 1983 (H.R. 3175). Often referred to as the Miller bill for its sponsor, Democratic Congressman George Miller of California, this act would have set up a program resembling workers' compensation; the benefits would have served as workers' exclusive remedy for asbestos-related exposures. Potential compensation would have been capped, but workers would have gained greater certainty of receiving compensation. Cases of mesothelioma would have been presumed to be asbestos-related. Lung cancer would have been covered by a similar presumption, provided that it occurred within ten years of the first job exposure. Funding would have been provided by a tax on employers linked primarily to relative market share rather than benefits awarded.

Although cost estimates are not available for this act, they are available for its antecedent, H.R. 5735.[54] Based on an intermediate-risk assumption, total compensation costs for occupational diseases related to asbestos exposure will be $28 billion (using a 2 percent real interest rate). If, however, all non-job-related cases of lung cancer for asbestos workers are compensated, as the act would ensure, the cost would reach $98 billion.

These statistics highlight the major danger of disease compensation programs. The inherent difficulty of distinguishing job-related from other illnesses will boost costs well beyond what can be reasonably afforded— in this case more than tripling the burden.

It is instructive to compare these estimates with likely court-ordered compensation costs estimated by MacAvoy (also based on a 2 percent discount rate).[55] If only lung cancers caused by job-related asbestos

---

54. Cost discussions are based on the findings in Frederick B. Siskind, "Cost Impact of the 1982 Miller Proposal (H.5735) for Compensating Accident Victims," Office of the Assistant Secretary for Policy, U.S. Department of Labor (November 1982). The principal change in the more recent version was that, instead of continuing indefinitely, benefits to widows compensated for only five years of income.

55. MacAvoy, "Economic Consequences of Asbestos-Related Disease."

exposures were compensated, the costs of the compensation bill evaluated at a comparable basis would be $10 billion less than court-ordered compensation. But if, as seems likely, almost all lung cancers among asbestos workers would receive compensation, the cost would triple to an amount well in excess of the estimated costs imposed by prospective products liability lawsuits. As a result, it would not be in the financial self-interest for asbestos producers and affected insurance companies to have such legislation supersede the present mechanisms for settling claims.

In fact, the financial burdens imposed by the proposed asbestos compensation legislation could not be borne by the asbestos industry. Some firms would shut down. Others would reorganize, and their asbestos-producing units would file for bankruptcy. To the extent that compensation burdens would be shifted to other firms in the industry, their financial viability would also be threatened. In short, the asbestos compensation proposal does not appear to be economically viable.

Even if the burden could be borne, the primary mechanism for funding would be an output-related tax. This tax would reduce the output of affected firms but would provide no incentive for risk reduction for diseases likely to be compensated in the next two decades, since these are the product of past decisions. Diseases that would have to be compensated beyond that point might create incentives for safety to the extent that the funding mechanism is linked to current job conditions.

Because of the difficulty of making any precise linkage of this type, one alternative would be to place a tax on current asbestos exposure levels. Such an externality tax could lead to an efficient level of risk and hence could supplant direct regulatory controls. Any additional costs needed to fund benefits for diseases already caused would be drawn from general revenues.

This approach, however, would address only a small segment of the occupational disease problem—new asbestos-related diseases. It would ignore the chief problem posed today by decades of asbestos exposure: paying for future claims arising from asbestos-related diseases already in gestation.

An Affirmative Policy Proposal

Gaps in information make it difficult to design an effective policy to address the problem of occupational disease. For diseases that have been already caused, no compensatory or regulatory system can alter safety incentives retroactively. The most that can be done is to provide efficient levels of insurance. There is no compelling rationale for policy involvement beyond existing social insurance efforts, since victims of occupational disease are no more deserving than victims of environmental exposures or risks of undetermined origin. To the extent that workers can prove a job link in a product liability suit or workers' compensation claim, there is at least some promotion of equity by making the companies involved pay the costs.

For the diseases not yet caused, the emphasis should be on regulatory measures, since these are targeted most directly at the risks. Workers' compensation and the civil liability system have a role to play in complementing this safety incentive and in providing adequate levels of compensation.[56]

Conclusion

The long-run functioning of the market for potentially hazardous jobs will continue to be governed by multiple institutions. Chief among these is the role of free market forces as worker preferences generate a powerful incentive to provide adequate job safety. The principal mechanisms to bolster market forces are government regulations to promote control of risk and workers' compensation to address income and medical insurance needs. The responsibilities of these institutions are so extensive that the civil liability system will be much less important with respect to job accidents and illnesses than for any other class of accidents. Indeed, the system's only current function is for third-party lawsuits.

This secondary function is, however, not inconsequential. For job-related diseases civil liability remedies have become increasingly prominent. The functioning of the legal system with respect to mass toxic torts is not entirely uncontroversial, but many of the problems that have been encountered are inherent to the problem area.

56. For a fuller discussion of policy remedies for occupational disease, see W. Kip Viscusi, "Structuring an Effective Occupational Disease Policy: Victim Compensation and Risk Regulation," *Yale Journal of Regulation,* vol. 2, no. 1 (1984), pp. 53–81.

CHAPTER SEVEN

Products Liability Law
and the Accident Rate

George L. Priest

W ITHIN the past three decades, products liability law has been transformed from a minor subfield of commercial law and negligence litigation to an exceptionally rich and diverse set of doctrines that constitutes perhaps the most prominent feature of modern civil jurisprudence. There is little need today to plead the importance of products liability law. No one conscious of the dwindling budget and meager accomplishments of the Consumer Product Safety Commission can pretend that the United States makes a serious effort to regulate product quality directly. Instead, our society relies on liability actions to police the manufacturing process. The prospect of liability judgments affects design and production decisions of all manufacturers, foreign and domestic, that sell to U.S. consumers.[1] And increasing numbers of corporate bankruptcies and reorganizations stem from such judgments. As recently as a decade ago, insurance for products liability was subsumed in general commercial liability coverage, of insufficient importance for separate categorization. Today it is a growing component of commercial underwriting—indeed growing at such a rate that foreign and domestic reinsurers have recently been frightened into withdrawing further coverage.

Along with medical malpractice law, products liability law is widely viewed as the most egregious source of modern legal uncertainty. Within the past two years, efforts to reduce these uncertainties and, more generally, the extent of liability have generated extraordinarily vituperative legislative battles among manufacturers, insurers, consumers, and trial

---

1. A recent study reported that 25 percent of the nation's 500 largest corporations had withdrawn products from the market because of liability or liability insurance problems. Nathan Weber, *Product Liability: The Corporate Response* (New York: Conference Board, 1987), pp. 4–7.

lawyers seeking to change the law or to preserve it. Some forty states have enacted tort reform legislation, and twenty of them, important tort reform legislation.[2]

Yet despite the tremendous controversy over modern products liability law, its goals have been uncontroversial. Virtually all courts and commentators have embraced the goals of accident reduction and insurance that correspond to the principal economic effects of the law. There are only two important economic effects of any legal rule: a rule can provide incentives to reduce the accident rate and, for accidents that cannot be prevented, a legal rule can provide a form of victim compensation insurance tied to product sales.[3] Although there are occasional references to fairness and equity, courts in products cases have largely focused on these two economic goals alone in their elaboration of the law.[4]

The current controversy instead stems from disagreement over whether the expansion of products liability law successfully achieves these objectives of deterrence and providing compensation insurance. Until recently, the debate has not been well focused on the goals the courts are striving to achieve. Critics of the law, including product manufacturers, have condemned the extent to which the law has disrupted their activities, but they have not shown that increased manufacturing costs and insurance premiums are inappropriate results of a demand for safer products. Consumer advocates have championed the higher levels of compensation awarded to injured consumers, but they have not shown that higher compensation is essential for obtaining safer products or that the compensation provided by litigation offers insurance that would not otherwise be available. A separate group of academic analysts, led by prominent law and economics scholars, has argued that modern products liability law promotes accident reduction efficiently, but the scholars have supported the claim only with models and have provided no empirical confirmation of any sort.

In recent years, however, many commentators have come to appreciate the need for more careful analytic focus on the insurance and accident reduction goals of the law. There has long been widespread skepticism

2. For a summary, see Michael Bird and Brenda Trolin, *Selected State Legislative Action Re: Affordability and Availability of Liability Insurance* (Washington, D.C.: National Conference of State Legislatures, 1986).

3. See George L. Priest, "Internalizing Costs," unpublished manuscript (Yale Law School, 1987).

4. For a discussion of the development of this judicial approach toward products liability law, see George L. Priest, "The Invention of Enterprise Liability: A Critical History of the Intellectual Foundations of Modern Tort Law," *Journal of Legal Studies,* vol. 14 (December 1985), pp. 461–527.

concerning the ability of a civil legal regime to provide effective compensation insurance because it was thought that the insurance provided by the law would never be sufficiently comprehensive.[5] The new criticism of the law's insurance function, however, argues that civil law should never attempt to provide insurance because of adverse effects on consumers. First it was demonstrated that the compensation insurance provided through contract law remedies was excessive.[6] The analysis was extended to tort law and to the problem of catastrophic injuries in particular.[7] Recently, it has been shown that the insurance provided in products liability law was inferior to what might be allocated by contract.[8] And more recently still, it has been demonstrated both that the expansion of liability on insurance grounds reduces insurance availability and that it harms most seriously poor and low-income consumers, exactly those that courts had hoped to help by the expansion of liability.[9] This work shows that the attempt to provide insurance through the law is largely responsible for the recent insurance crisis and that insurance availability could be increased and poor and low-income consumers benefited if the insurance component of modern law were excised completely. Chapter 2 of this volume demonstrates these effects analytically.

This chapter represents an attempt to evaluate the other of the two goals of modern products liability law: the effect of the law on product safety. The first discusses the implications of data concerning trends in products liability claims and judgments and in product-related accidents. The second part approaches the question analytically. It describes the current understanding of the effects of the standard of strict products liability dominant in modern law and economics scholarship, and it performs an empirical test of the efficient accident reduction characteristics of the law, suggesting that much of the modern economic approach is simplistic and misdescriptive of the law. The third part looks carefully at the most basic doctrines of modern products liability law affecting product manufacture, design, and warning. It attempts to show why, in their

5. Guido Calabresi, *The Costs of Accidents: A Legal and Economic Analysis* (Yale University Press, 1970).

6. Samuel A. Rea, Jr., "Nonpecuniary Loss and Breach of Contract," *Journal of Legal Studies,* vol. 11 (January 1982), pp. 35–53.

7. Patricia M. Danzon, "Tort Reform and the Role of Government in Private Insurance Markets," *Journal of Legal Studies,* vol. 13 (August 1984), pp. 517–49.

8. Richard A. Epstein, "Products Liability as an Insurance Market," *Journal of Legal Studies,* vol. 14 (December 1985), pp. 645–69.

9. George L. Priest, "The Current Insurance Crisis and Modern Tort Law, *Yale Law Journal,* vol. 96 (June 1987), pp. 1521–90.

Table 7-1. *Federal Products Liability Cases Filed, 1974–86*

Year	Cases filed	Percent change from previous year
1974	1,579	...
1975	2,886	83
1976	3,696	28
1977	4,077	10
1978	4,372	7
1979	6,132	40
1980	7,755	26
1981	9,071	17
1982	8,944	−1
1983	9,221	3
1984	10,745	17
1985	13,554	26
1986	13,595	0.3

Sources: *Annual Report of the Director of the Administrative Office of the United States Courts,* various issues.

current formulation, these doctrines depart substantially from rules that would more adequately control the accident rate. There is little dispute that the accident rate can be most effectively controlled by application of very rigorous cost-benefit analysis of product design issues. This part also attempts to set forth how modern products liability doctrines could be redrafted to better achieve the accident reduction goal.

Trends in Products Liability Litigation and in Accident Rates and Their (Questionable) Implications for Evaluation of the Law

Much of the severe disagreement over the ultimate effects of the expansion of modern products liability stems from differing interpretations of changes in the volume of products liability litigation. Table 7-1 shows that products liability filings in federal courts have increased from 1,579 in 1974 to 13,595 in 1986.[10] It is this 861 percent growth in twelve years that suggests the great increase in the effect of products liability law on manufacturing operations. Annual filing rates increased substantially in 1975

10. For a fuller discussion of these statistics, see U.S. Department of Justice, *Report of the Tort Policy Working Group on the Causes, Extent and Policy Implications of the Current Crisis in Insurance Availability and Affordability* (Washington, D.C., 1986). See also Priest, "Current Insurance Crisis," pp. 1532–34.

Table 7-2. *Products Liability Trials and Verdicts, Cook County, Illinois, and San Francisco, 1960–84*
Awards in thousands of 1984 dollars

Trials	1960–64	1965–69	1970–74	1975–79	1980–84
Number of jury trials					
Cook County	73	140	219	212	177
San Francisco	54	88	127	101	49
Percent of total trials					
Cook County	2	3	5	7	5
San Francisco	4	5	8	8	6
Mean award					
Cook County	265	287	578	597	828
San Francisco	99	194	145	308	1,105
Median award					
Cook County	103	118	178	196	187
San Francisco	27	72	51	81	200
90th percentile award					
Cook County	710	532	727	1,132	n.a.
San Francisco	429	n.a.	n.a.	817	n.a.
Percent of total trial awards					
Cook County	6.4	11.0	22.0	23.7	10.0[a]
San Francisco	6.0	12.0	8.0	14.0	16.4[a]

Sources: For number of trials, percent of total, and mean and median awards, author's calculations based on Mark A. Peterson, *Civil Juries in the 1980s: Trends in Jury Trials and Verdicts in California and Cook County, Illinois,* R-3466-ICJ (Santa Monica: Rand Corp., 1987). For 90th percentile awards and percent of total trial awards, author's calculations based on Mark A. Peterson and George L. Priest, *The Civil Jury: Trends in Trials and Verdicts, Cook County, Illinois, 1960–1979,* R-2881-ICJ (Rand Corp., 1982); and Michael G. Shanley and Mark A. Peterson, *Comparative Justice: Civil Jury Verdicts in San Francisco and Cook Counties, 1959–1980,* R-3006-ICJ (Rand Corp., 1983). The figures reported in Peterson do not correspond to those reported in Peterson and Priest or Shanley and Peterson for unspecified reasons.
n.a. Not available.
a. Derived by author from Peterson, *Civil Juries in the 1980s,* table 4.6.

and 1976, again in 1979 and 1980, and in 1985. Curiously, the volume of filings remained virtually constant between 1985 and 1986.

Table 7-2 shows changes in products liability jury trials and judgments since 1960 in Cook County, Illinois, and San Francisco.[11] The absolute number of jury trials and the proportion of products liability trials in civil litigation increased rapidly in both jurisdictions from 1970 to 1974 but have been declining since. Regardless of number, the mean plaintiff judg-

11. For fuller discussions of these data, see Mark A. Peterson and George L. Priest, *The Civil Jury: Trends in Trials and Verdicts, Cook County, Illinois, 1960–1979,* R-2881-ICJ (Santa Monica: Rand Corp., 1982); Michael G. Shanley and Mark A. Peterson, *Comparative Justice: Civil Jury Verdicts in San Francisco and Cook Counties, 1959–1980,* R-3006-ICJ (Rand Corp., 1983); and Mark A. Peterson, *Civil Juries in the 1980s: Trends in Jury Trials and Verdicts in California and Cook County, Illinois,* R-3466-ICJ (Rand Corp., 1987).

ment in these trials has skyrocketed, with extraordinary increases in Cook County in 1970–74 and 1980–84 and in San Francisco in 1975–79 and 1980–84. Judgments in the largest cases have been the primary influence on the increase in the average award. As a percentage of total trial judgment dollars awarded, products liability awards expanded in Cook County and San Francisco, respectively, from a relatively insignificant 6.4 percent and 6 percent of judgment dollars in 1960–64 to nearly 24 percent and 14 percent of judgment dollars in 1975–79. From 1980 to 1984, however, this proportion dropped substantially in Cook County (to 10 percent), although it increased in San Francisco (to more than 16 percent).

It might be thought at first glance that the data concerning litigation trends for the past decade are contradictory, since they show large increases in filings and trial judgments yet decreases in the number and proportion of products liability trials and in the proportion of trial awards. All trial statistics, however, must be interpreted with the influence of litigants' settlement decisions in mind.[12] Only 4 to 5 percent of all claims are ultimately litigated to trial; thus 95 to 96 percent are settled without entering public records. Indeed, products liability defendants have strong incentives to settle suits because adverse judgments will affect manufacturing operations beyond the award's dollar amount.[13]

Increases in the average judgment and, presumably, in the likelihood of a plaintiff's success because of the expansion of manufacturer liability may very well lead to an increase in suits filed. Defendants, however, are likely to have greater interests in settling these suits to avoid the larger impact of adverse judgments. Indeed, as the implications of adverse judgments become broader and more far-reaching, manufacturers' incentives to settle increase. Thus the decline in the number and proportion of trials and trial dollars, coupled with an increase in filings and in average awards, may well reflect a substantial rise in the rate of products liability settlements.

Tables 7-3 through 7-6 show trends in product-related accidents. The relationship between these accident data and the litigation data of the preceding tables is complex. If the expansion of products liability has had an important impact on product safety, we should observe a decrease in the injury rate in the years after the expansion.

---

12. See, generally, George L. Priest and Benjamin Klein, "The Selection of Disputes for Litigation," *Journal of Legal Studies*, vol. 13 (January 1984), pp. 1–55.

13. For a model and both simulation and direct empirical support for this approach, see ibid.

Table 7-3. *Deaths per 100,000 Resident Population, by Accident Type, Selected Years, 1950–80*

Accident type	1950[a]	1955[a]	1960	1965	1970	1975	1980
Possibly product related							
Motor vehicle	23.1	23.4	21.3	25.4	26.9	21.3	23.5
Railway	1.4	0.8	0.6	0.5	0.4	0.3	0.3
Fires and flames	4.3	3.9	4.3	3.8	3.3	2.8	2.6
Firearms	1.4	1.3	1.3	1.2	1.2	1.1	0.9
Explosive material	n.a.	n.a.	n.a.	n.a.	0.3	0.2	0.1
Hot substances, corrosive liquids	0.6	0.5	0.2	0.2	0.1	0.1	0.1
Poisoning by drugs and medicines	n.a.	n.a.	n.a.	n.a.	1.2	1.5	1.1
Poisoning by other substances	1.1	0.9	0.9	1.1	0.6	0.7	0.3
Poisoning by gases	1.2	0.7	0.7	0.8	0.8	0.7	0.5
Medical procedures	0.4	0.5	0.6	0.8	1.8	1.5	1.1
Nonproduct related							
Accidental falls	13.8	12.3	10.6	10.3	8.3	6.9	5.9
Accidental drowning	3.2	3.1	2.9	2.8	3.1	3.1	2.7
All other accidents	10.1	9.5	8.9	8.8	8.4	7.6	7.6
Total	60.6	56.9	52.3	55.7	56.4	47.8	46.7

Source: U.S. Bureau of the Census, *Statistical Abstract of the United States*, various issues.
n.a. Not available.
a. Excludes Alaska and Hawaii.

As table 7-2 shows, the greatest growth in products liability trials occurred between 1965 and 1974. If this litigation were stimulated by an increase in the injury rate, one should observe the increase between 1962 and 1970, given the typical three- to five-year delay between accident and trial. Trial volume declined after 1974. If the decline reflected an increase in product safety rather than in settlement behavior, the product-related injury rate should have dropped after 1970. Indeed, given the substantial increase in median awards after 1969, the injury rate should have dropped rapidly after 1970 if the decline in trial volume reflects an increase in product safety.

Tables 7-3 through 7-5 report accidental death and injury rates in the United States, of which, of course, deaths or injuries that are the consequence of products constitute only some proportion. Table 7-3 presents accidental death rates by the context of the accident. Death rates in almost all accident categories have been declining steadily but not sharply since 1950. There is little evidence of a sharp decrease in accident rates after 1970 that might be attributed to the deterrent effect of products liability law. The substantial decline in the death rate between 1970 and 1975 in the motor vehicle category can be more confidently attributed to the increase in gasoline prices and adoption of the

Table 7-4. *Worker Job Deaths per 100,000 Workers and Total Disabilities, Selected Years, 1945–83*

Year	Deaths	Disabling injuries (millions)	Year	Deaths	Disabling injuries (millions)
1945	33	2.00	1976	14	2.20
1950	27	1.95	1977	14	2.30
1955	24	1.95	1978	14	2.20
1960	21	1.95	1979	13	2.30
1965	20	2.10	1980	13	2.20
1970	18	2.20	1981	12	2.10
1973	17	2.50	1982	12	1.90
1974	16	2.30	1983	11	1.90
1975	15	2.20			

Source: U.S. Bureau of the Census, *Statistical Abstract of the United States, 1985*, p. 425.

fifty-five mile per hour speed limit than to products liability law.[14] Moreover, the rate of auto deaths rose between 1975 and 1980, a finding inconsistent with any deterrent effect of expanding products liability law. There was also a sharp decline between 1965 and 1970 in the death rate attributed to poisoning by "other substances," but this occurs too early to be the result of products law. Similarly, the decline in this category between 1975 and 1980 is isolated. From these data it is difficult to credit the expansion of products liability with much deterrent effect.

Table 7-4 shows death and disabling injury rates for workers. Again, the data do not indicate the proportion of injuries caused by products, although it is well known that injuries on the job form a very large component of total products liability claims.[15] Worker death rates have declined steadily since 1945, although the rate of decline seems to have slowed after 1960. The rate of disabling injuries has been far more variable, increasing from 1960 through 1973 and remaining roughly constant from 1974 through 1981. Although it declined somewhat in 1982, even in 1982 and 1983 it was only slightly less than the rate in 1950.

14. See Transportation Research Board, *55: A Decade of Experience* (Washington, D.C.: National Academy Press, 1984).

15. According to studies of products liability claims involving large losses, in 1979 workers comprised 59.2 percent of bodily injured claimants and in 1985, 60.1 percent; Alliance of American Insurers, *Highlights of Large-Loss Product Liability Claims* (Schaumberg, Ill., 1980); and Lawrence W. Soular, *A Study of Large Product Liability Claims Closed in 1985* (Schaumberg, Ill.: Alliance of American Insurers and American Insurance Association, 1986), p. 26.

Table 7-5. *Disabling Work Injuries per Million Employee Hours, by Selected Industry, Selected Years, 1950–70*

Industry	1950[a]	1955[a]	1960	1965	1970
Manufacturing					
Food products	18.9	18.6	21.1	23.4	28.8
Textile mill products	11.0	9.7	9.2	9.6	10.4
Lumber and wood products	50.2	40.5	38.0	36.0	34.1
Chemicals	11.1	8.0	7.4	7.5	8.5
Petroleum products	9.3	6.5	6.8	8.6	11.3
Fabricated metal products	19.0	15.4	15.4	18.1	22.4
Machinery (excluding electrical)	13.8	11.1	10.8	11.9	14.0
Coal mining	n.a.	n.a.	42.5	44.7	41.6
Contract construction	41.0	34.5	31.5	28.3	28.0
Transportation and public utilities					
Local rail and bus	n.a.	11.8	14.3	15.8	23.9
Trucking	34.5	28.7	32.3	29.2	35.3
Electric and gas	13.8	8.2	6.2	5.3	6.6
Wholesale and retail trade	12.3	12.6	n.a.	11.8	11.3
State government hospitals	n.a.	n.a.	16.3	21.0	21.4

Sources: U.S. Bureau of the Census, *Statistical Abstract of the United States, 1960*, p. 232, and 1972, p. 239.
n.a. Not available.
a. Excludes Alaska and Hawaii.

Table 7-5 shows work injuries by industry calculated against worker hours rather than against the size of the work force. The results are mixed. The injury rate declined between 1965 and 1970 in only four industries: lumber and wood products, coal mining, contract construction, and wholesale and retail trade. For all others the rate has increased progressively since 1960, although in many it had been decreasing from 1950 to 1960. In the few industries in which there were declines, the declines were modest. There is no evidence in either table 7-4 or table 7-5 of a reduction in the injury rate of a magnitude corresponding with the expansion of products liability.

Finally, table 7-6 shows the annual number of product-related injuries requiring hospital emergency room treatment. These data present the most detailed correlation of injuries according to specific product type, but they show only the absolute number of injuries rather than injury rates adjusted according to the number of products in use, the number of users, or the extent of use. In addition, they are vastly overinclusive for my purposes because they report all injuries related to products, not just those related to product manufacture or design features that are affected by the law. Thus, for example, according to the full reports of the Consumer Product Safety Commission, the nation's most injurious consumer product is stairs (662,000 injuries in 1980), followed by bicycles (526,000), baseball equipment (432,000), and

Table 7-6. *U.S. Product-Related Injuries Requiring Hospital Emergency Room Treatment, Fiscal Years 1974–81*
Thousands

Product	1974	1975	1976	1977	1978	1979	1980	1981[a]
Playground equipment	140	143	158	164	151[b]	165	162[b]	178
Ladders	61	73	81	85	83[b]	98	89[b]	98
Power lawn mowers	56	63	57[b]	61	69	74	63[b]	71
Swimming pools	53	56	69	68[b]	68	89	116	124
Power saws	41	58	59	60	68	71	73	79
Cleaning agents	35	36	40	35[b]	40	38[b]	32[b]	38
Electrical fixtures	25	22[b]	26	28	26[b]	34	32[b]	41
Chain saws	23	27	28	35	48	51	62	64
Space heaters	20	7[c]	8	10	10	16	23	25
Electric power tools	13	13[b]	16	16	14[b]	22	25	28
Tractors	6	7	7	10	9[b]	10	13	13

Sources: *Annual Report of the Consumer Product Safety Commission,* various issues.
a. Calendar year.
b. Indicates reduction from previous year.
c. CPSC begins to differentiate among three heater categories

football equipment (425,000). Even beds generate more injuries a year (168,000) than any of the products reported in table 7-6. I have therefore culled from the complete tables those products for which injuries are most likely to be the consequence of technological design or manufacturing features affected by the expansion of products liability.

Table 7-6 shows that for most products and most years, the number of injuries increased steadily between 1974 and 1981.[16] As is evident, declines are infrequent (sixteen of a possible seventy-seven). If products liability had remained constant over the period, one might expect that the number of injuries would increase as product use increased in a growing economy and would decline as technological advances made products safer (see, in particular, tables 7-3 and 7-4). Given the expansion of products liability litigation over this period and the increase in damages awarded, it is surprising that there is no evidence of a systematic decrease in product-related injuries. Indeed, these data present no evidence of even a slowing in the growth rates of these injuries.

What do these statistics tell us about the effects of the expansion of products liability litigation? Little more than the obvious: that there has been an enormous expansion of products liability. They cannot tell us whether the expansion has been beneficial or harmful.

16. After 1981 the Consumer Product Safety Commission modified its reporting method, presenting statistics much less variegated by product type and deleting reports of many products. See *Annual Report of the U.S. Consumer Product Safety Commission, 1981,* and later years.

The injury and death statistics in tables 7-3 through 7-6 are mysterious. Although they are admittedly crude, they provide no evidence that the expansion of litigation has affected the injury or death rate. This conclusion corresponds to findings of the small number of careful empirical studies of specific products, each of which shows little accident-reduction effect of either expanded products liability litigation or greater direct regulation of product quality.[17]

If this conclusion is accurate, it is disquieting. The expansion of products liability has led to the withdrawal of large numbers of products from consumer markets and large increases generally in product prices.[18] Most commentators presume that products withdrawn from the market are relatively more risky than others and that product prices have been increased in response to greater manufacturer investments in product safety. Both effects, however, should result in sharp reductions in the injury rate, reductions that appear not to have occurred.

The quality of empirical data is so poor, however, that no confident conclusion can be reached about the success of products liability law in establishing incentives for the manufacture of safer products. The law appears to have had no significant effect, but more careful research on the issue is needed. The remainder of this chapter attempts to find other ways to determine whether the law has influenced product safety.

The Economic Argument for Strict Products Liability Evaluated

How Strict Products Liability Is Thought to Generate Optimal Accident Reduction

The central principle of modern products liability law is the strict liability standard adopted for defective products by the *Restatement of Torts (Second)* in 1965 and by the various states shortly thereafter.[19]

17. For example, W. Kip Viscusi, *Regulating Consumer Product Safety* (Washington, D.C.: American Enterprise Institute, 1984); and Sam Peltzman, "The Effects of Automobile Safety Regulation," *Journal of Political Economy,* vol. 83 (August 1975), pp. 677–725.

18. For withdrawals, see Weber, *Product Liability.* For prices, see Priest, "Current Insurance Crisis."

19. See *Restatement (Second) of Torts,* § 402A (1965). For a discussion of the adoption of the section and for the state response to the adoption, see Priest, "Invention of Enterprise Liability," pp. 511–19.

Although many doctrinal details in the products field depart from strict liability, the standard remains the benchmark from which all new doctrinal developments derive. Almost universally when courts are faced with novel products problems requiring new doctrines or new applications of earlier doctrines, they will return to the central distinction between the rejected negligence standard and the now-dominant strict liability standard to infer a solution. This approach has received nearly unanimous scholarly support, and there has been no serious conceptual criticism of the strict liability standard since its original announcement.[20]

The most sophisticated justification of strict products liability is that of law and economics. In its early years law and economics scholars emphasized the efficiency of negligence, especially as the standard was applied in the nineteenth century, and one might have expected some disapproval of modern strict liability.[21] As commitment to the efficiency-of-the-law hypothesis grew, however, greater efforts were made to determine ways in which strict products liability itself could be efficient. In 1970 Guido Calabresi provided important encouragement for expanding manufacturer liability; in more recent work by Steven Shavell and by William Landes and Richard Posner, the law and economics movement has embraced products liability law on the grounds that strict liability creates incentives for optimal accident reduction, as do the other doctrines in the field that essentially adopt an economic cost-benefit approach.[22] Indeed, strict liability is now commonly considered as efficient as negligence in terms of reducing accidents and, in the context of products, superior to the negligence standard on several subsidiary grounds.

Although it could not be claimed that the recent direction of the law is the result of sophisticated economic analysis, the discovery of the

20. But see Richard A. Epstein, *Modern Products Liability Law: A Legal Revolution* (Westport, Conn.: Quorum Books, 1980). Epstein's criticism of strict products liability has been confused by his more general theoretical embrace of the strict liability standard; see "A Theory of Strict Liability," *Journal of Legal Studies*, vol. 2 (January 1973), pp. 151–204. He attempts to clarify his theory in "Products Liability as an Insurance Market," *Journal of Legal Studies*, vol. 14 (December 1985), p. 660.

21. For the efficiency of the negligence standard, see Richard A. Posner, "A Theory of Negligence," *Journal of Legal Studies,* vol. 1 (January 1972), pp. 29–96; for disapproval of strict liability, see Posner, *Economic Analysis of Law* (Little, Brown, 1972).

22. See Calabresi, *Costs of Accidents;* Steven Shavell, "Strict Liability versus Negligence," *Journal of Legal Studies,* vol. 9 (January 1980), pp. 1–25; and William M. Landes and Richard A. Posner, "A Positive Economic Analysis of Products Liability," *Journal of Legal Studies,* vol. 14 (December 1985), pp. 553–66.

seemingly benign economic effects of strict products liability has generated a sense of confidence in the law's current direction.[23] Much of this confidence stems from the fact that courts have embraced the economic goals of accident reduction and insurance in developing the products liability field.

The economic analysis of the effects of liability rules on the accident rate is straightforward.[24] To establish efficient incentives for accident reduction, a legal rule should place liability on the party that could most easily have prevented the accident, as long as the accident was worth preventing. More precisely, liability should be placed on the party for whom marginal prevention costs are lower, again as long as marginal prevention costs are lower than the marginal benefits of prevention. Courts achieve this result in practice by evaluating the accident to compare what the alleged tortfeasor and the victim could have done to have prevented the accident. Since potential parties to accidents will know that they can avoid all liability if they take cost-justified accident prevention precautions, the accident rate will achieve the efficient level. Incentives will be established to prevent every accident that is worth preventing.

According to the analysis, in the products context a negligence standard will achieve efficient accident reduction if manufacturers are held to be negligent, and thus liable for resulting injuries, if they fail to make all cost-justified investments in accident avoidance. This view of negligence compels consumers to bear all losses in those instances in which manufacturers have not acted negligently, a burden that places incentives on consumers themselves to take all cost-justified precautions. Thus in terms of accident prevention, the negligence standard will induce efficient preventive investments by both parties.

The strict liability standard, however, can achieve identical effects. Strict liability is presumed to hold manufacturers liable for product-related injuries unless the consumer is found to be contributorily negligent.[25] The contributory negligence standard will establish incentives for consumers to take cost-justified precautions as long as the rule is defined in terms of relative marginal costs and benefits of consumer prevention.

---

23. But see Epstein, *Modern Products Liability Law*.
24. This analysis was first presented in Posner, *Economic Analysis of Law*. See also John Prather Brown, "Toward an Economic Theory of Liability," *Journal of Legal Studies,* vol. 2 (June 1973), pp. 323–49; and Shavell, "Strict Liability versus Negligence."
25. Ibid. But see chapter 2 in this volume.

If it is, then because manufacturers are required to bear all losses when consumers are not contributorily negligent, manufacturers themselves will take precautions solely to reduce their own costs.

The key to the standard economic approach is that courts adopt cost-benefit definitions of negligence and, under strict liability, of contributory negligence. The accident rate will be as low as it can efficiently be as long as courts carefully review the marginal costs and benefits of manufacturer and consumer prevention. Accidents may still occur because of error or oversight or because some types of accidents are simply not worth preventing. But the accident rate will be as low as it can efficiently be.

Strict liability, according to this analysis, is simply the converse of negligence in terms of residual responsibility for losses that cannot be efficiently prevented. That is, the only difference between negligence and strict liability is responsibility for those losses that occur despite the cost-justified preventive investments of both parties. Under the negligence standard, consumers bear responsibility for these losses, and under strict liability, manufacturers.

In the years since the articulation of this approach, advocates have developed subsidiary accident reduction grounds for preferring the strict liability standard.[26] In a famous article, Guido Calabresi and Jon Hirschoff proposed shifting from a legal rule that requires precise comparison of marginal prevention costs and benefits to a simpler standard based on a determination of which of the parties is in the better position to make the cost-benefit analysis. Thus the proposed rule would have a court or jury place liability on the party best able to make the cost-benefit judgment rather than have the court or jury make the cost-benefit judgment itself. In various examples, Calabresi and Hirschoff suggested that product manufacturers are typically in better positions than consumers to make these calculations, thus justifying a standard of strict manufacturer liability.[27] More recently, Landes and Posner have

26. Of course, there are several grounds for preferring a strict liability standard that are unrelated to accident prevention. One is alleged administrative savings, since the negligent act need not be proved. See Alan Schwartz, "Products Liability Reform: A Theoretical Review," working paper 65 (Yale Law School, Program in Civil Liability, August 1987). A second is the greater level of insurance provided by a strict liability standard. See Priest, "Current Insurance Crisis."

27. Guido Calabresi and Jon T. Hirschoff, "Toward a Test for Strict Liability in Torts," *Yale Law Journal,* vol. 81 (May 1972), pp. 1055–85. For a notable example, see the discussion in which the authors justify manufacturer liability to a passerby injured when a consumer mowing a lawn hits a rock (p. 1064).

defended various applications of the strict liability standard for product defects on similar grounds.[28] This approach, of course, endorses the cost-benefit standard but differs from what I have called the standard economic analysis chiefly in the level of cost-benefit application.

A second ground for preferring a strict liability standard in products cases is to offset consumer misperceptions about product quality.[29] According to this analysis, consumers may underestimate or overestimate product risks and as a consequence purchase products that are either more or less risky that they would prefer if fully informed. These consumer misperceptions, however, will have consequences only under a negligence standard, where consumers bear liability for accidents not worth preventing. Under a strict liability standard these risks will be built into the product price, leading consumers to make efficient product choices.

These grounds for preferring strict liability, however, are highly controversial. First, the approach has very carefully defined limits. The analysis concedes that consumer misperceptions are irrelevant to the basic safety characteristics of products. Products will be designed and manufactured efficiently in terms of accident reduction because, under either negligence or strict liability, manufacturers will bear accident costs if they fail to make all cost-justified investments in product safety. Consumer misperceptions are therefore relevant only with respect to product accidents that are not worth preventing. That is, consumer misperceptions become a policy concern only after courts have completed rigorous cost-benefit judgments of the relative accident prevention abilities of injurer and victim.

Second, adopting strict liability to offset consumer misperceptions will increase consumer welfare unambiguously only when the negligence and strict liability standards are exactly equivalent in terms of their insurance consequences. It is now strongly suspected that the insurance consequences of strict liability are adverse to consumer welfare.[30] The benefits to be achieved by internalizing costs to offset consumer misperceptions may thus be remote.

Finally, there are many reasons to doubt that consumers systemati-

28. Landes and Posner, "Positive Economic Analysis." This approach is discussed later.

29. See Michael Spence, "Consumer Misperceptions, Product Failure and Producer Liability," *Review of Economic Studies,* vol. 44 (October 1977), pp. 561–72; and Shavell, "Strict Liability versus Negligence." See also chapter 2 of this volume.

30. See Priest, "Current Insurance Crisis."

cally underestimate risks (the source of the problem). Risk-averse consumers, especially, will invest to avoid misperception, and very large proportions of product sales represent repeat purchases by consumers with both information and experience in the characteristics of the specific product.[31]

Recently, an effort has been made to apply the standard economic analysis of strict liability to the more particular doctrines of products liability law. In a 1985 article Landes and Posner reviewed the rules of products liability law and showed that the "current doctrinal structure" of the field is *"in the main* consistent with efficiency."[32] They reasoned that in cases involving component or process failures (more typically, manufacturing defects), strict liability is efficient because consumers can do nothing to prevent such defects and because strict liability creates incentives for manufacturers to invest in research to reduce their frequency. In cases involving design and warning defects, strict liability is efficient because, in application, the standard closely resembles negligence: courts have explicitly adopted "risk-utility" standards that the authors believe are indistinguishable from weighing marginal prevention costs against benefits. Similarly, the concept of unavoidably dangerous products is efficient because courts employ it chiefly when consumer information costs are high or when manufacturers can best search for ways to make products safer. Products liability law incorporates "the general range of defenses based on victim misconduct," which, of course, is crucial to the efficiency claim. Moreover, products law "contains at least one interesting refinement that seems economically justified": a consumer can still pursue manufacturer liability, even though the dangerousness of the product was obvious, when the manufacturer could have cheaply redesigned or shielded the dangerous characteristic.[33]

Landes and Posner admittedly do not attempt to justify every products liability rule or decision, and there are some very obvious omissions. They do not explain the role of the concept of defect, nor do they address those jurisdictions that have explicitly rejected the contributory negligence defense in strict liability actions. They express reservations about, but do not carefully analyze, the developing doctrine of manu-

31. See Schwartz, "Products Liability Reform"; and U.S. Federal Trade Commission, *Market Facts, Warranties Rules Consumer Follow-Up: Evaluation Study Final Report* (Washington, D.C.: FTC, 1984).

32. Landes and Posner, "Positive Economic Analysis," p. 535.

33. Ibid., pp. 553–61.

facturer liability for foreseeable consumer misuse.[34] But again, they purport only to claim that products liability law is "in the main" efficient.

The influence of the economic defense of products law should not, however, be underestimated. In its first years the expansion of manufacturer liability was defended as a means of redistributing income by those who preferred burdening manufacturers rather than injured victims.[35] Indeed, the redistributional defense has seemed the preeminent example of the debate between those seeking to employ the law to achieve equitable ends and those seeking to achieve efficiency, a debate that has dominated legal scholarship since the 1960s.[36] The most sophisticated students of the effects of law, however, have resolved this debate by making equity and efficiency into allies where products are concerned. The expansion of products liability is claimed both to benefit consumers and to create optimal accident reduction incentives. This conception thus cements the foundation of modern products liability law in a way unknown to any other modern field of legal scholarship. But how realistic is the argument for the efficiency of products liability law?

The Efficiency of Strict Products Liability

The standard economic approach is crucial to the defense of modern products liability law because it provides the only reason for believing that the law establishes incentives for efficient accident reduction. Therefore, it is important that the approach be carefully examined. The standard analysis of strict products liability has several implications. First, as under the negligence standard, courts should be observed to be focusing their attention on the marginal costs and benefits of accident prevention by the parties; under strict liability, they should, in particular, be focusing on costs of prevention to victims. Second, courts should be resolving disputes in accord with the efficiency standard. They should be accurately evaluating the relative costs and benefits of prevention and should be holding the manufacturer liable only when the marginal prevention costs to the victim are relatively greater than to the manufacturer.

Can these implications be tested empirically? It is easy to evaluate the

---

34. Ibid., pp. 560–63.

35. See Calabresi, *Costs of Accidents.*

36. For an example in the products liability field, see "Symposium on Products Liability: Economic Analysis and the Law," *University of Chicago Law Review,* vol. 38 (Fall 1970), pp. 1–141.

first by examining whether courts are in fact focusing on the relative costs and benefits of accident prevention. The second implication, however, poses more troublesome empirical problems. It is extremely difficult to evaluate independently whether cost-benefit decisions are actually efficient. Courts, surely, have access to more detailed and reliable information about marginal costs and benefits than do commentators who must rely on the courts' descriptions of the facts.

Yet a third implication of the standard economic approach provides some independence for examining courts' determinations of efficiency. As described earlier, the economic approach defines the strict liability standard as equivalent to the negligence standard with respect to accident prevention; strict liability is different only in assigning insurance responsibility for accidents not worth preventing. Indeed, with respect to control over the determinants of the accident rate, the two standards not only have identical effects, they *are* identical. According to the standard law and economics approach, under both negligence and strict liability the judge or jury weighs the relative marginal costs and benefits of prevention to injurer and victim and, if either one or both could have prevented the accident in a cost-effective manner, assigns liability to the party for whom marginal prevention costs are lower.[37]

It follows that except for cases in which neither party could have prevented the accident, the assignment of liability in similar disputes should be similar under negligence and strict liability.[38] Thus we can evaluate the consistency of courts' cost-benefit decisions by comparing the resolution of factually similar disputes under the two standards. If courts are focusing on the marginal costs and benefits of prevention and are assigning liability similarly under negligence and strict liability, we can be confident that accident reduction incentives are efficient as pro-

37. See Brown, "Economic Theory of Liability."
38. There may be very small differences in terms of litigation—settlement incentives. In disputes in which courts or juries are uncertain as to relative marginal prevention costs, courts decide in favor of injurers under negligence (that is, finding no negligence) and in favor of victims under strict liability (that is, finding no contributory negligence). This may lead to a slightly different set of cases being litigated when evidence is problematic. But these differences are probably small, since the underlying basis for decision under the two standards remains the same. There may be also a wealth effect attending the shift from using negligence as a basis for decision to using strict liability. See Donald Wittman, "Is the Selection of Cases for Trial Biased?" *Journal of Legal Studies,* vol. 14 (January 1985), pp. 185–214; and George L. Priest, "Reexamining the Selection Hypothesis: Learning from Wittman's Mistakes," *Journal of Legal Studies,* vol. 14 (January 1985), pp. 215–43.

posed by the standard economic approach. But if these implications fail to hold, we cannot be assured, and it will become necessary to examine these incentives more carefully.

I have attempted to compile sets of factually similar cases in typical products liability contexts decided first under the negligence standard and then after judicial adoption of the strict liability standard. I have selected negligence cases decided shortly before the adoption of strict liability to minimize the significance of technological changes over time. Obviously, cases involving manufacturing defects will be decided differently under the two standards. I also present examples of cases involving design defects and allegedly inadequate warnings.

Consider first some typical cases of consumer injuries implicating lawn mower design. In a 1964 negligence decision, *Murphy* v. *Cory Pump and Supply Co.*, a seven-year-old child was injured when she slipped on the grass and fell in front of a rotary mower operated by an older sister. The plaintiff claimed that the mower was inherently dangerous and had been negligently designed because it had no front guard; indeed, it was without a front screen or bar lower than eight and three-quarters inches from the ground. The court held as a matter of law that there was no manufacturer negligence because the mower would have caused no harm without the independent act of the victim and because the manufacturer "should not be required to anticipate or protect against any such accident."[39]

Compare the strict liability decision of the Supreme Court of California eight years later in *Luque* v. *McLean,* in which the adult owner of a lawn mower had slipped on wet grass and fallen, inserting his hand in a small hole for grass ejection that had been labeled "Caution." The court reversed a jury verdict in favor of the manufacturer, noting that ordinary contributory negligence does not bar recovery under strict liability nor does the latent character of the alleged defect.[40] Similarly, in 1975 in *Rogers* v. *Toro Manufacturing Company*, a Missouri court of appeals reversed a jury verdict in favor of a manufacturer in a case in which a child was injured when the child's father left the machine running but unattended, despite warnings in the product pamphlet: "Never Leave Equipment Unattended," "Keep Children or Pets Away,"

39. 197 N.E.2d 849 (Ill. App. Ct. 1964), p. 858.
40. 501 P.2d 1163 (Cal. 1972). Quoting from *Greenman* v. *Yuba Power Products, Inc.,* 377 P.2d 897, 901, the court held that the objective of strict liability is to impose the costs of injuries resulting from defective products on manufacturers rather than injured persons powerless to protect themselves (p. 1169).

and "Always Shut Off Engine When Removing or Reinstalling Bags." The court held that the warning was defective since it did not indicate that the mower might engage if left unattended. According to the court, a plaintiff's contributory negligence is no defense for the manufacturer under strict liability.[41]

Do these decisions establish efficient incentives for accident prevention? The decisions under the negligence and strict liability standards cannot both be efficient since they clearly resolve these disputes differently. Under negligence the court ruled in favor of the manufacturer as a matter of law on the ground that the victim's slipping constituted an independent act. Under strict liability one court (in *Luque*) overturned a jury verdict in favor of a manufacturer in a case despite the victim's slip (and despite the much more carefully guarded machine); another ruled out any reference to the victim's contributory acts.

If the standards are not equally efficient, does negligence or strict liability appear the relatively more efficient in reducing accidents? None of the courts in these cases seems to have been focusing carefully on the relative marginal costs and benefits of accident prevention. Perhaps one could interpret the court's decision in *Murphy,* under the negligence standard, as reflecting a comparison of marginal prevention costs in the court's conclusion that the seven-year-old could have avoided falling under the mower. But the court gave no consideration to preventive investments by the manufacturer such as safer product design, concluding baldly that the manufacturer has no duty to protect against such accidents. *Murphy* is not atypical in this regard. The open and obvious danger defense was a prominently applied doctrine in products cases under the negligence standard. Yet it is equally difficult to regard the decisions made under strict liability as reflecting a weighing of marginal costs and benefits. There is little consideration of alternative precautions available to either of the parties.

It is also implausible that the decisions under either negligence or strict liability are efficient in fact. Who can believe that a rotary blade unprotected for eight and three-quarter inches (*Murphy*) represents efficient product design, especially in comparison with the heavily protected blade described in *Luque* only eight years later? Similarly, however, it is difficult to regard the strict liability decisions as establishing efficient accident prevention incentives. The standard economic approach presumes that the determination of efficiency under strict liability

41. 522 S.W.2d 632 (Mo. Ct. App. 1975).

will be implemented through the definition of the victim's contributory negligence. But in both *Luque* and *Rogers* courts refused to regard victims' contributory negligence as determinative. Indeed, in *Rogers* the court denied the availability of contributory negligence as a defense under strict liability.

Consider, next, typical cases of design defect litigation involving worker injuries. *Messina v. Clark Equipment Company* in 1959 concerned a worker who was killed when the bucket on an earthmover fell as he was getting out of the cab. In his claim of negligent design the plaintiff had proved that it was customary among other manufacturers of such machines to install guards and protective devices to prevent an operator from leaving the cab while the bucket was raised. Despite this seemingly uniform practice, however, the court affirmed summary judgment against the plaintiff on the grounds that there was no hidden defect or concealed danger.[42]

Compare the 1978 strict liability decision in *Barker* v. *Lull Engineering Company, Inc.,* in which a high-lift loader operator was injured as he jumped out of the cab when the load began to fall. The plaintiff claimed that the loader was defectively designed because it did not have seat belts or a roll bar and because it was without outriggers appropriate for the steep slope on which the load was being negotiated. The manufacturer claimed that the employer had chosen the wrong machine for the job. The regular operator of the lifter had unsuccessfully recommended a different machine and ultimately had called in sick because he believed that the lift was too dangerous. The Supreme Court of California reversed a jury decision in favor of the manufacturer on the grounds (among others) that the plaintiff should not have to prove that the machine was unreasonably dangerous.[43]

Do these decisions establish incentives for efficient accident prevention? Again, despite the factual similarity of the disputes, the judgments are radically different, so both cannot be efficient. In addition, as before, judicial analysis of relative prevention costs and benefits seems perfunctory at best. In *Messina,* the negligence decision, the court ruled against the plaintiff on grounds that he knew or should have known of the danger, but it gave little attention to alternative product designs that the manufacturer could have chosen. In *Barker,* the famous strict liability decision, the court reversed the jury decision in a case in which,

42. 263 F.2d 291 (2d Cir. 1959).
43. 573 P.2d 443 (Cal. 1978).

though there had been substantial testimony with respect to product design, there were also many concerns about the misjudgments of the victim or of the victim's employer.

Once again, it is very difficult to regard either decision as establishing efficient incentives for accident reduction. In *Messina* the court exonerated the manufacturer even though its machine was alleged to be inferior in terms of safety precautions to *all* other such machines in the trade. In *Barker* the jury verdict was overturned and a new trial ordered despite the substantial evidence implicating worker contributory negligence and improper product choice. Again, according to the standard economic analysis, the chief focus in strict liability cases should be on the victim's contributory actions. In *Barker* the court ignored the victim's precautions despite the jury verdict against him.

Finally, consider typical cases involving employee injuries from exploding or breaking grinding wheels in which the principal legal issue was the manufacturer's failure to warn of product dangers. In *Oettinger v. Norton Company,* decided in 1957 under the negligence standard, an employee was injured when an abrasive spindle exploded and penetrated the safety goggles he was wearing. The plaintiff alleged that the manufacturer had failed to warn of the appropriate point speed on the product itself or on the product container. The court affirmed a judgment for the manufacturer (thus reversing a jury decision for the worker) on the grounds that the manufacturer's distribution of a pamphlet to the employer was legally sufficient.[44]

Compare two similar cases decided under the strict liability standard. In 1973 in *Young v. Aro Corporation,* a worker was killed when a grinding wheel disintegrated, allegedly because of excessive grinder speed. The grinder carried a warning on a nameplate indicating that workers should check grinder speed with each wheel change. The court reversed a jury decision for the manufacturer on grounds that the trial judge had failed to instruct the jury that sometimes particular job requirements may keep workers from reading nameplates. According to the court, the jury should have been instructed that reasonable men should read nameplates, but in practice reasonable men whose employers have habituated them to particular risks may not read them. The warnings made available to the employer were not regarded as relevant to the issue.[45] Even more clearly different, in 1976 in *Haugen v. Min-*

44. 160 F. Supp. 399 (E.D.Pa. 1957).
45. 111 Cal. Rptr. 535 (Ct. App. 1973).

nesota Mining and Manufacturing Company, a court affirmed a judgment against a manufacturer in a case in which a grinding wheel exploded, striking in the eye a worker who was not wearing safety glasses. The court ruled that the manufacturer was strictly liable for failing to warn the worker of the need to wear impact-resistant safety goggles.[46]

These decisions, too, show dramatic differences between judgments based on negligence and strict liability, and they show substantial distance between the careful evaluation of marginal prevention costs necessary for optimal accident prevention. Weighing costs and benefits in warning cases is inherently difficult because effective methods of transferring information and securing its reception are poorly understood. But the respective courts made little effort to formulate efficient incentives. The decisions under both standards were formulaic. In *Oettinger,* under the negligence standard, the worker wearing safety goggles was held contributorily negligent for failing to act on information appearing in pamphlets provided to his employer. There is little concern with relative abilities to provide or receive information. The court's ruling was simply that the manufacturer fulfilled its duty by giving the employer pamphlets. The strict liability decisions, however, are no more sensitive to relative prevention costs. In *Young,* although the manufacturer had installed a plate warning of proper wheel speed, the court overturned the jury verdict for the manufacturer on grounds that in some circumstances victims might not read the plates, yet it did so without reference to alternative warning methods the manufacturer might practicably have adopted. Similarly, in *Haugen* the court affirmed a verdict against the manufacturer, apparently to give manufacturers incentives to warn grinding wheel workers to wear safety goggles, a warning that seems obvious and hardly necessary.

It is too strong to conclude definitively that all these decisions were inefficient. But they certainly departed significantly from the conditions defined by the standard economic analysis for efficient accident prevention. Under both negligence and strict liability, courts devoted little attention to the marginal costs and benefits of accident prevention and none to the careful weighing of costs and benefits necessary for establishing optimal accident reduction incentives.

Moreover, these decisions are typical of negligence and strict liability decisions in the products field. They strongly suggest that the effectiveness of modern products liability law in controlling the accident rate is

46. 550 P.2d 71 (Wash. Ct. App. 1976).

blunt at best. And they provide additional grounds for confirming the empirical finding that there has been no substantial reduction in the accident rate despite the extraordinary increase in products liability litigation.

A final implication of these cases is perhaps more important. They show, at the least, that products liability law could have a much greater effect on the accident rate. The doctrines of the law only crudely address accident prevention. They could be substantially reformed to focus more carefully on accident reduction.

Reforming Products Liability Law

This part describes the principal doctrines of modern products liability and shows more carefully why they are largely ineffective in controlling the rate of product accidents. It also suggests how these doctrines could be reformed to achieve more successfully the accident reduction goal. Again, it is uncontroversial that the accident rate can be reduced to the level optimal for society by determining at trial whether there was a specific cost-effective action that either party could have taken to prevent the accident and by placing liability on the party that could have prevented the accident more effectively. Assigning liability in this manner will create incentives for optimal future accident reduction.

The doctrinal foundation of modern products liability law is the *Restatement (Second) of Torts,* section 402A, which was adopted by virtually all state courts in the decade following its adaptation in 1965.[47] Under section 402A a manufacturer is liable for a product-related injury only when a product is found to be both unreasonably dangerous and defective. That the injured consumer must demonstrate that the product is unreasonably dangerous establishes a limitation of manufacturer liability short of absolute liability. The requirement that the product also be defective is redundant in many cases, but serves to distinguish a product such as a chain saw that is inherently dangerous but fully and adequately operational.

Although the distinction was only vaguely understood in 1964, it is the common view today that a product can be defective and unreasonably dangerous in three ways: it can deviate from the standard production run (a manufacturing defect); it can be misdesigned in a way that makes all items of the production run equally defective (a design defect); or it

---

47. See Priest, "Invention of Enterprise Liability," for a discussion of this history.

can be inadequately labeled or explained in terms of characteristics that could be harmful (a defect in product warning). Section 402A appears to establish strict liability for injuries resulting from each of these types of defects. Following section 402A, all jurisdictions have adopted strict liability for manufacturing defects. Some have quibbled over whether the standard for design and warning defects is negligence or strict liability,[48] but regardless of the nominal standard, virtually all jurisdictions have shifted design and warning standards by focusing principal attention on the role of the manufacturer and away from preventive actions of the consumer and by openly disregarding as irrelevant the actions of the manufacturer in place of evaluating the alleged dangerous character of the product.[49]

Defects in Manufacturing

Liability for manufacturing defects today is absolute, a principle that was Prosser's most important objective in drafting section 402A. The principle is an extension of nineteenth century warranty liability, in particular of the implied warranty of merchantability. Indeed, it was Prosser's conception that the chief effect of section 402A would be to expand warranty liability beyond the express obligations offered voluntarily by manufacturers.[50]

Absolute liability for manufacturing defects, however, has no clear relation to accident reduction. In most cases involving manufacturing defects, there is no justification for manufacturer liability in terms of potential accident prevention. For this purpose the issue is not whether the product deviated from the manufacturer's own specifications but whether the manufacturer could have efficiently prevented the deviation. It is important to establish incentives for manufacturers to adopt those production methods and systems of quality control that do most to reduce the accident rate. But all manufacturing processes will necessarily involve some deviations from the standard run. As consumers, we want manufacturers to make all practicable efforts to reduce the incidence of such deviations, and we reward them in the marketplace if they are

48. See Louis R. Frumer and Melvin I. Friedman, *Products Liability* (New York: M. Bender, loose-leaf service), for a review of this case law.

49. See George L. Priest, "The Disappearance of the Consumer from Modern Products Liability Law," in E. Scott Maynes, ed., *The Frontier of Research in the Consumer Interest* (Columbia, Mo.: American Council on Consumer Interests, forthcoming).

50. See George L. Priest, "Section 402A: The Original Intent," unpublished manuscript (Yale Law School, 1987).

successful in doing so: reliability is a very highly regarded product characteristic. But no manufacturer can make the production process perfect, nor is it worthwhile to consumers for manufacturers to do so—consumers are typically not willing to pay for perfection.

Landes and Posner, following Calabresi and Hirschoff, have argued that absolute liability for manufacturing defects is efficient because only the manufacturer can influence the manufacturing process; with respect to manufacturing defects above all, consumers are powerless to prevent injuries.[51] This proposition ignores the factual difficulty in many cases of distinguishing manufacturing from design defects. More importantly, absolute liability for manufacturing defects ignores adverse insurance effects. When a manufacturer has made all practicable investments in the manufacturing process and in quality control, liability for remaining defects involves only insurance. Absolute liability for manufacturing defects is an insurance doctrine. The only issue in such cases is who should insure for losses attributable to the manufacturing process that cannot be efficiently prevented.[52]

It is increasingly clear that consumers are harmed when social policy attempts to provide insurance through the tort system.[53] It follows that absolute liability in cases involving manufacturing defects should be relaxed. In terms of accident prevention, the legal distinction between manufacturing and design defects is no longer tenable, and the problem of manufacturing defects should be addressed by applying standards for design defects. Optimal quality control or the best choice of manufacturing materials or components of the manufacturing process is a design question. The accident rate from manufacturing defects can be effectively controlled without adverse insurance effects by adopting a rule that holds manufacturers liable only when there are alternative methods of manufacture that could have efficiently prevented the accident.

Design Defects

The standard for evaluating design defects is central to modern products liability. Initially, the drafters of the *Restatement (Second) of Torts* saw strict liability as an extension of warranty law, although this view

---

51. Landes and Posner in "Positive Economic Analysis," pp. 555–56; and Calabresi and Hirschoff, "Strict Liability in Torts." See also Schwartz, "Products Liability Reform," who supports absolute liability for manufacturing defects to save litigation expenses.

52. Landes and Posner, "Positive Economic Analysis," explicitly ignore insurance effects.

53. See Priest, "Current Insurance Crisis."

is obsolete today. Nevertheless, the interpretive "Comments to the Restatement," which are far from obsolete, define the design defect standard in terms that resemble contract law principles of agreement and consent, that is, in terms of the interests and preferences of the relevant product consumers. "Defective condition" is defined in comment (g) as "a condition not contemplated by the ultimate consumer, which will be unreasonably dangerous to him." Similarly, "unreasonably dangerous" is defined in comment (i) as "dangerous to an extent beyond that which would be contemplated by the ordinary consumer who purchases it, with the ordinary knowledge common to the community as to its characteristics."

THE CONSUMER EXPECTATION STANDARD. In the first years following the *Restatement,* many courts looked to consumer expectations as a standard for the definition of defective design. Problems arose immediately, however, because it was unclear under a consumer expectation standard how courts could differentiate the new doctrine of strict liability from negligence. Most troublesome were cases in which the dangerous characteristics of the product were fully obvious to the user. The safety characteristics of these products could not be claimed to violate the user's expectations. Rather the claim was that the products should have been designed with greater safety protections. If the consumer expectation standard were to be taken seriously, manufacturers would be exonerated when the dangerous character of the product is obvious, in exactly the manner that the "open and obvious danger" defense had exonerated manufacturers under negligence.[54]

It is not surprising that courts generally, although not universally, have rejected the consumer expectation standard. The rejection coincides with judicial efforts to better achieve control over the accident rate by employing risk-utility analysis, discussed later. In some jurisdictions, however, the standard has survived, either exclusively or as part of a multipronged test.

Some courts enforce pure consumer expectation standards, delegating to the jury all questions of the appropriateness of product design based on the jury members' appreciation of community standards.[55] The Supreme Court of Connecticut, for example, affirmed a jury verdict against a manufacturer by finding the design of a two-year-old auto unreason-

---

54. See the discussion of *Murphy* and *Messina* earlier.
55. See, for example, *Heaton* v. *Ford Motor Company,* 435 P.2d 806 (Or. 1967); and *Holm* v. *Sponco Mfg., Inc.,* 324 N.W.2d 207 (Minn. 1982).

ably dangerous. At the time of the accident allegedly caused by the design, the car had been driven 46,000 miles, was alleged by two previous owners to pull to the left, but was described by a mechanical engineer as having broken spot welds. According to the court, this evidence was sufficient for the jury to have concluded that the design was defective because the consumer expectation standard allows "the jury [to] draw its own reasonable conclusions as to the expectations of the ordinary consumer and the knowledge common in the community at large."[56]

Other courts have adopted standards that resemble a consumer expectation standard. The Supreme Court of Oregon evaluates claims of design defects by examining whether a reasonable person would have put the product into the stream of commerce knowing of its harmful characteristics.[57] According to the court, this standard of manufacturer judgment coincides with what consumers might expect.

Still other courts retain elements of a consumer expectation standard within a multifaceted standard. The Supreme Court of California allows the plaintiff to establish defective design either by showing that the product design deviates from consumer expectations or that product risk exceeds its utility.[58] In jurisdictions employing multifaceted standards, the implementation of the consumer expectation element closely resembles that in the pure consumer expectation jurisdictions. For example, in a case involving a claim of a defectively designed bus the Supreme Court of California held that there was sufficient evidence to support a verdict for the plaintiff by the introduction of nothing more than photos of the bus and the victim's account of the injury. A rider who had fallen out of her seat alleged that the bus was defectively designed because there was no grab bar. According to the court, "the need for a 'grab bar' or pole to steady oneself when a bus turns a sharp corner is a matter within the common experience of lay jurors. . . . Since public transportation is a matter of common experience, no expert testimony was required to enable the jury to reach a decision."[59]

56. *Slepski* v. *Williams Ford, Inc.*, 364 A.2d 175, 178 (Conn. 1975). See also *Giglio* v. *Connecticut Light and Power Company*, 429 A.2d 486 (Conn. 1980).
57. *Phillips* v. *Kimwood Machine Company*, 525 P.2d 1033 (Or. 1974).
58. *Barker* v. *Lull Engineering Company, Inc.*, 573 P.2d 443 (Cal. 1978).
59. *Campbell* v. *General Motors Corporation*, 649 P.2d 224, 232–33 (Cal. 1982). For a similar decision, see *Moorer* v. *Clayton Manufacturing Corporation*, 627 P.2d 716 (Ariz. Ct. App. 1981). For other cases of the same nature, see *Brady* v. *Melody Homes Manufacturer*, 589 P.2d 896 (Ariz. Ct. App. 1978); and *Hohlenkamp* v. *Rheem Manufacturing Company*, 655 P.2d 32 (Ariz. Ct. App. 1982).

As these examples illustrate, the consumer expectation standard pays no careful attention to the determinants of the accident rate. And because consumer expectations are largely insensitive to safety design potential except, perhaps, with respect to grossly dangerous product features, the standard is likely to have no coherent influence on the rate of product-related accidents. Even if one were to presume that consumer expectations were an important measure of optimal product design—a presumption, incidentally, at odds with most of defective-product warning law—the standard is not presented to juries in a way that allows informed design evaluation. Juries in these cases are given nothing in the way of research on the operation of consumer product markets. Nor are they instructed in how to consider the formation of consumer expectations, the determinants of consumer product selection, or the influences on consumer product use, all factors relevant to optimal product design.

THE RISK-UTILITY STANDARD. Except for the small number adopting the consumer expectation standard, jurisdictions have adopted a variation of the risk-utility standard for determining whether a product's design is defective. The risk-utility standard is widely advocated as establishing efficient incentives for accident reduction on the grounds that it is equivalent to cost-benefit analysis, the dominant tool of modern governmental regulatory policy, and because it resembles the classic formulation in the law and economics literature for establishing efficient accident reduction incentives.[60] How well does the risk-utility standard control the accident rate?

The most widely adopted formulation of the standard is that of John Wade, one of the architects of the *Restatement*. Wade lists seven factors for determining whether a product design is abnormally dangerous:

1. The usefulness and desirability of the product—its utility to the user and to the public as a whole.
2. The safety aspects of the product—the likelihood that it will cause injury, and the probable seriousness of the injury.
3. The availability of a substitute product which would meet the same need and not be as unsafe.
4. The manufacturer's ability to eliminate the unsafe character of the product without impairing its usefulness or making it too expensive to maintain its utility.

60. See Landes and Posner, "Positive Economic Analysis," pp. 553–54. See also Posner, *Economic Analysis of Law.*

5. The user's ability to avoid danger by the exercise of care in the use of the product.

6. The user's anticipated awareness of the dangers inherent in the product and their avoidability, because of general public knowledge of the obvious condition of the product, or of the existence of suitable warnings or instructions.

7. The feasibility, on the part of the manufacturer, of spreading the loss by setting the price of the product or carrying liability insurance.[61]

Typically, courts allow parties to introduce evidence bearing on any of these seven factors and then refer some version of the list to the jury for the determination of whether the product design was defective and unreasonably dangerous. Of course, it is impossible to know exactly how juries employ the list. None of the factors can be said to be irrelevant to product design, yet the vague and overlapping character of the factors suggests a range of possible judgments that may only occasionally help establish incentives to reduce the accident rate. Even at the most basic level, for example, it can never be certain that the jury will be able to distinguish the statistical evaluation of risk and utility for the set of product consumers as a whole from the risk faced (and suffered) by a particular injured claimant.

Yet, though one cannot determine how juries are in fact applying Wade's seven factors, it is possible to evaluate how closely the seven factors themselves correspond analytically to what would be necessary to establish appropriate incentives for accident reduction. And here it is evident that the factors bring a level of analytical confusion to the issue of design defect that would make it extremely difficult for even the most diligent jury to establish coherent incentives to reduce the accident rate.

First, the seven factors are not equally relevant to all types of design defect cases. The first factor, product usefulness, and the second, product risk, for example, may help evaluate general product utility but are meaningless when a plaintiff claims that a specific alternative design should have been adopted. In the context of alternative designs there is no reason to calculate product utility net of product risk.

Factors 3 through 6 refer to alternative ways to prevent the accident by manufacturers and consumers. Factor 4 loosely suggests reference to alternative methods the manufacturer might have chosen to design the

---

61. John W. Wade, "On the Nature of Strict Tort Liability for Products," *Mississippi Law Journal,* vol. 44 (November 1973), pp. 837–38.

product to reduce the accident rate. Factors 3, 5, and 6 refer to alternative actions that consumers might take. Factor 5 most clearly addresses what efficiency analysis refers to as the consumer's contributory actions to the occurrence of the injury. Factor 6 addresses the information available to the consumer about the product. Factor 3, oddly, brings up the possibility of using a safer product to achieve the same end. Perhaps this was meant to suggest that the consumer might choose the wrong product for the intended use, much as in the claim in *Barker* that the high-lift loader was inappropriate for the job. Alternatively, factor 3 might be thought to duplicate factors 1 and 2, that is, to condemn products altogether if there are equally effective but safer products on the market.

Perhaps it might be thought that factors 3 through 6 together raise the considerations needed to evaluate whether the manufacturer or consumer could have taken some specific action to prevent the injury, the calculus that all commentators concede is appropriate. But Wade's formulation, again, is excessively diffuse. It is much more direct and effective to ask simply: could the manufacturer or consumer have taken some specific action that would have efficiently prevented the accident? The in part disconnected and in part redundant character of Wade's factors undoubtedly introduces significant variation into juries' decisions that weakens the influence of the law as an incentive for efficient design.

There is a further confusion in the list. It is difficult to know how a jury's evaluation of factors 3 through 6 will interact with its consideration of factors 1 and 2, which are broader and more general. Factors 1 and 2, in referring to the general utility and riskiness of products, are relevant only to the now-growing number of cases in which courts entertain allegations that a product is so dangerous that liability for injuries related to its use should be absolute. Very recently, several courts have defined liability categories of this nature. One has created a category of products unreasonably dangerous per se.[62] Another, somewhat more subtly, has allowed a jury to find a generic class of products unreasonably dangerous, which amounts to essentially the same result.[63] Other courts approach similar conclusions by employing hindsight standards of defectiveness, according to which all products that still function but whose design is obsolete can be found defective.[64] The judicial rejection of the state-of-the-art defense has the same

62. *Halphen* v. *Johns-Manville Sales Corporation,* 484 So.2d 110 (La. 1986).

63. *O'Brien* v. *Muskin Corporation,* 463 A.2d 298 (N.J. 1983).

64. *Barker* v. *Lull Engineering Company, Inc.,* 573 P.2d 443 (Cal. 1978).

effect.[65] Moreover, this category of cases is the subject of a rising number of claims against manufacturers of guns, alcohol, and cigarettes, among others. The claim of the Indian government that Union Carbide should be liable for all losses resulting from the Bhopal disaster on grounds of cost internalization is similar.

There is a fundamental incoherence in applying Wade's risk-utility factors to claims of generic product defectiveness. To illustrate the problem, imagine how the evaluation of utility versus risk of a generic product might proceed—that is, how a careful jury would implement Wade's factors 1 and 2.

First, though empirically difficult, it is conceptually straightforward to calculate generic product risk (Wade's factor 2). A jury must estimate the likelihood of injury from particular product uses and then estimate the expected costs of these injuries. The multiple will equal expected product risks.

Calculating product utility (Wade's factor 1) to set against risk, however, is substantially more difficult. The term *utility* typically refers to the subjective value or satisfaction that consumers obtain from product use. It is never possible to put a precise dollar value on absolute personal satisfaction from consumption. Economists routinely calculate relative consumption values by measuring marginal rates of substitution among commodities. But relative values equal absolute values only at the margin.

One possible measure of product utility is the maximum amount that any single person or the set of consumers as a whole would pay for the product, represented by the area under the economist's demand curve. This measure is not precise because utility does not equal willingness to pay but rather willingness to pay discounted by the marginal utility of income. Such a measure can serve as an approximation of product utility, however, on the assumption that the marginal utility of income equals 1 (surely an overestimate). A first approximation of product utility, then, is the area of an estimated demand curve, bounded by the quantity of the product actually sold.

An alternative, lower-bound estimate of consumer utility can be obtained by looking at the actual amounts paid by consumers for the product. This is a lower-bound estimate because, of course, all consumers place a higher value on the product than its price or they would not

65. See, generally, Commerce Clearing House, *Products Liability Reporter* (1987, looseleaf service).

buy it. The difference between full product value to consumers and product price is referred to as consumer surplus, which again is measured by subtracting the price consumers have paid from the area under the product demand curve. The alternative estimate of product utility, then, is total sales revenues, which again is a lower bound because it ignores consumer surplus.

There is some ambiguity when social utility is at issue in looking even at total sales revenues because some philosophers and many judges question whether corporate profits should enter into the measure of social utility.[66] To some, profits are a return for taking entrepreneurial risks. To others, profits are only transfers of assets from one group (consumers) to another (shareholders) and do not reflect a gain in social utility.

If profits are not to be considered, then the best lowest-bound approximation is production costs.[67] Production costs include wages, taxes, and capital asset investment. There is a further, more substantial conceptual foundation for using production costs as a surrogate for consumer utility. In perfect competition, economic profits (returns higher than those necessary to generate continued investment) are negligible; price equals marginal costs. Thus the aggregate lowest-bound level of consumer utility is equal to the sum of production costs. Again, the relevance of evidence on production costs is not that production benefits measure utility but that they are one of the measures to be referred to when precise estimates of consumer satisfaction are unavailable.

These three measures, then—the area under the demand curve, total sales revenues, and production costs—seem to be the only possible coherent measures of product utility for which any empirical basis might exist. But each measure would lead to a seriously erroneous conclusion if employed to determine product utility to be set against product risk. With respect to product risks, each is a measure of net consumer utility, not gross utility as anticipated by the risk-utility test. The price a person is willing to pay for a product represents the utility of the product to the person net of expected ancillary costs, such as the expected risk of injury or the expected risk of damage to health. Injury or health costs associated with product use, obviously, are meant to enter into the calculation of product risks considered in Wade's factor 2, not in product utility, Wade's factor 1.

66. *Cippolone* v. *Liggett Group, Inc.,* 644 F. Supp. 283 (D.N.J. 1986).
67. Of course, if manufacturer profits are ignored, then it would be conceptually inconsistent to give credit to consumer surplus.

Yet, if we measure utility by willingness to pay or by total sales volume, then to the extent consumers are informed about expected product or health risks, the risks of the product have already been taken into account. The product demand curve is defined with respect to consumer expectations of product risks. The value of the product to consumers incorporates the deduction of product risks. To then again subtract the cost of product risks pursuant to the risk-utility standard would count product risks twice. Put differently, for products alleged to be unreasonably dangerous per se, factor 1 is all that is necessary for the analysis. Factor 2 is redundant.

The point is that consumers themselves engage in risk-utility analysis of generic products. If I refuse because of concerns for safety to allow my teenage son to purchase a motorcycle, I am concluding that the expected risk of the product exceeds its expected utility. Similarly, if I decide to forgo the pleasures of hang gliding, I am concluding that the expected risk of the product exceeds its expected utility. Those consumers who choose to buy such products are making different calculations. As long as they have information about expected product risks, their continuing purchase represents the best estimate of the utility of a product relative to its risk.

Of utmost importance to this point, of course, is that consumers be informed of product risks to make effective risk-utility calculations. Consumer product demand is an accurate measure of product utility net of product risks only when consumers are well informed about risks. This qualification, however, does not justify the use of Wade's seven (or even his first two) factors in the evaluation of generic product risk-utility. The issue in cases in which consumers lack information about product risks is one of appropriate product warning, an issue entirely different from that of appropriate product design or manufacture. When consumers lack product risk information, the accident rate can be reduced only if incentives are created for the dissemination of appropriate product warnings. It follows that there are no circumstances in which the risk-utility calculation can be effectively implemented with respect to claims of generic product dangerousness.

Defects in Warnings

Current doctrines defining the manufacturer's duty to provide warnings about product dangers seem, perhaps, the most congruent with the liability standard that I have proposed to control the accident rate.

Many jurisdictions today hold manufacturers liable when the court believes that a warning could have been offered that would have prevented the accident.[68] Warning law, however, has also been greatly influenced by the insurance goal of modern law and by the empirical presumption that the manufacturer is almost always in the best position to prevent injuries. As a consequence, although the doctrinal foundation of warning law is consistent with the accident reduction objective, the implementation of the law could be greatly reformed to better establish accident prevention incentives.

The leading cases of modern warning law have employed the duty to warn to fulfill insurance objectives. The furthest reach of warning law is *Beshada* v. *Johns-Manville,* in which the Supreme Court of New Jersey held the manufacturer liable for failing to warn, despite the court's admission that it was impossible for the manufacturer to have known of the product danger at the time it breached its warning duty.[69] The court explicitly justified its conclusion on insurance grounds (although it alluded vaguely to research and development incentives). Because it is inconceivable that a manufacturer can actually warn of some danger that it does not know about, and of which it is impossible to know, the *Beshada* rule can have no important influence on actual accident reduction.[70] Indeed, the Supreme Court of New Jersey has itself retreated from the rule, although hardly in a principled fashion.[71]

Modern warning law departs from the objective of defining effective incentives for accident prevention in many additional respects. Courts have struggled mightily to define a distinctive strict liability standard for warning cases. Toward this end, legal presumptions have been adopted that impair accident prevention incentives. For example, many courts presume that manufacturers have or should have knowledge of all product dangers, of which they must inform consumers.[72] This presumption deflects attention from the judicial inquiry as to how manufacturers can effectively obtain and impart information about product dangers. There are no effective incentives created for accident reduction by holding manufacturers liable for failing to take actions that they could not in

68. *McCormack* v. *Hankscraft Company,* 154 N.W.2d 488 (Minn. 1967).
69. *Beshada* v. *Johns-Manville Products Corporation,* 447 A.2d 539 (N.J. 1982).
70. See Alan Schwartz, "Products Liability, Corporate Structure, and Bankruptcy: Toxic Substances and the Remote Risk Relationship," *Journal of Legal Studies,* vol. 14 (December 1985), pp. 689–736.
71. See *Feldman* v. *Lederle Laboratories,* 479 A.2d 374 (N.J. 1984), apparently limiting *Beshada* to asbestos-like circumstances.
72. For example, *Phillips* v. *Kimwood Machine Company,* 525 P.2d 1033 (Or. 1974).

fact have taken. Thus the presumption of manufacturer knowledge provides no important accident reduction effects.

In a similar effort to articulate a strict liability standard for warning cases, some courts have adopted the legal presumption that, had a warning been provided, the consumer would have read it and acted on it.[73] This presumption too detracts from the effort to create realistic incentives for accident prevention. In many circumstances, consumers have limited capacities to read and comprehend warnings. Manufacturer liability for failing to provide a warning in such circumstances achieves no effective preventive function. The presumption also ignores the complicated issue of the definition of the consumer group to which a particular product warning should be directed. The most important issue in warning cases is identifying the appropriate consumer groups, since most modern products are used in many different ways. Except for the simplest products, one cannot presume a single warning will be equally effective for all consumers or for all uses.

It is a similar error to presume that complicated or multivariate warnings—designed to warn of wide ranges of product danger—will be effective. Many modern warning cases involve accidents in which the product was used in such an unusual manner or in a manner so distinctly within the control of the injured consumer that manufacturer liability for the failure to warn serves no effective accident reduction purpose. Manufacturers, for example, have been held liable for breach of the warning duty where teenage girls were injured from pouring cologne on a lighted candle, where a bystander was hit by a champagne cork exploding from a bottle, and where a four-wheel-drive vehicle was being driven on a slope so extreme that the vehicle flipped end to end.[74] In such cases the accident would probably not have been prevented if the respective manufacturers had issued more specific warnings. Put differently, the respective product users would probably not have been sufficiently sensitive to warnings detailed enough to incorporate notes of caution about these and the wide range of analogous unusual uses to reduce the likelihood of injury significantly.

The multiple presumptions that the manufacturer has all knowledge about product dangers, that it may warn of these dangers easily and cheaply, and that all consumers will read, comprehend, and act on the

73. See Schwartz, "Products Liability."
74. *Moran* v. *Faberge, Inc.*, 332 A.2d 11 (Md. 1975); *Shuput* v. *Heublein, Inc.*, 511 F.2d 1104 (10th Cir. 1975); and *Leichtamer* v. *American Motors Corp.*, 424 N.E. 2d 568 (Ohio 1981).

warnings lead warning law toward absolute liability. Except with respect to intentionally self-inflicted injuries, all product-related losses can be regarded as deriving from insufficient information about product risks. Initial cases in the warning field involved injuries in contexts where no warnings at all were provided. Thus it may have seemed plausible that courts could improve accident prevention incentives by adopting these presumptions. But it is a short step from the presumption that some warning is better than none to the presumption that the existing warning can easily be made more effective. If a court presumes that a consumer will always respond to warnings, yet the consumer is injured despite an existing warning, the warning must have been inadequate. Thus these presumptions propel the duty to warn toward absolute liability for all but intentionally self-inflicted injuries.[75]

This expansion of the duty to warn serves no helpful accident reduction purpose. Crucial to every warning case is a causation issue: whether any effective warning, or a warning drafted in some particular way, would have led this particular consumer to have avoided the injury. Without the rigorous evaluation of warning content, courts are only providing insurance by expanding manufacturer liability, an insurance function that is counterproductive. Moreover, such action blunts the instructive function that courts can serve in guiding manufacturers to develop clear and effective warnings. Thus courts must examine with greater care and rigor exactly which warnings would have been effective for which consumer product uses.

The Standards Evaluated

There are, then, significant discrepancies between each of the basic standards of modern products liability law and rules that would create incentives for optimal accident prevention. The standard of absolute liability for manufacturing defects extends liability far beyond what is necessary for accident control. The consumer expectation standard for design defects is likely to exert no systematic influence on the accident rate. The risk-utility test, though suggesting the flavor of cost-benefit analysis, is formulated so loosely and in some contexts so incoherently that its effect on the accident rate is likely to be minimal. The presumptions of warning law lead toward absolute liability and not toward an

---

75. Indeed, some courts have ruled that assumption of risk is inapplicable in an action involving duty to warn. See *Heil Company* v. *Grant, 534* S.W. 2d 916 (Tex. Civ. App. 1976).

effective focus on how to draft warnings to prevent accidents. It is, therefore, little surprise that aggregate statistics show no substantial reduction in product-related accidents since 1970 despite the enormous expansion of products liability.

The failure of the basic doctrines of products liability law to control the accident rate is peculiar because commentators universally agree that accident reduction is a central goal of the law, and economists, lawyer-economists, and policy analysts agree that rigorous cost-benefit analysis is the most effective way to achieve it. This failure should be attributed to the misleadingly simplistic claims of efficiency-of-the-law scholarship. These claims have diverted the attention of economists and lawyer-economists from the dismal economic performance of modern products liability law.

The program for reform is straightforward. If courts want to work seriously to create incentives for accident prevention, they must adopt standards that place liability on manufacturers only when it can be shown that there was some practicable method for the manufacturer to have prevented the accident. If there was nothing the manufacturer could have done, manufacturer liability will serve only an insurance effect, an effect that has been shown to harm consumers, and poor and low-income consumers most of all.[76] At the most basic level, this standard can be implemented by adopting rigorous cost-benefit analysis in every products case. The distinction between manufacturing and design defects must be abandoned. The risk-utility test may survive, but only if it is substantially sharpened and its focus made more precise. The causation issue in warning cases must not be presumed away.

Some might object that a simple standard asking whether it is possible to identify any specific cost-effective action that either the manufacturer or consumer could have taken that would have prevented the accident closely resembles the negligence or fault standard, which virtually every court has repudiated in most products liability contexts. But such a conclusion is grossly incorrect and again betrays the unfortunate influence of the efficiency-of-the-law school. As the many negligence cases described earlier demonstrate, the standard in force in the products field until the early 1960s was crude and paid no careful attention to the determinants of the accident rate. There is little reason to believe that the negligence standard required even cost-effective investments by manufacturers. The adoption of the strict liability standard may very likely

---

76. See Priest, "Current Insurance Crisis."

have improved accident prevention incentives. But modern strict liability itself can be improved. To the extent that courts are seriously interested in accident reduction—as they should be—they must strive to create rules and standards more sensitive to the determinants of the accident rate.

The Stakes in Products Liability Law

This chapter has attempted to show that modern products liability law fails to provide adequate control over the accident rate involving products because it fails to establish sensible and effective incentives for accident prevention. There is no empirical evidence whatsoever of an effect of the tremendous expansion of products liability on the number or rate of product-related accidents. Judicial decisions under either the negligence or strict liability standard have been insensitive toward the determinants of the accident rate. And the basic doctrines of modern law largely neglect the most effective methods of accident control.

The implications of these failings are extremely unfortunate. Manufacturer and consumer investments in accident prevention are complements over some range but substitutes at the margin. It follows that erroneous decisions in cases involving manufacturing and design defects increase the rate of product-related accidents.[77] Increasing manufacturer liability may lead to products that, in some mechanical sense, are safer, products that, if they were accompanied by a constant level of consumer safety investment, would generate a decrease in the accident rate. But courts cannot guarantee the constancy of consumer safety or care investments. Many studies have shown that consumers respond to an increase in manufacturer safety investments by conserving on investments of their own.[78] That the expansion of liability increases the accident rate is a direct implication.

Our society has a stake not in a unidirectional expansion of manufacturer liability but in creating incentives to optimize safety investments. The more rigorous formulation of cost-benefit standards for products liability law is essential to this objective.

77. For an elaboration, see George L. Priest, "Punitive Damages and Enterprise Liability," *Southern California Law Review,* vol. 56 (November 1982), pp. 123–32.

78. See, for example, Viscusi, *Regulating Consumer Product Safety;* and Peltzman, "Effects of Automobile Safety Regulation."

CHAPTER EIGHT

Policy Options

Robert E. Litan and Clifford Winston

THE POLICIES proposed to address the recent crisis in the insurance and liability systems fall into three major categories: modifying regulation of the property-casualty insurance industry; limiting compensation through the tort system, popularly labeled "tort reform"; and augmenting or replacing the tort system with new compensation devices, coupled with alternative measures for deterring accidents.

Based on the analyses in the foregoing chapters, none of the proposals unambiguously solves the problems of rising liability insurance premiums and cutbacks in coverage. John Calfee and Clifford Winston demonstrated in chapter 2 that on theoretical grounds it is extremely difficult to identify the mix of institutions that best achieves both the deterrence and compensation objectives of the liability system. Moreover, there are no comprehensive empirical estimates of the costs and benefits of the current system. The total costs of the tort system, for example, are not known: although premium costs for insurance are available and estimates of the administrative cost of the tort system exist, we do not know the magnitude of liability costs for those individuals and corporations who self-insure nor the costs of steps they may take to avoid or prevent injury. Even less is known about the benefits of the current tort system in terms of costs saved through deterrence. Consequently, it is difficult to assess the comparative costs and benefits of supplementing or replacing the current system with other compensation and deterrence mechanisms.

Nevertheless, certain recommendations are supported by the data and theoretical research that are available. Equally important, a number of proposals clearly are not advisable and could even be counterproductive.

Modifying Insurance Regulation

Given the explosion in insurance costs and cutbacks in availability, it is not surprising that many critics have directed their reform proposals at the property-casualty insurance industry itself. One class of suggestions, advanced at the state level where property-casualty insurers are regulated, would strengthen regulation of premiums and policy cancellations, or at a minimum impose additional requirements on insurers to report data. Table 8-1 summarizes these types of reforms enacted by various states just since 1986. The premise for more extensive regulation is that the industry is imperfectly competitive; only with vigilant control will consumers be protected against excessive premium increases or cancellations.

A second possible reform, currently being considered in Congress, is to repeal or significantly scale back the antitrust exemption afforded property-casualty insurers by the McCarran-Ferguson Act.[1] Since 1944 the act has immunized from the antitrust laws the joint activities of insurers—primarily the sharing of loss-collection data and analysis—provided that the business of insurance is regulated by the states. The premise underlying proposed reform is that insurance markets are inherently competitive but that antitrust immunity enables insurers to act collusively to set rates at excessive levels or to withdraw coverage that would otherwise be made available. Indeed, several major property-casualty insurers have recently been charged with conspiring with their rating bureau to limit the coverage available to policyholders. A definite resolution of the issues raised in these lawsuits may not occur for many years, if ever. In the meantime, it is prudent to make policy on the basis of the information that is available.

Harrington demonstrates in chapter 3 that the conventional indicators of market behavior and performance—many competitors, low levels of market shares, and the absence of abnormally high profits—indicate that the property-casualty insurance industry is highly competitive. The limited evidence available suggests that, at least in auto insurance markets, insurers tend to set rates independently despite the sharing of loss data. Rating bureaus do influence rates charged by smaller auto insurers, but these

---

1. S. 80, introduced in the One-hundredth Congress by Senator Howard Metzenbaum of Ohio, would repeal the McCarran-Ferguson Act but grant a two-year moratorium on civil antitrust litigation against insurers to give them time to adjust to the new legal environment.

Table 8-1. *State Insurance Reforms, January 1986–May 1987*

State	Data collection[a]	Rate setting and review[a]	Notice requirements (cancellation or nonrenewal)[a]
Alabama	...	2	...
Alaska	...	...	1
Arkansas	1	2	1
California	1	...	2
Colorado	2	1	1
Connecticut	2	...	1
Delaware	3	...	1
Florida	...	1	1
Georgia	...	1	1
Hawaii	...	1	1
Idaho	...	...	1
Illinois	...	...	1
Indiana	...	...	1
Kansas	1	2	2
Louisiana	...	...	3
Maine	...	...	1
Massachusetts	...	2	...
Michigan	2	1	...
Minnesota	...	1	...
Mississippi	...	1	...
Missouri	...	1	1
New Hampshire	...	2	1
New Mexico	...	2	1
New York	...	...	1
North Carolina	1	...	...
North Dakota	...	1	1
Ohio	1	...	...
Pennsylvania	1	...	1
Tennessee	...	1	...
Vermont	1	...	...
West Virginia	...	1	2
Wisconsin	1	...	2
Wyoming	...	...	1

Sources: Rand Corporation, draft (Rand Corporation, 1987), pp. 77–78; and National Conference of State Legislatures, *Liability Insurance* (Denver and Washington, D.C., 1986 summary and May 1987 summary).

a. 1 is applicable to almost all insurance suits; 2 is applicable only to particular types of cases; and 3 is applicable to most insurance suits and specifically to particular parties and types of cases.

carriers also benefit most from the cost savings produced by the joint activities allowed by the exemption.

The objective indicators of the competitive nature of the property-casualty insurance industry weaken the case for more stringent state regulation of premiums and policies. Stricter regulation of rates may, of course, hold premiums down, as it apparently has done in states where auto insurance rates have been regulated. But in a nation in which state regulation of insurance has long been a tradition, tighter regulation by some states will only induce carriers in those states to reduce the coverage they offer or even to withdraw entirely.[2] The recent attempt by Florida, for example, to limit premiums charged by insurance companies has apparently driven almost all providers of medical malpractice insurance from the state. Moreover, it is far from clear whether the repeal of McCarran-Ferguson would even have a significant impact on the behavior of insurers. Under the "state action" doctrine, the states could choose to exempt the joint activities of insurers from the antitrust laws.[3]

The only way in which regulation of the property-casualty industry might be significantly improved is to strengthen solvency regulation by state insurance agencies. Like banks, insurance companies are typically required to maintain specific levels of surplus (equivalent to capital) and to operate in a sound manner. State insurance departments supervise insurers to make certain these standards are met. In recent years, however, insolvencies in the property-casualty insurance industry have risen sharply; indeed, 59 out of 140 insolvencies from 1969 to 1986 occurred after 1983.[4] While the trend in insolvencies has paralleled the recent deterioration in the industry's financial performance, questions have long been raised about the quality of supervision conducted by state insurance departments, many of which lack the staff to adequately fulfill their mission.[5] Rather than institute stiffer rate or policy regulation, states should improve supervision of the financial and business practices of the insurers they regulate.

2. Resa W. King, "The Damage Is Mounting in Property and Casualty," *Business Week* (August 10, 1987), p. 32.

3. In *Southern Motor Carriers Rate Conference, Inc.* v. *United States,* 471 U.S. 48 (1985), the Supreme Court held that state regulation of collective ratemaking by intrastate motor carriers exempted the joint activities of the participants in the rating bureau from the antitrust laws. By the same reasoning, state supervision or regulation of the collective ratemaking practices in the insurance industry could be sufficient to insulate those functions from the antitrust laws under the state action doctrine even if the McCarran-Ferguson exemption were removed.

The removal of the antitrust exemptions for collusive ratemaking in the motor carrier industry in 1980 offers some instructive lessons in the context of property-casualty insurance. There is some evidence that restoring the motor carrier exemption would reduce information costs to shippers, while competition would keep rates from rising. See Jerry A. Hausman, "Information Costs, Competition, and Collective Ratemaking in the Motor Carrier Industry," working paper (Massachusetts Institute of Technology, August 1982).

4. U.S. General Accounting Office, *Insurer Failures: Property/Casualty Insurer Insolvencies and State Guaranty Funds*, GAO/GGD-87-100 (Washington, D.C., 1987).

5. King, "Damage Is Mounting."

Tort Reforms

The most widely discussed solutions to the insurance crisis involve reforms of the tort system: statutory changes in liability doctrines and limits on the damages juries can award. These suggestions respond to the contention, generally supported in this volume, that insurance costs have spiraled upward because compensation provided through the tort system has both increased and become more uncertain. But before identifying some sound proposals, it is useful to review the full range of reforms that have been advocated at both the federal and state levels.

Federal Reform Proposals

To date, Congress has concentrated its tort reform efforts on product liability laws. Early proposals, such as the legislation introduced by Senator Robert Kasten of Wisconsin in the Ninety-seventh Congress (S. 666), would have created a new system of products liability at the federal level, one based largely on negligence rather than standards of strict liability, that would have preempted state law. Manufacturers could have escaped liability if their products met applicable federal safety standards. In addition, punitive damages would have been limited, joint and several liability would have been eliminated for noneconomic damages (unless defendants acted in concert), and the statute of limitations would have required the dismissal of cases brought more than two years after the plaintiff reasonably could have discovered both the harm and its cause. Although the Kasten bill was vigorously supported by the business community and the liability insurance industry, it was strongly opposed by consumer organizations, the organized bar, and political interests favoring states' rights. The opponents prevailed; Senator Kasten's proposal never emerged from the Senate Commerce Committee.

Senate advocates of product liability reform have attemped to combine proposed revisions in various Kasten-type bills with the introduction of an expedited alternative to products liability litigation for plaintiffs who choose to forgo major awards for pain and suffering. The most recent product of this marriage was the Product Liability Reform Act of 1986 (S. 2760), which the Senate Commerce Committee approved in 1986 by a vote of 16 to 1 but which was never voted on by the full Senate.[6]

6. Proposals similar to S. 2760 were introduced in 1987 and referred to the Senate Judiciary Committee, including S. 687 and S. 688 (sponsored by Senator John Danforth

The liability proposals given most attention in the House generally take a somewhat different tack. At one extreme are bills that would modify products liability standards only for specific products. An example is H.R. 2238 sponsored by Congressman Dan Glickman of Kansas, which would apply only to aircraft manufacturers. At the other extreme are generic product liability reform proposals in the Kasten mold, now most prominently represented by the Uniform Product Safety Act of 1987 (H.R. 1115) introduced by Congressman Bill Richardson of New Mexico. Unlike the Kasten bill, however, the Richardson proposal would retain strict liability for product defects, though it would allow a number of defenses. Manufacturers would not, for instance, be liable if they used state-of-the-art production methods or if the harm were caused by an inherent characteristic of the product. They would also be exempt from liability if the plaintiff were under the influence of alcohol or drugs when using the product and if that condition were responsible for more than 50 percent of the plaintiff's injury. At this writing the Richardson bill had been marked up by the House Energy and Commerce Committee but had not yet been voted on by the full House.

It is unclear whether, based on current approaches, Congress will be able to fashion a compromise on products liability reform legislation. Private-sector support for federal reform originally came mainly from the liability insurance industry. But with the recent improvements in the financial condition of the industry and the apparent leveling off of premium increases, the urgency appears to have gone. Moreover, the property-casualty insurance industry has itself become a target for legislation, weakening both the intensity of the industry's interest in tort

---

of Missouri). Among other things, S. 2760 would have established a new settlement procedure for products liability claims by authorizing expedited resolution if a defendant manufacturer offers the plaintiff payment for his or her economic losses (net of compensation from other sources) and up to $100,000 for noneconomic (or dignatory) losses. If the plaintiff refuses such an offer and proceeds with litigation, he or she would bear costs and attorneys' fees if the final award were less favorable than the settlement offer. Although the bill would not preempt liability standards applicable to manufacturers, it would make clear that any seller (other than a manufacturer) could be held liable only for negligence or breach of warranty. The bill would also raise the evidentiary standards for granting punitive damage awards, impose a two-year statute of limitations running from the time a party discovers both the harm and the cause, require payments received under workers' compensation to be deducted from damage awards, and eliminate joint and several liability for noneconomic damages (instead allocating damages by degree of responsibility among the various defendants).

reform and the receptivity of legislators to the industry's arguments favoring reform.

Tort Reform in the States

Table 8-2 summarizes tort system reforms adopted by the states between January 1986 and May 1987. Among the more popular are the elimination of joint and several liability (primarily for noneconomic damages), limits on contingency fees collected by plaintiffs' attorneys and sanctions on attorneys for filing frivolous lawsuits, and limits on the liability of governmental entities and their employees. Less widespread are amendments to the collateral source rule, which currently prohibits juries and judges from decreasing tort damage awards by the amount of compensation the plaintiff receives from other sources; permission for defendants to pay judgments over time rather than in lump sums; and so-called dram shop legislation limiting the liability of liquor store owners or individuals serving alcoholic beverages in their homes.

Table 8-3 lists states that have imposed statutory ceilings on damage awards. Most of the amendments apply to all awards for noneconomic damages in tort cases, but a few states have imposed damage caps for medical malpractice awards only. As discussed later in this chapter, it is unclear if damage caps will survive constitutional challenges that they deprive citizens of due process of law.

Assessment

Virtually all the tort reform measures would reduce compensation available through the system. In fact, there is evidence, at least for medical malpractice cases, that tort reforms have already reduced the frequency of claims and the growth rate of insurance premiums.[7] But deterring injury is also an objective of tort law, and reducing compensation could weaken deterrence. The problem facing policymakers is that relatively little empirical information is available to indicate how tort compensation could be modified without compromising deterrence.

Nevertheless, the foregoing chapters suggest that certain reform measures are more likely to meet this concern than others. They are most usefully summarized in three categories: those affecting plaintiffs'

---

7. See chapter 5; and Tort Policy Working Group, *An Update on the Liability Crisis* (Washington, D.C., 1987), pp. 91–96.

Table 8-2. State Tort Reforms, January 1986–May 1987[a]

State	Comparative and contributory negligence	Joint and several liability	Punitive damages	Attorney's fees and miscellaneous sanctions	Collateral source rule changes	Interest and taxes on judgments	Periodic payment of judgments	Dram shop liability	Government liability
Alabama	…	…	…	…	…	…	…	…	2
Alaska	…	1	…	…	1	1	1	…	…
Arizona	…	1	…	1	…	…	…	2	…
Arkansas	…	1	…	…	…	…	…	…	…
California	…	1	1	…	1	…	…	2	2
Colorado	…	1	…	…	1	…	…	2	2
Connecticut	1	1	…	1	1	…	1	…	…
Delaware	…	…	…	…	…	…	…	…	…
Florida	…	1	1	…	1	…	1	…	2
Georgia	…	…	…	1	1	…	…	…	2
Hawaii	…	1	1	3	1	…	2	…	2
Idaho	…	1	…	1	1	…	…	2	…
Illinois	1	1	1	1	1	…	…	…	2
Indiana	…	…	…	1	1	1	1	2	2
Iowa	…	…	3	1	…	…	1	2	2
Kansas	…	1	…	3	…	…	2	…	…
Louisiana	…	…	…	…	…	…	…	2	…
Maine	…	…	…	2	…	…	2	2	2
Maryland	…	…	…	…	…	…	1	…	…
Massachusetts	…	…	…	2	2	…	1	2	…
Michigan	…	1	…	1	3	1	1	2	2

State							
Minnesota			1	1			
Mississippi		1					1
Missouri							2
Montana							2
Nebraska			1	1			
Nevada	3	1					1
New Hampshire	1	1				2	2
New Mexico	2					2	
New Jersey	1	1					
New York	1	1	1	1	1		
North Dakota	1	1					
Ohio	1	1	1	2			
Oklahoma	2	2	2		2		
Rhode Island							2
South Carolina	2	2	1	1	1		2
South Dakota	1	1				2	1
Tennessee	1	1	2		2	2	1
Utah		2	2	2	2		2
Virginia	1	1	1		1		2
Washington	2	3					2
West Virginia	3	3					3
Wisconsin	1	1				2	2
Wyoming							

Source: National Conference of State Legislatures, *Liability Insurance* (May 1987 summary), pp. 173–80.
a. 1 denotes most insurance and liability suits; 2 applies only to particular types of cases; and 3 applies to most suits and specifically to particular parties and types of cases.

Table 8-3. *Damages Caps Adopted by the States,*
January 1986–May 1987

State	Noneconomic damages generally	Medical malpractice
Alaska	$500,000 based on separate injury or accident	. . .
Arkansas	$25,000–50,000 for motor vehicle death	. . .
	$15,000 for property damage, $5,000 if by minor	
Colorado	$250,000 for noneconomic loss; $500,000 if is "clear and convincing" evidence	. . .
Connecticut	$20,000 per person, $50,000 per incident selling liquor to intoxicated person	. . .
Florida	$450,000 for damages in civil actions	. . .
Kansas	$250,000 against health care providers	Damages against health care providers capped at $1 million. Supplemental awards asked for up to $3 million
Maine	$250,000 for negligent serving of minor or intoxicated person	. . .
Maryland	$350,000 cap	. . .
Michigan	. . .	$225,000 in medical malpractice unless case involves death or other serious medical problems
Minnesota	$400,000 cap on intangible losses	. . .
Missouri	Environmental damages and cleanup capped at $1 million for one person and $3 million for all persons	. . .
New Hampshire	$875,000 cap on pain and suffering awards	. . .
	Liability cap of $500,000; and for municipalities $150,000	. . .
New Jersey	Judgments against public entity: $500,000 per claimant, $1 million per occurrence	. . .
South Carolina	Monetary liability on state and political subdivisions of $250,000 per incident and $500,000 per occurrence	. . .
South Dakota	. . .	$1 million cap
Utah	$100,000 per incident and $300,000 per occurrence on dram shop liability	. . .

Table 8-3 (*continued*)

State	Noneconomic damages generally	Medical malpractice
Virginia	$25,000 cap in damages by an uninsured motor vehicle if serious injury is inflicted	. . .
	Recovery of noneconomic damages limited to 3 times the amount awarded for economic damages, or $350,000, in personal injury and wrongful death cases	Recovery of noneconomic damages limited to 3 times the amount awarded for economic damages, or $350,000
Washington	$117,000 to $493,000 cap according to the formula: 0.43 × expected annual wage × plaintiff's life expectancy	. . .
Wisconsin	$1 million cap	. . .
	$250,000 cap on damages recoverable for negligent operation of municipally owned vehicle	. . .

Sources: National Conference of State Legislatures, *Liability Insurance* (1986 summary and May 1987).

eligibility for damages through tort law, those relating to the amount of damages plaintiffs receive, and those tending to reduce the heavy transactions costs of the system.

ELIGIBILITY CRITERIA: FINE-TUNING TORT DOCTRINES. Not everyone who files a tort action deserves compensation. Over time, judges and legislatures have established certain standards for screening worthy plaintiffs from those less deserving. But critics of recent trends in tort law argue that these standards have become too porous and too removed from the objective of encouraging safety and deterring injury.

For example, critics have charged that judges are increasingly moving away from the principal screening device, the negligence doctrine, and toward a standard of strict liability. The analysis in chapter 2 is sympathetic with this criticism. Nevertheless, the discussion in the later chapters suggests that the gains from moving toward a negligence standard are uneven.

As Patricia Danzon explains in chapter 4, while medical malpractice cases purportedly have long been governed by the negligence doctrine, concern has arisen that some courts are in effect using a strict liability standard. Danzon urges that the use of the negligence standard be made clear and, in particular, that the relevant standard of care should be the customary or usual practice at the time of the allegedly wrongful conduct. A state-of-the-art rule would ensure that courts are not imposing liability with twenty-twenty hindsight, which may provide compensation to unfortunate plaintiffs but produces no deterrence—precisely the kind of result the tort system should avoid.[8]

The authors of chapters 5 through 7, however, provide somewhat less sanguine assessments of the value in practice of returning to a negligence standard. In chapter 5, for example, Peter Huber shows that the major expansion of liability in toxic tort cases has arisen primarily from expansive notions of causation rather than the adoption of strict liability standards by judges. Yet Huber is skeptical that judges or legislatures will be amenable to tightening causation tests by imposing rigorous standards of proof. Moreover, he points out that at a sufficiently aggregated level, given all of the external costs imposed by industrial activities, even the current liberal attitudes toward causation may result in too little environmental liability rather than too much.

Kip Viscusi in chapter 6 notes that in cases of injury on the job, the negligence standard has long been supplanted by strict liability in the form of workers' compensation. Here the adoption of strict liability standards appears to have had the expected effects: a diminution of employers' incentives to implement safety measures. Nevertheless, there is little realistic prospect that workers' compensation laws are going to be repealed. The more problematic issues for occupational injury relate to worker exposure to toxic substances such as asbestos. But as just noted, Peter Huber documents that the principal issue in toxic tort litigation is the standard of causation rather than the doctrinal differences between negligence and strict liability. Viscusi does provide some support for allowing defendants to be excused from liability when their conduct, products, or equipment meets applicable government regulations. But he also correctly notes that such a defense may have limited

8. An effective state-of-the-art rule or defense would also significantly mitigate the insurance problems associated with the newer statutes of limitation, which run from the time of discovery rather than from occurrence of the injury. As Danzon points out, these liberal statutes create the risk that courts will impose new standards of liability on defendants retroactively, resulting in compensation that has no deterrence value. However, if defendants are permitted a state-of-the-art defense—that is, if they can show that their conduct was reasonable judged by the standards applicable at the time it occurred—this risk of retroactive application would be substantially reduced.

application: while most regulations are written to cover a broad class of factual circumstances, many tort suits involve highly fact-specific hazards or situations that are often not precisely covered by a particular regulation.

In chapter 7 George Priest argues that neither the negligence nor the strict liability doctrines, as they have been applied by judges and juries in products liability cases, have efficiently deterred behavior that causes accidents. He suggests that judges abandon the old negligence and strict liability terminology and require juries to decide products liability cases by weighing the costs and benefits of the specific type of behavior. Producers would thus be liable for injuries only when plaintiffs could establish that there was some practicable way producers could have prevented the accident at a lower cost than the plaintiff.

LIMITATIONS ON DAMAGES. A major reason for the increase in costs of liability-related litigation is an apparent rapid rise in jury awards, expecially for noneconomic damages. One logical reform, therefore, would be to limit noneconomic damages, as a number of states have already done (see table 8-3). But as Patricia Danzon points out in chapter 4, flat caps on noneconomic damages are discriminatory because they tend to penalize the younger, more severely injured parties who often receive little compensation from other sources. In addition, a number of state courts, including those in Florida, Kansas, and Virginia, have struck down flat caps as inconsistent with constitutional guarantees of due process of law.

Danzon offers a better alternative: *scheduled* limits on noneconomic damages in malpractice awards, based on the age of the plaintiff and the severity of the injury. To take account of inflation and growing real incomes, these limits could be indexed to increases in medical costs, wages, or the GNP. There may be good grounds for applying this suggestion to all tort cases. Scheduled limits for pain and suffering would remove much of the lottery element that now characterizes the tort system; damage awards would become more predictable, thus removing much of the uncertainty that has plagued liability insurers. But would scheduled limits on noneconomic damages stand any better chance of surviving constitutional challenge than flat caps? One reason they might is that they would take into account the relevant differences in injuries and potential suffering among plaintiffs. In this respect, they are much like the new federal guidelines for criminal sentencing that establish sentences according to a defendant's past criminal record and the severity of the crime.[9] Still, there is no way of stating with certainty that scheduled limits would be deemed constitutional in all states.

There are good arguments both for and against most of the other commonly discussed reform proposals. One popular suggestion is to eliminate the collateral source rule, which currently allows claimants to recover costs from public or private insurers as well as from tort defendants. But as Danzon notes, eliminating this rule would weaken deterrence because it would permit defendants to escape liability for some portion of the damage caused by their risk-creating behavior. A possible alternative would give all public and private insurers the right to recover from successful tort plaintiffs the amount of compensation the insurers had previously paid. This would preserve the deterrence objective of the system because the defendant would still be obligated to pay in full, but it would also result in further litigation, adding to the already heavy transactions costs of the system.

Another suggestion often mentioned is to allow or require tort awards to be paid periodically as annuities rather than in a lump sum. Such a requirement clearly would cushion the financial burden on unsuccessful defendants, but it would not lower the total cost of tort awards if heirs of successful plaintiffs have rights to the unpaid balance of the annuities.

Yet another proposal would limit punitive damages, perhaps by tightening the standard of evidence required to prove the bad faith that normally triggers a punitive award or by placing a flat cap on punitive damage awards. It is not clear that tightening the evidentiary standard would make a difference in decisions to award or withhold punitive damages. There is a stronger case for a cap, since these damages are analogous to civil or criminal fines, which are subject to statutory limits. In addition, there are grounds for channeling the proceeds of any punitive damages assessed against defendants to state or federal governments rather than to plaintiffs. Awarding such damages to successful plaintiffs provides excess compensation. Giving them to the government would preserve both the compensation and deterrence objectives of tort law.

Finally, many have urged the elimination of the doctrine of joint and

9. For a description of these new rules, see Jon O. Newman, "Federal Sentencing Guidelines: A Risk Worth Taking," *Brookings Review* (Summer 1987), pp. 29–33. The sentencing guidelines were struck down by a federal appeals court in 1988, not for substantive reasons but instead on the grounds that the commission that developed them violated the constitutional doctrine of separation of powers.

several liability, which has led to the "deep pockets" problem: wealthy defendants responsible for a disproportionate amount of the damages in cases involving multiple defendants, some of whom are less wealthy. Clearly, this doctrine excessively deters wealthy businesses because it promotes accident avoidance measures that must account for costs beyond those for which the firm may be responsible. However, eliminating the doctrine could leave many successful plaintiffs uncompensated. Primarily for this reason, most of the relevant proposals would remove joint and several liability only for noneconomic damages, ensuring that successful plaintiffs are at least compensated for their medical costs and lost income.

REDUCING TRANSACTIONS COSTS. One of the few subjects on which proponents and critics of tort reform agree is that the current system is extremely expensive to administer. There is also a growing consensus about certain measures that would reduce costs. For example, some judges have shown interest in requiring opposing litigants in complex cases to complete a minitrial before proceeding. At these minitrials, lawyers summarize their arguments to juries without presenting witnesses. Nonbinding judgments are then rendered. There is some evidence that such proceedings perform a valuable educational function for the parties and thus tend to promote less costly settlements.[10]

It is also widely recognized that attorneys must be discouraged from filing frivolous lawsuits. The federal discovery rules were recently amended to require stiffer sanctions for such suits.[11] Table 8-2 indicates that many states have adopted similar measures.

Other proposals to reduce high transactions costs are more controversial, however. A number of states have placed limits on the percentage of a tort recovery that plaintiffs' attorneys may receive as a contingency fee, and the Justice Department's Tort Policy Working Group has suggested a schedule.[12] Clearly, such caps would discourage lawsuits with smaller potential damages and those resting on untested, innovative legal theories, which would reduce both the total transactions

10. See *Wall Street Journal,* December 1, 1986.

11. Thus under the amended rule 11 of the Federal Rules of Civil Procedure, federal courts may award expenses, including attorneys' fees, to a litigant whose opponent acts in bad faith in initiating or conducting litigation.

12. The group recommends that contingency fees be limited according to a sliding scale: no more than 25 percent of the first $100,000 of a verdict or settlement, 20 percent of the next $100,000, and so on down to a 10 percent ceiling on any increments above $300,000. See Tort Policy Working Group, *Update on the Liability Crisis,* p. 87.

costs of the tort system and the amount of compensation processed through it. But there is no reliable empirical research indicating how significant these benefits might be; we simply do not know how the volume of litigation or its deterrence effects respond to attorneys' fees.

Ultimately, the most effective way of avoiding much of the transactions cost would be to provide ways of compensating injured parties that do not require the high fact-finding expenses often characteristic of tort litigation. This suggests a trade-off: relaxed standards for eligibility but limits on compensation, especially for noneconomic damages. The Product Liability Reform Act of 1986 (S. 2760) offers the trade-off within the tort system itself by giving plaintiffs incentives to accept manufacturers' settlement offers that have limited noneconomic damage components.

The approach in S. 2760 could be generalized to all types of tort cases. By penalizing plaintiffs who fail to obtain jury verdicts as generous as defendants' settlement offers, S. 2760 would clearly raise the stakes for any plaintiff who desires to continue a case. Compensation and transactions costs would thus probably go down. But at the same time, because the expedited settlement alternative in S. 2760 also offers a way for defendants to minimize their exposure to loss, it might encourage them to settle poorly justified lawsuits. Given current information about plaintiffs' and defendants' behavior, however, it is difficult to determine whether an expedited settlement process would result in net savings.

Alternative Compensation Mechanisms

A final set of proposals seeks a more efficient method of compensating injured parties outside the tort system. The method would perhaps be modeled on workers' compensation programs, which entitle persons injured on the job to recover for medical costs and a portion of their lost wages without proving that their employers are at fault. The workers' compensation system is largely administrative, and relatively few cases land in court.

Other countries have experimented with even more ambitious nontort compensation devices. New Zealand's, perhaps the most comprehensive, provides medical insurance for all residents. In addition, three major programs compensate residents for lost income and, to a limited extent, for pain and suffering caused by accidents. An earner's program financed by a tax on employers compensates all workers for accidents occurring on or off the job. A motor vehicles program financed by a flat tax on all automobile owners compensates nonearners injured in auto accidents. And a supplementary compensation program financed by general revenues compensates nonearners injured in accidents not involving automobiles.[13]

There are no comprehensive assessments of how New Zealand's programs have worked—specifically whether they have reduced the compensation and transactions costs of the tort system the programs replaced in 1967. In any event, New Zealand's experience is likely to be of limited value to the United States, which is far larger and has a much more heterogeneous population. Moreover, New Zealand's compensation programs do not cover disease or sickness. Yet as both Peter Huber and Kip Viscusi point out in their chapters, the potential sums that may eventually be required to compensate individuals in the United States through the tort system is staggering—an estimated $38 billion for product liability claims related to asbestos alone.

Precisely for this reason, Huber anticipates that compensation for diseases plausibly due at least in some respect to environmental causes utimately will be processed outside the tort system, perhaps through an expansion of the Superfund program (the program does not currently cover personal injury lawsuits). But as he, Viscusi, and Danzon point out, any broad effort to provide compensation for disease is likely to be highly susceptible to cost explosion; the expansion of eligibility criteria over time could increase costs far more than any attempt to limit the amount of damages per claim.

If alternative compensation programs were to replace significant elements of the tort system, it is far from clear whether more intensive regulation could efficiently deter the risky behavior that would be created. Much of the environmental, health, and safety regulation in the United States has been carried out through detailed rules rather than through marketlike techniques such as taxes or performance standards. As numerous commentators have observed, detailed commands and controls tend to be inefficient because they do not permit private actors to search for and implement the cheapest methods of reducing the risks

13. For a description of New Zealand's system, see Sheila A. M. McLean, "Accident Compensation Liability Without Fault: The New Zealand Experience," *Journal of Social Welfare Law* (January 1985), pp. 31–45.

that regulatory programs are designed to reduce.[14] Even where performance standards have been established, they have often entailed substantial costs relative to their desired objectives, as Viscusi demonstrates for
many Occupational Safety and Health Administration regulations.

The tort system also performs a valuable informational function that
regulators often cannot duplicate. The virtue of tort law is that it provides a decentralized mechanism for determining the hazards in substances, product designs, or behavior that in many situations may be
superior to relying on centralized government regulation. The judicial
reporting services are littered with cases in which lone individuals, not
governmental agencies, induced significant changes in private behavior
through successful litigation—cases involving defects in automobile and
airplane design, asbestos, and dangerous medical practices, to name just
a few. In short, we simply do not know whether society would be better
off if the process of identifying risks and hazards were further centralized by replacing the tort system with more intensive regulation.

Conclusion

Obviously the problems caused by the recent explosion in insurance
premiums for certain types of liability have no easy solutions. This book
shows that the recent trends in these markets reflect the more intensive
use of the liability system by plaintiffs, judges, and juries to compensate
individuals for their misfortunes. Although many states have recently
enacted reform measures that may slow these trends, it is unlikely that
they will be fundamentally reversed.

Policymakers at both state and federal levels must struggle against
imperfect information about the economic effects of the current liability
system. We know roughly how many dollars flow through the tort
system and how much it costs to process tort claims. But we know little
about how much deterrence the system provides and ultimately whether
the benefits of deterrence outweigh the costs. Clearly, research in this
area is far from complete.

Even with this limited empirical base, however, it is possible to reach
some conclusions. First, stiffer regulation of liability insurance rates or
policies will not solve the liability crisis and conceivably could be coun-

14. See Charles L. Schultze, *Public Use of Private Interest* (Brookings, 1977).

terproductive. Second, judges should encourage juries to evaluate the costs and benefits of the behavior of both plaintiffs and defendants in tort cases in deciding which parties should bear the loss from the accident or event at issue. Third, there is a strong case for limiting noneconomic damages in tort cases, but only in a way that takes into account the age of the injured party and the severity of the injury. Finally, while some may be disappointed by the failure of Congress to enact comprehensive tort reform legislation, the experiments now being conducted by the states may prove more useful in the long run. Given the uncertainties about the economic effects of different legal rules, we may one day be grateful that reform proceeded in the relatively uncoordinated fashion that it has in recent years. Today we simply know too little to be confident that any major overhaul of the U.S. tort system would produce more benefit than harm.

Index